THE CHRISTIAN APPROACH
TO THE BIBLE

THE CHRISTIAN APPROACH TO THE BIBLE

(La Lecture Chrétienne de la Bible)

BY

DOM CELESTIN CHARLIER

Translated from the French by
HUBERT J. RICHARDS, L.S.S.,
and
BRENDAN PETERS, S.T.L.

Preface by
THE RT. REV. MGR. JOHN M. T. BARTON,
D.D., L.S.S., F.S.A., F.R.S.A.

PAULIST PRESS DEUS BOOKS

NEW YORK   GLEN ROCK   WESTMINSTER
TORONTO   AMSTERDAM

Published by Paulist Press
Editorial Office: 304 W. 58th St., N.Y., N.Y. 10019
Business Office: Glen Rock, New Jersey 07452

Printed and bound in the United States of America by Our Sunday Visitor Press

CONTENTS

FOREWORD

FOR too long now Christian spirituality has subsisted on a diet of substitutes. It is to-day becoming increasingly evident that such poor fare does not satisfy the discerning appetites of educated men, who are eager to go back to the true source of Christian life which is the Bible. The aim of this book is to act as their guide.

This is not the first book that has set out to teach people how to read the Bible. In fact there have been so many books with so many different approaches that people are bewildered and some have lost heart. There are books which are so utterly technical that an ordinary man is out of his depth, and the spiritual nourishment he set out to find is lost under a blanket of erudition. There are other books which advise him to forget about science and leave everything to intuition, an approach which he finds equally unsatisfactory and, if he has any common sense, unacceptable. A third kind of introduction to Scripture has tried to combine both methods, but this strange mixture of scientific apologetics and sentimental piety is still far removed from the living Truth and true Life which is the object of his search.

This book refuses to make a choice between science and piety, or to treat them as two separate things. It does not promise an easy solution to the problem of bringing the Bible back to the people. The Word of God cannot be understood without some familiarity with the form in which it took flesh, and this study of the Bible's historical and literary problems demands much patient hard work. Nor can this science alone put the reader in touch with the divine content of the Bible. His knowledge must be permeated by a deep faith if he is to be caught up in the rhythm and the Spirit of the sacred writers. A synthesis of this sort demands a refashioning of our modern mentality, the gradual integration of faith and technique. Science must blossom into Wisdom, and knowledge pass from the world of abstraction to the world of concrete reality. This was the ideal in mind when this book was written.

In fact this book is the outcome of a series of discussions which took place among friends and students drawn by a common desire to give thanks for the riches of God's Word. The author is no more than the spokesman of a larger experience shared by the whole group. To all those who were of one mind with him and who now wait for the final Vision, he dedicates this work.

This book has therefore no technical pretensions. It is simply based on a firm conviction born of experience that the Bible belongs to everyone, and has the power to transform the life of one who will read it with an informed mind and a ready heart. Our purpose is to outline the intellectual, moral and religious dispositions that such a reading of the Bible requires. No page here should be beyond the understanding of the ordinary person. Certainly nothing here is superfluous if the divine message is to be fruitfully read.

We do not promise that this book will be easy or light reading. Many of the problems dealt with are very complex indeed. Some of them will not mean very much until the reader has gained long and living familiarity with the Bible. Our aim is not only to encourage him to read the Bible, but also to accompany and help him in the task. By making him free of what we have ourselves found, we wish to show him what he may gain from his biblical experience, and help him to give expression to the fullness he receives. Like the Bible which our book is meant to serve, we ask for patience, generosity and confidence.

We have, finally, no intention of setting up the Bible as an absolute. All we aim to do is to define its rightful place in the economy of salvation through the Church. The Word of the Bible will pass. Its only purpose is to nourish man in the bosom of the Church and to sustain him in his pilgrimage on earth. In heaven the Word of God himself sings to the Father the eternal thanksgiving of the Spirit.

MAREDSOUS,
September 3rd, 1949.

PREFACE

by

THE RIGHT REV. MONSIGNOR JOHN M. T. BARTON,
D.D., L.S.S., F.S.A., F.R.S.A.

English Consultor, Pontifical Biblical Commission; Past President (1952), Society for Old Testament Study; Sometime Professor of Holy Scripture, Hebrew and Liturgy, St. Edmund's College, Ware.

IT is, as always, a pleasure to commend a book on Holy Scripture that is likely to be of service to the large number of people who are anxious to be better informed about the Bible and its background. The work that has been done in recent years by the late Mgr. Ronald Knox in his complete translation of the Bible, and by the Catholic Truth Society in issuing, only last year, its excellent cheap edition of the Douay Bible, has led, one is glad to think, to an appreciable increase in the reading of the Bible among Catholics. As one who is frequently asked to name a volume that will assist all earnest readers of the Bible, I have constantly recommended, since its first appearance in 1949, the French original of Dom Charlier's book, and I now give the warmest welcome to this scholarly, lively, and extremely readable translation entitled *The Christian Approach to the Bible*, the joint work of one of my successors at Ware, Fr. Hubert Richards, and of Fr. Brendan Peters.

Writing in 1923, in his stimulating book *Every Man's Story of the Old Testament*, an Anglican professor, Dr. Alexander Nairne, declared in regard to the famous fifty-third chapter of the prophet Isaias: "Here is a Gospel before the Gospel. Cool criticism, comparison of religions, analysis and tracing of the history of faith; we are almost scared to remember such occupations of our leisure when we turn from them to the Old Testament itself and become again readers of the Bible"

9

(p. 286). It is the purpose of Dom Charlier's work to give the help that is needed for an intelligent understanding of the Bible, but, above all, to lead his readers to recognize the truth of St. Jerome's phrase: Ignorance of the scriptures is ignorance of Christ. The book is sure to be widely appreciated.

JOHN M. T. BARTON

SS. Peter & Edward, Palace St., S.W.1.
Feast of St. Edmund, King and Martyr, Nov. 20, 1957.

CHAPTER I

THE PROBLEM

THE simplest and shortest form of introduction to the Bible for a modern Christian is to show him that the very reading of the Bible poses a problem. The fact that he is a Christian will mean that he admits its divine authority and the permanence of its message. This in itself imposes an obligation on him—it is his duty to read it. But he immediately finds the path of duty barred by obstacles. If he sets out to make the Bible his rule of faith he loses sight of the Church. If he approaches it in the Spirit of the Church he finds that the wealth of technical qualification required is altogether too much for him.

If we are to put him back on the right road we must unravel the tangled threads of biblical history during the last few centuries, because it is there that this problem began to take on its present form. Somewhere there the solution is to be found.

I

BIBLICAL JANSENISM

Decline of the Bible among ordinary people; beginnings of prejudice; rise of the lay spirit in the thirteenth century; the Reformation and its consequences.

IF A Gallup poll were to be taken among Christians on the question: " What sort of a person do you think is qualified to read the Bible? " some of the answers would be very illuminating. They would bring to light the widespread ignorance and apathy among God's people for God's Word.

Of these two, ignorance is the more widespread. · It is a long cry from here to St. John Chrysostom but a quotation from him does throw our situation into relief. In one of his homilies he

11

berated his people for not knowing how many Epistles St. **Paul** had written. Their ignorance was a pointer to their lack of zeal. One wonders what words he would have used to castigate some of our good practising Catholics. Some of them could hardly tell him who St. Paul was! We must be frank about this. Many Catholics to-day have a knowledge of the Bible which has not gone beyond the two or three vague questions they learned from their Catechisms. They have never looked into a complete Bible nor do they spend much time on the New Testament. If they read the Gospels at all it is in the form of a Life of Christ. They remember a few of the 'old faithfuls' like the Flood, the Fall of Jericho and Jonah's Whale, because they were the stories chosen for illustration in their Bible Histories. If this is a true picture of their knowledge we cannot be surprised that the only reaction that the Bible arouses in them is either a frank scepticism or a childish anxiety.

This ignorance is not confined to Catholics: Protestants are not much better off, even in those countries which are officially Protestant. The older people among them are still faithful to their 'readings' but the younger elements are riddled with rationalism and pietism. To these the Bible means no more than it does to the average Catholic, in fact not so much, because the Catholic does maintain some sort of contact with the sacred text in the liturgy. People are fast becoming unchristian. Among Protestants this shows itself in a loss of feeling for the Bible, among Catholics in a lack of real interest in the liturgy.

Such ignorance is deplorable, but there is a worse evil—prejudice and downright blindness. It is not unusual to hear Catholics (even priests) say: "Read the Bible? Only Protestants read the Bible!"[1] Many priests and religious, with the best of intentions, do their utmost to deter people from reading it, the Old Testament especially. "You will lose your faith," they say, "it is not edifying; it is forbidden." Certainly there are many who question the use of reading the Bible. "What for?" they say. "The Church teaches us all we need to know.

[1] Dom Charlier speaks of his own country, Belgium. However, even in England it is not so long ago that Cardinal Manning said: "How I wish I could convince my flock that the Bible is *not* on the *Index.*" (Tr.)

The Gospel has supplanted the Old Law. You just read the Bible stories, learn the Catechism and listen to the Sermon! "

We need not be surprised to find that only one priest in a hundred (and one religious in a thousand) has read his Bible from cover to cover. Nor should we wonder that the favourite spiritual reading of the layman is not the Bible or the Missal, but the *Imitation of Christ*, beautifully bound and sweetly illustrated, given to him when he made his First Communion. We do not wish here to criticize the *Imitation*; it is a wonderful book, but it is no substitute for the living and life-giving Word of God.

THERE we have a fair appraisal of what is wrong. We still have to find out why it went wrong. We cannot put all the blame on the great wave of irreligion which is sweeping the world, because the disease is rife even among fervent Catholics. It will be necessary to go back to the sixteenth century and even further to find the root cause. Further back even than the Renaissance, whose cry of humanism and emancipation was itself an echo of the late Middle Ages. The moral crisis of the Renaissance and the development of rationalism were simply the consequence of the gradual divorce which had been growing for some time between thought and action, between the individual and society, between man and God. The whole structure of Christian integrity was crumbling. The decline of the Bible, the lack of active participation in the liturgy, the excesses of Nominalism, the moral corruption of Churchmen—these were just the fruits of that collapse. For four hundred years it went on, from the thirteenth to the sixteenth century, until finally the Protestant crisis broke on the world. By now the Bible had ceased to be what it had been, the living framework of the Church's liturgy and the proper source of its prayer and thought and inspiration.

The assault of the sixteenth century Reformers was fierce. All the same, they themselves suffered from the disease which they were trying to cure. They prescribed a return to the Bible as the remedy which would cure the ills of a declining scholasticism. Unfortunately, instead of simply reforming the vices of the corrupt ecclesiastics, they rejected the whole social structure of the Church. In advocating a return pure and simple to the Bible as the only source of faith, the Reformation gave itself away as belonging to a new school of thought. Its very simplicity was deceptive: it aimed at a return to the pristine purity of the early Church, but it led to a way of life which was essentially new. The Reformation was very much a reflection of the age.

The Church at that time had men within her ranks who were not altogether untouched by the prevailing humanism, but that did not stop her from recognizing the Reformation as a definite break in the historical unfolding of the Christian message. It was therefore an instinct of self-preservation and not of innovation that inspired her own Counter-Reform. She saw that the Bible in Protestant hands (i.e. out of its proper context) would be a most dangerous tool. Her immediate problem was how to safeguard tradition. With this in mind, the Council of Trent restricted the use of the Bible. Its decrees affirmed the authenticity of the Vulgate and forbade the reading of the Scriptures in the vernacular unless there was an accompanying explanation which conformed to Catholic teaching.

This was the only wise thing to do. All through the ages the Church has steadfastly maintained that she alone is the true guardian of the Scriptures, and her tradition the only true guide to interpretation. It was unfortunate that the results of these measures went far beyond what the Council had intended. There grew up a distrust of the Word of God which outlived the religious strife of the time. In the seventeenth and eighteenth centuries Catholics read the Bible less and less. They suspected it of being the root cause of all the various shades of Protestantism. There grew alongside this feeling of distrust a lack of appreciation of the liturgy, and the Bible lost the context which gave it life and meaning. It is not to be wondered at that the nineteenth century eventually lost all faith in the Scriptures under the impetus of historical criticism, the child of private judgment and rationalism. Nor is it difficult to see how twentieth century Modernism (for that is what it grew into) could put the last touches to the conviction that all heresy comes from reading the Bible.

There was a distinct parallel at the beginning of this century between the problem of the Bible and the problem of the Eucharist. The Jansenists wanted to reserve the incarnate Word of God for the few who were worthy to receive it. It was basically the same movement that wanted to reserve the pre-incarnate Word for an even smaller intellectual clique who were qualified to read it. In both there was the same tendency to exaggerate the subjective and moral aspects of Christianity and to sacrifice the deeper aspects of revelation and supernatural life. Catholic reaction against Protestantism had come full circle to Protestantism's own starting point: Christianity was no more than an attitude of mind.

II

BIBLICAL SCIENTISM

Its origin in Germany; its growth and effects on Protestant-ism and Catholicism; the crisis of Modernism.

WE MADE reference above to the birth of the new critical out-look and the growth of science which at the end of the nine-teenth century upset the older ways of thinking and modes of approach. It was this, even more than the cultural changes of which it was born, that was responsible for another revolution in the Christian attitude to the Bible. The ordinary people lost interest in the Bible and the specialists took over. What had once been the living manifesto of revelation now became a mere historical document; the very source of religious life degenerated into a subject for technical research.

Already the Protestant crisis had reduced the problem of the Bible to an historical level by making the principle of evolution the issue at stake. The Reformers protested against the gulf which they believed existed between the " pristine purity " and the " embroideries of Rome ". Catholic apologists maintained in defence that despite these changes the continuity of biblical revelation had run unbroken through the patristic age. Such was the work of men like Baronius, Bellarmine, and the brilliant forerunner of biblical criticism in the seventeenth century, Richard Simon.

But it was really in the nineteenth century that the new historical approach won the day in all branches of western culture. Preoccupation with the idea of time played an all-important part in the philosophy of Hegel, as it did in the evolutionary view of science. The political changes and the social consequences of the French Revolution gave sympathy to this intellectual revolt. It was not only the discoveries of archaeology, the development of linguistic studies and the new methods of education that aroused this interest in the past. More responsible than these was the new-found spirit of independence that was in the air, a spirit which was untrammelled by tradition.

Protestant Germany first applied the method to the Bible. Private judgment, in the name of biblical history, had already passed sentence on the tradition of the Church. In the name of scientific history it would now pass sentence on the Bible. To give even a summary of the unbelievably large number of works and systems to which this gave rise is beyond the scope of this book. We can do no more than unravel the main threads.

DURING the first, or *Philosophical Period*, the approach was entirely subjective, and its whimsical erudition soon ran to extremes. It set out to find in Christianity some justification for the opinions of such men as Hegel and Schleiermacher. From these came the Mythical School (Strauss +1874) and the Tübingen School founded by Baur (+1860). For them the supernatural was impossible because it was both inconceivable and unverifiable.

The *Documentary Period* saw some appreciable progress. It was more scientific and objective in approach. Graff and Wellhausen set out to unravel the various literary sources which they maintained were at the basis of the Pentateuch (1889), and after them came a whole multitude of scholars who, with varying success, subjected the sacred books to a piercing literary and linguistic analysis. However, they so dissected the texts that their method gained little widespread respect. They were heirs to the school which preceded them in that they rejected the supernatural. They were hampered too by the confines of the Germanic approach. Still, their work did produce a number of conclusions which could not be disregarded. Literary criticism, as a method, had made its mark.

A further method which came in towards the end of the

century, the *History of Religion*, might have restored the balance. It got away from the over-rigid Documentary School, but unfortunately veered towards the subjective method of the Philosophical School. There were three or four main schools in this group. The " Pan-Babylonian School " represented by Winckler and Delitzsch explained the characteristics peculiar to the Jewish religion as the result of an interplay between the religious ideas common among all Semitic peoples in the Ancient East. After them, the "Hellenistic School" saw Christianity as the spontaneous growth on Greek soil of an original Jewish myth. Variously they related it to the official cults, mystery religions, Hermetic or Mandaean sects. The "Eschatological School " judged Christianity to be the only child of an otherwise barren Jewish nationalism. Others tried to make a synthesis of all these trends by selecting here and there. In all this there was plenty of science and imagination, but it was spoilt by a lack of common sense and of objectivity. Texts were manipulated and facts were twisted.

In spite of that (or perhaps because of that), the effects were far-reaching, especially among Protestants. The intellectuals threw over all dogma, and salvaged their religious life only by cutting out all pretence to precise historicity. The great names of Harnack and Goguel gave a certain amount of weight to this *Liberal Protestantism*. Christianity for them was no more than the best of natural religions, and Christ no more than the most perfect of men.

Among Catholics the crisis came later, but more suddenly and violently. For the greater part of the nineteenth century the leaders of Catholic thought had held aloof from this movement of new ideas which was changing world opinion. They took up a defensive attitude. Never in all its long history was the Church's biblical exegesis so wilfully conservative and at times even retrogressive. Nothing at all was known of the work done in Germany except that it was extremist. Renan's *Life of Christ*, which wrecked the faith of a whole generation, only made this work more suspect, and it was rejected wholesale in the name of a tradition which was blinded by fixed and narrow ideas. It was for Leo XIII to broaden this narrow outlook. His encyclical *Providentissimus* (1893) encouraged many to get to grips with independent criticism. In 1890 Père

B

Lagrange formed the Ecole Biblique in Jerusalem with the resolute intention of providing an exegesis based on a sound historical method. The Catholic Congress of Fribourg in 1897 was another vigorous step in the same direction.

Unfortunately most people were unprepared for this sudden change of direction. So divergent were the conflicting attitudes between the older schools and the new criticism that tension was inevitable. Lacking the protection afforded by a sound and open-minded theology, many took fright, and retired in confusion to cover their unprotected flank. These came to be known as the *Strict School*. The rest found themselves bracketed together under the name of the *Wide School*. It included those like Pere Lagrange and his followers whose faith was firm and who did not fear the truth, because they knew that it could not do anything but a service. But it included others too, skilful men, but not skilful enough to avoid the rocks of rationalism. They were fascinated by the new criticism, but they had not sufficiently mastered it to see any way out of their dilemma other than to separate Faith from History. They lacked the necessary philosophical and theological training to do otherwise. In 1902 the Abbé Loisy produced his famous "little book", *L'Evangile et l'Eglise*, thinking in all sincerity that he had thereby rescued Catholicism from Harnack's naturalistic exegesis. In fact, by making Christ's Resurrection a matter of faith and not a historical fact, he had agreed with his adversary and effectively compromised revelation.

ALTHOUGH we stand only some fifty years from these events, we can hardly appreciate the confusion caused in the minds of the faithful of those days. The violent contrast outlined above throws some light. Eyes accustomed to narrow and rigid limits had suddenly to focus themselves on the boundless perspectives of the new science, where established fact jostled with arbitrary hypothesis. It was thus that a whole brilliant generation of our young people died of a kind of intellectual indigestion.

This fact cannot be too heavily underlined—it should be taken as a warning. The Church, especially in her more golden periods, has always frowned on those who, through cowardice and lack of confidence, try to stifle the legitimate development of her tradition. In this respect a diehard conservatism is as harmful as an irresponsible liberalism. And there were Catholics in the nineteenth century who compromised the faith precisely by their negative attempts to safeguard it. They must be counted partly responsible for the crisis of Modernism.

Pius X happily and quickly brought matters to a head. In a series of documents of which the most notable was the encyclical *Pascendi* (1907), the Pope denounced Modernism in all its shapes and forms. Perhaps the movement did not have very much shape about it. Therein lay its danger. Its very lack of precision made it all the more difficult to nail down. About the same time, the Pope promulgated a number of disciplinary measures to dispel the prevailing uncertainty which was in itself possibly more dangerous than the ideas which had already been given expression. He separated into two distinct channels what had all previously been called Modernism. At least now the rebels were seen in their true colours. There followed a period of uncertainty. For a while much was hidden under a cloud, but eventually the integrity of the true sons of the Church was made clearer by their submission.

We shall always be indebted to Pius X for making this courageous stand. The shock was a brutal one, but it brought to light many things that had been hidden. The foundations of the Christian faith which had been brought into question were in fact strengthened. However, the peace which should have followed on this spontaneous action of the Church, inspired as it was by the Spirit of God when the mission of his Church was compromised, was not immediately evident. The crisis of Modernism gave rise to much bad feeling. Some, the " Integrists ", relapsed into a state of suspicion and mistrust. The rest were intimidated and simply dispersed. Many abandoned the movement altogether, and preferred to exercise their critical powers in the more specialized fields of textual criticism, philology and archaeology, where there was not so much danger. Others took refuge in duplicity, teaching in private what they would not admit in public. By far the greatest number sought sanctuary in a kind of intellectual dishonesty, quick to employ the critical method when there was nothing much at stake, and equally quick to double back to a safe position when they were not so sure of their ground.

In spite of everything peace did come, helped not a little by the atmosphere after the 1914-1918 war. In the immediate post-war years the slow work of distillation began. Independent criticism began to put its own house in order. Some theses which had once been thought irrefutable were now rejected. Others were corrected and their emphasis modified. Those which had weathered the passage of time were reaffirmed and polished. It was here that biblical theology made its appearance, forced by these well-established facts to find a less abstract approach. It was a gentle penetrative movement that introduced it to the findings of historical evolution. Little by little the anxious concern for apologetics faded and disappeared. People grew more confident, and as time passed Modernism was seen in perspective as something premature. Thanks to the rugged wisdom of the Church, Catholic exegesis again found its feet and developed as it should, along the lines of its own tradition, despite the attempts of Modernism to misdirect it.

The present controversy about the spiritual interpretation of the Bible has shown the inadequacy of much of this exegesis. Even those whose aim it is to popularize the Bible have confessed their inability to satisfy the requirements of the younger elements in the Church to-day. Their plea for the authentic living truth is not being heard. This of course is partly inevitable; it is one of the limitations of scientific specialization to lay emphasis on the technical aspects of a problem at the expense of other aspects. But that is not the whole trouble.

The real trouble is to be found in the field of philosophy and theology. Our exegetes have followed the rules of logic which were developed for and by the western mind. Their procedure in the sciences is conditioned by this western approach. They have not thought it necessary to transpose their thought or to strip it of its idiom. Generally they have presupposed that the minds of all people were moulded, as theirs were, in the idiom of Aristotle, Descartes and Kant. They have applied western standards of philology, psychology and logic to texts which were conceived in a totally different atmosphere. Not enough notice has been taken of a whole world of thought and feeling which is radically different from their own world. What is even more unpardonable, no real attempt has been made to get inside that world to appreciate its pecularities. This is the real barrier which has kept men from that vital truth which the Bible has to give.

To add a few pious paragraphs to a soulless scientific analysis is no real way to solve the problem. Nor does exegesis become "objective" and "impartial" by making faith a mere blue pencil. The whole intellectual approach needs to be re-created from the inside. For a Christian it means that his faith must be the living yeast which will leaven the whole truth.

Such an approach admittedly condemns the greater proportion of books on the Bible produced in the last fifty years. Nearly all of them have taken no account of the one rule essential for sane exegesis, namely that the full import of a given text can be appreciated only when the mentality in which the text was conceived is appreciated. The mentality of the Bible is one of challenge, one which demands commitment, and it is necessary to get inside that mentality. That is precisely what these people have failed to do. They think that if they are to be scientific they must remain detached. By so doing they have failed miserably. They have not provided the vital truth which our people want. They have not even been faithful to the first principles of their own scientific method.

III

BIBLICAL PIETISM

Reaction against scientism; origins and lay character; tendencies and ambiguities.

THIS attempt to thread the maze of nineteenth century biblical history will have left the reader in two minds. He may be put off by all the quarrels and controversies and say "What is the use of trying to read the Bible? Apparently I need to be highly skilled if I am to preserve my faith in it." Or he may wonder "Is there any meaning at all in talking about the inspired message of the Bible? All these scholars, all these learned books, some of them Catholic, and not a mention of the inspired message among them." Swayed by each opinion in turn he may well leave the Bible to the experts and then complain that it is they who have set up a barrier between him and God's Word.

That is the dilemma which faces Christians to-day. The majority have solved it by rejecting the Bible. They do not know the full story of the scandals, apostasies, condemnations and quarrels, but they have got it firmly into their heads that biblical study is the school for heresy. Others, and their number grows daily, are beginning to reject science. They feel that, since it has compromised the Bible, it would be better to leave it alone and go back to the pious simplicity of Christian tradition. This point of view is presented in various ways, but they all boil down to a reaction against science.

THIS is a good sign and the reaction should be welcomed. It shows an awakening interest in our young people, and promises a confident return to God's Word.

It is difficult to explain the reasons for this return, because they are so complex. In origin they are religious, a result of the new spiritual environment which has grown out of the ruins of humanism. During the years between the wars, and perhaps even before, the world of the specialist, the rationalist and the individualist had begun to fall to pieces because of its own inherent weaknesses. The new outlook has its own gods admittedly, but the idol is no longer the individual. More insistence is being put on social values. The appreciation of real values is bringing the world of ideas out of the clouds and getting it more in line with the world of action. The outlook is changing, and in many ways it has an affinity with the mentality of Christian society before the sixteenth century and especially with the biblical world which gave that society its impetus.

Although it is a subconscious development, it is affecting the movement which is driving our Christian leaders back to the sources of faith. It is all the more remarkable in that it is helping to reunite (albeit slowly) those Churches which split up at the Reformation. Spurred on by their reading of the Bible, sincere Protestants are beginning to realize the value of the unity and liturgy of the true Church. The ecclesiastical awakening in Sweden, the Cluny community, writers like

Cullman and de Dietrich, all these are furthering the findings of K. Barth and Kierkegaard. They are realizing that the Bible cannot live or give life unless it is seen in its proper context, the Church. At one end of the scale Protestants are finding through the Bible a tradition; at the other end Catholics are being led back to the Bible through the liturgy.

The spiritual appetite of both has become a little jaded by the test-tube fare (not always pure fare) which has been served up to them ever since the sixteenth century. Now they are eager to find a diet which is nourishing and honest. Instinctively they look to the traditional spirituality of the Church.

Catholic and Protestant alike have the same destination in mind, although they take different routes. Steeped in his Bible, the Protestant discovers that his efforts to find the Spirit of God are baulked by the barriers of technical analysis and private interpretation. He seeks to make the Bible his prayer and is led unwittingly to the prayer of the Church. His movement was originally biblical but has now become liturgical. The Catholic on the other hand starts off with the liturgy. He finds his prayer right at the heart of the Church, in the Missal. The liturgy gives him an appetite for the whole Bible of which the Missal gives him only samples. Furthermore he realizes that if he is to live the liturgy he must do more than merely follow his Missal. The strange atmosphere which it exhales is altogether different from what he has been used to. If he is to enjoy it in all its richness he must sooner or later go to the Bible. In this way the various movements, liturgical, biblical, patristic and ecumenical, all come to the same thing in the end—a return to Christianity at its strongest and most vital.

THIS movement back to the Bible is not peculiar to any one country, although it would seem that Bible-conscious Germany, the homeland of community, must be given credit for initiating it. From the beginning the Bible and the liturgy have always been linked closely together there. One of their chief Catholic periodicals was called *Bibel und Liturgie*. In France there is no specially organized movement, but everywhere the beginnings of such a movement are present in the different existing groups. It is noteworthy that the movement is getting all its impetus from the laity. The priests remember scarcely anything of their Scriptural course in the seminary except that it was boring, technical, and had an apologetic purpose about it. They too feel that Christianity needs a new lease of life and they are demanding a new approach. But something far more fundamental is needed—a complete reorganization of traditional teaching.

We are seeing therefore a surprising return to the Bible by the laity. As yet, only a small group is involved, and they are chiefly literary men (in France anyway). Poets like Péguy and Claudel, writers like Denys Gorce and Jacques Maritain, to name only the best known, have all found appreciative audiences when they have advocated a return to the Bible. The success of the recent books of Daniel Rops shows that they are fulfilling a real need.

Some wide-awake theologians have been impressed by the movement. They have accepted its challenge and are giving it the benefit of their direction. Many of the periodicals produced by the religious orders keep their readers in touch with the movement by means of articles on biblical interpretation. A plan is beginning to unfold; it needs an objective but its scope is clear. As yet no general strategy has been worked out: it is every man for himself, and it is not surprising to find that these views and methods are sometimes in opposition. But at least they have a common aim.

FIRST and foremost, there is an ardent desire to discover the living meaning of the Bible. This is based on a rediscovery of the divine origin of the Bible. If the Bible comes from God then it is for all men. And if every Christian should read the Bible, then it is *ipso facto* accessible to all.

Such a supposition involves a reaction against everything which in recent years has clouded the divine sense of Scripture. Nearly everybody agrees in putting the blame on the purely scientific treatment of the text, of which even Catholics have been guilty. In his *Introducion to the Book of Ruth* (1938) Paul Claudel drew up a formidable charge against such exegesis. Tired of the "thin milk" it had served him, he called for a return to the spiritual interpretation which he believed was to be found in the Fathers. Others put the blame on the barrenness of science, but with less violence. They do not condemn science outright—they even give it a passing salute —but they prefer to read the Bible without its help. They keep faith and science in strictly watertight compartments. Some others have made laudable attempts to use scientific findings, but they do not understand the mysteries of science and they apply it timidly and uneasily, not sufficient masters of their subject to take the full benefit of the scientific technique.

There is a third tendency and this has found favour among intellectuals. They say that if science has been found wanting, and with it the literal interpretation in its scientific sense, then we must go back to early tradition and wrest the secret of spiritual interpretation from the Fathers. Small monographs, sometimes hastily produced and not really very penetrating, have been written on some of the Fathers. Translations of their works have been produced which underline the world of difference between their rich spiritual interpretation and the dry-as-dust scientific efforts.

To sum up, there is an insistence on the religious interpretation, a mistrust of science, and a desire to get back to the Fathers with their supremacy of the spiritual sense over the literal. These are the three inter-connected pivots on which the whole of the new biblical revival turns.

NOT everything in this programme is of equal value. There are veiled differences of opinion and clouded ambiguities, but at least the starting point is clear. Anything which prevents a Christian from reaching the living waters of God's Word in the Bible is to be heavily censured. In the last analysis the only thing that matters is the divine meaning enshrined there, its message of life in God and its revelation of the Father's truth and love. From this point of view the reaction against the biblical science of the last century is largely justified. Too often exegetes, Catholic ones included, have allowed themselves to be so fascinated by the sheen on the skin that they have forgotten to taste the divine fruit itself. They have shut themselves up behind their technical wall and have neglected their plain duty to the people they should have been trying to reach. They were responsible for divorcing science from life when they divided the Bible into two compartments: a scientific reading for the clever ones, a devotional reading for the rest.

All the same, the grave shortcomings of scientific exegesis do not justify a swing to the other extreme. The over-insistence on the human aspect of the Bible in the past does not mean that this aspect can now be neglected. The scientific method has a great contribution to make, and it cannot be ignored simply because of its inevitable faults. Every human gain has its place in Christianity, and the nineteenth century has earned its place in the hall of fame by bringing to our notice two very important things—Time and Evolution. If the Church should ever disregard that, she would be failing in her mission to sanctify men as they are.

We must be particularly careful to watch out for religious sentimentality. Writers on the Bible sometimes give the impression that there is no need to worry about anything else as long as piety is served. The real meaning of the text is not important: a sense is true if it fosters devotion. Such sentimentality is purely subjective and has no roots. It certainly does not come from the Fathers, even though the authors may imagine that it does. The Fathers were ever deeply aware of the necessary connection between love and truth. It is disconcerting to see such irresponsible articles coming from the pen of serious writers. "Open the Bible anywhere," they say, "and there you will find a text where God speaks direct to your soul." Given this sort of attitude, there is no need for the Church, dogma or sacraments. On these terms, we are back where we started in the sixteenth century, with the Bible opposed to the Church.

This anti-scientific trend in an important section of the biblical world is dangerous. It might very easily resolve itself into that anti-intellectual pietism of the Renaissance period, which neglected dogma, historical fact, and the whole sacramental aspect of a teaching and mediating Church, and left nothing in its place save a vague religious sentimentality. The natural reaction against modern materialism is giving this anti-intellectual trend a certain amount of popularity in our own days. We must be careful. The man who divorces his religious life from all contact with truth is asking for trouble. Similarly if the return to the Fathers is seen as an escape into the past it must be qualified. The past is over and done with, and means nothing unless it is transposed into a modern key. The abuse of texts by scholars and the contradicting interpretations made by the Fathers call for special care, particularly when these are quoted to further a purely subjective method based on a false understanding of inspiration. Pious imaginings and ingenious private interpretations should not be canonized into principles of exegesis.

To sum up then, the whole problem of the Bible is contained in the one question: "Who should read the Bible?" Most people will say "Nobody". The scholar will say "Only specialists". The enthusiast will say "Everyone". Their answers imply that they have already answered another set of questions: "Who is the author of the Bible?" "How is it inspired?" "What is its purpose?" "How is it to be understood?" The expert will be more concerned with the inspired writer. He knows that the Bible was written in a certain idiom which needs a specialist to understand it. The pietist on the other hand will concern himself only with the God who inspired the writer. He concludes that there must be a divine and eternal message which is directly intelligible. The one treats the Bible as a record of the past which may still have its usefulness. The other treats it as a personal and intimate communication from God, indispensable and valid for all time. Which of the two is right? Only the Church can give us the answer, in the constant and unchanging principles of her tradition.

IV

THE BIBLE AND TRADITION

Sources of biblical tradition; patristic methods; perennial themes of traditional interpretation.

FIRST of all we must determine precisely where some indication of what the Church thinks about the Bible may be found. The Conciliar decrees and the encyclicals give us some idea of the Church's official teaching on the matter, but we will get a deeper insight into her mind if we examine the actual use she makes of the Bible. It is her textbook and her prayer book, as the Fathers and the liturgy bear witness.

The twofold use of the Bible

FOR the sake of clarity we must here make an important distinction. The Church uses the Bible in two ways, for a *doctrinal* purpose and for a *pastoral* purpose. In practice these two are often combined, but we must bear the distinction in mind; the two uses are absolutely distinct.

In the former case, the Church consults the Bible *ex professo* as the divine source of all her thought and life, in order to teach her children and bring them to God. In the other case, she applies what she has thus learned to all branches of her redemptive work, even when they have no direct connection with the Bible. Here she uses the inspired words to express not the divine message itself but her own thought. The liturgy uses the language of the Bible in this way, for its own end. The Fathers also, in their homilies and controversies, frequently clothe their own thought in biblical language. But they use this simply as a consecrated language, a Christian way of putting things, and to regard it as biblical interpretation would be to misunderstand them. If we find it difficult to see how they could take this liberty, the fault is ours: we are not so much in our element with the Bible as they were. They were so much at home that they could only express themselves happily in biblical phrases, and this was true even when they were not specifically dealing with the Bible. The lover talks in and out of season in the accents of his beloved. The Fathers, and the Church in her liturgy, do the same.

It will be enough here to give one small illustration of this. When St. Benedict (in the Rule) wanted to stir up the enthusiasm of a novice, he urged him to ponder the text *Ad quid venisti?* . . . " My friend, what have you come here to do? " Everybody knows that Christ used these words to reproach Judas. One can hardly suppose that St. Benedict looked upon every novice of his as another Judas. It is simply that he has used Christ's words as an invitation to repentance.

This example was chosen deliberately to illustrate the fact that the pastoral method does not boggle at using the text in a sense which is absurd from the point of view of exegesis. It is not usually so. More often a wide use is made of the Bible by the Fathers precisely because it is an extension of the primary meaning. After all, the Church has nothing to say which does not in some way stem from the Bible, and, since her own thought is only a blossoming of God's thought in the Bible, it is altogether natural that she should use its words to express herself.

What are usually called the "accommodated sense" and the "allegorical sense" are not strictly speaking biblical senses at all. They are familiarities, pleasantries. They can be regarded as part of that affectionate understanding that exists among members of a family. Psychologically they are justified: they are part of the intimate feeling of being "in" on a secret. We who do not know the secret must be careful not to mistake "what seems" for "what is". Nor have we the right to use these pleasantries until we are ourselves familiars of that circle.

Literal and Spiritual Schools of Interpretation

BEARING in mind the important distinction between the doctrinal and pastoral use of the Bible, we can now proceed to a further point. We must be careful to avoid arbitrary generalizations when we talk of patristic exegesis. Even apart from the pastoral use, there is still plenty of variation in strict exegesis among the Fathers. It is worth remembering that with the exception of a few verses there is no unanimity to be found among them. Deeply aware that God has hidden his richest thoughts in the Bible, they knew that the man who would quarry there must be prepared for constant hard work and expect little reward.

In the main there were two methods of approach. In the third and fourth centuries, the disciples of Clement of Alexandria came to the Bible by way of symbolism after the manner of the commentators on the pagan poets. The school of Antioch aimed at a more positive exegesis and insisted on the immediate meaning of the text. In the West the great Doctors of the Church (St. Augustine for example) had the same deep concern for the immediate sense, and proceeded only along the lines of the well established principles of Christian interpretation. But where a man like St. Augustine was obviously more attracted by the doctrinal content, others like St. Jerome showed that they were only really at home with textual criticism.

These two main trends or schools continued down through the Middle Ages and were identified by their allegiance to St. Augustine or St. Jerome. They represent two legitimate and indispensable aspects of exegesis, and it would be wrong to think of them as opposed or to separate them rigidly into literal and spiritual schools. Whether they followed Alexandria and Augustine or Antioch and Jerome, the patristic writers used both methods of approach. Only in general can one school be called doctrinal and the other literal or textual.

It is impossible therefore to pretend that the opinion of the Fathers was unanimously in favour of either method. What we must look for in their commentaries is a frame of mind rather than an opinion. What is common to them all and obvious from their writings is their same love for Scripture and their same basic outlook. When they deal with the Bible, they all have certain themes in common.

The Bible, the only source of faith in the Church

A COMPREHENSIVE study of the Scriptural thought of the Fathers has not yet been made. It would involve a complete study of their theology, which alone may explain why this immense labour has not yet been undertaken. But if that study ever is made, we may be surprised to discover how very closely the Bible was knit into the structure of Christian life. These people were not afraid to go all the way; the Bible for them was the book of Christian doctrine and the only guide to true living. As St. Athanasius put it, "All Sacred Scripture is the mistress of virtue and true belief." Without the Bible there could be no teaching, no life. In fact all Christian literature should either defend or comment on Sacred Scripture.

It would be a mistake for us to let their high esteem for the Bible lead us to rash judgment. The Fathers were lavish with their praise, but it was never their intention to deify the Book itself, nor would they have thought that anyone would level such a charge against them. Their confidence in the Bible was identified with their faith in the Church. When they thought of the Bible it was always in its proper context, the Church. It does not quite reflect their thought to say that they subordinated the Bible to the Church's tradition. The affinity between the Bible and the Church in their minds was much more subtle than that. The Bible that they esteemed so highly as the only true measure of faith and life was not a dead thing; it was the living Bible, owing its vitality to the tradition of the Church. In other words it was the Spirit of the Church which informed the letter of the Bible. Without that informing mind the letter was dead and brought death. The criterion of faith therefore was never the bare text of the Bible, but the Spirit living in the mind of the Church.

If there is any doubt that this was their true opinion, one has only to study their treatment of those heretics who from the second century attacked the traditional faith in the name of the written letter. St. Irenaeus (against the Gnostics) and St. Augustine (against the Donatists) were fierce in their condemnation of this sacrilegious outrage, this attempt to set God against himself. If the Church has anything at all to give her children it is the flesh and teaching of the incarnate Word of God, and it is only in the Church that they will be found. A quotation from St. Clement of Alexandria (third century) makes this point clear:

It is sheer pride that makes people deliberately evade the divine meaning of the inspired words by clever argument. To set up human teaching against divine tradition is to fall into heresy. (*Stromata,* VII, ch. 16.)

Christ the Synthesis of the two Testaments

S T. C L E M E N T develops this in another passage. He identifies the Bible and tradition and formulates another principle of patristic exegesis:

Once a man has turned against the tradition of the Church, and has let himself be deceived by the human opinions of the heretics, he has broken his loyalty to the Lord and has ceased to be a man of God. But when he leaves his error, to listen to the voice of Scripture and to open his mind to the Truth, he is no longer a mere man. He has in some way become God. The Lord alone is the source of all doctrine. It is he who leads us to all knowledge, first and last, from the Prophets down to the Gospels and the Apostles. (*Ibid.*)

This attitude, which is common to all the Fathers, can be summed up by saying that Scripture is no more and no less than Christ expressed in words. Witness the well-known saying of St. Jerome: "Not to know the Scriptures is not to know Christ." That is a fair example of the rich and vibrant thought that is to be found on almost every page of the Fathers.

Their whole attitude is Christological. It is their foundation and common starting point. They may develop that thought along their own different lines, but it is their central theme that the Old Testament is the starting point of the New, and the New Testament is the realization of the Old. The two Testaments are complementary. There is no discord between them but a deep harmony, no superiority but a mutual subordination to Christ. In this way Scripture throws light on Scripture: it is a unified and organic whole. Its different parts are not equivalents; each has its own significance, but the one completes the other, and together they form the gradual expression of that unique revelation which is the Word incarnate.

The "Somatic" and "Pneumatic" Points of View

THIS correlation between the two parts of the Bible was appreciated right from the beginning of Christianity. St. Paul, St. John and even the Synoptics saw it as the expression and proof of Christian truth. So it was that the Fathers based their distinction between the "somatic" and the "pneumatic"[1] interpretation of Scripture on Christ himself. For them it was a distinction of the utmost importance. Since Scripture shows its fullest meaning only in Christ, it is obvious that before the coming of Christ Scripture was capable only of an immediate and less pregnant interpretation (somatic); its rôle was to provide an introduction and support for the fuller meaning which would follow later (pneumatic). St. Jerome writes:

> There is a brilliant sheen on the surface of what we read in the sacred Books, but the full sweetness lies beneath. You must break the shell before you can taste the nut. (Ep. 58.)

From the Greek *soma*, body, and *pneuma*, spirit.

Theodore of Mopsuestia, of the same so-called literal school, wrote similarly:

> Much of what happened in the Old Testament was arranged by God in a way that would not only help those who experienced it, but also point to what was to happen later, and at the same time make it clear that the later event excelled the former. In this divine plan, the earlier reality must be seen as a kind of type of the later. It is not simply that the earlier event and the later event played similar rôles in their times. The earlier event actually proclaims its own subordination to the later. (Beginning of *Comm. in Jonam*.)

This text is particularly valuable because it introduces us to another of those basic themes common to the Fathers, namely that the Christian import of the Scriptures will be fully appreciated only by a searching examination of the literal sense. If modern exegetes have so rarely perceived that, it is because they mistake the homiletic language of the Fathers for spiritual exegesis. St. Augustine has suffered from such misinterpretation, yet it was he who wrote:

> It is a mistake to give the Scriptures a meaning different from the one intended by the writers, even when such an interpretation serves to foster charity and so stays in the realm of truth. . . . It is like someone wandering off the path, and reaching by a cross-country route the place to which the path would have taken him. He should be corrected and shown that it is better not to leave the path at all, for fear that this should become a habit and eventually lead him astray. (*De Doctrina Christiana*, I, ch. 35.)

And later on:

> To understand the divine oracles properly, there must be a constant effort to reach the mind of the author. It is through him that the Holy Spirit has spoken. (*Ibid.*, III, ch. 27.)

C

St. Athanasius wrote similarly:

Here, as in all passages of Scripture, we must observe the occasion of the Apostle's utterance, and note carefully and accurately the person and the subject which were the cause of his writing. Ignorance or error concerning these points can lead us to misconceive the meaning of the author. (*Contra Arianos*, I, 54.)

The Bible and Time

THIS does not mean that the Fathers are the forerunners of the modern historical method. The scientific discoveries of the nineteenth century, the importance of the Time-factor and the concept of Evolution all brought about a profound revolution of thought, and as a result both psychology and philosophy have been deeply affected. But the Christian has nothing to fear from this revolution. Revelation cannot be added to, but that does not mean that it is dead. It lives and adapts itself to the changing needs of those to whom it must bring salvation. To do this it develops its inherent riches under the constant action of external forces. All human truth is of its nature Christian. Revealed truth transcends human truth but it is built on it and in fact welds both together in man. Every advance in human understanding and science does a service to the Church in so far as it prompts the Church to be more aware of the latent aspects of her unchanging revelation. Christian dogma does not change, and yet it develops and grows in stature more perfectly than any mere human thought.

There is then nothing incongruous in admitting that present day exegetes are better equipped than the Fathers were; but such an admission does not imply that the traditional conception of the Bible must go by the board. If we had to choose between the historical method and the patristic method as between two incompatibles, we should undoubtedly reject science and go back several hundred years. Happily no such choice has to be made: these two methods are two successive ways of applying the same principles under the guidance of the

same Spirit.   The seed of the entire historical method is already
present in St. Augustine:

> Anything that history has to teach us about past events
> can only lead us to a better understanding of the sacred
> Books, even though apart from the Church such knowledge
> would be mere erudition.   (*De Doctrina Christiana*, II,
> ch. 28.)

The Modernity of the Fathers

T H E Fathers did not have the advantage of modern scientific
research, nor did they need it.   It is not surprising then that they
had no realization of the far-reaching consequences of this
principle of St. Augustine.   All the same, we should do them
an injustice if we thought that they were completely devoid of
a sense of evolution.   Their minds were steeped in the biblical
mentality; in fact they were a natural continuation of it, and
this more than made up for any deficiency in technique.   We
have lost this awareness of historical continuity, not so much
because of the distance that separates us from them but because
of the general intellectual upheaval.   Our reason-dominated
culture lost touch with biblical culture.   It has however invented
the science which to some extent will help us to rediscover it.
In restoring to us a sense of evolution, it is making good the
break for which it was responsible.

The Church therefore has the right and duty to integrate all
the legitimate conquests of the human mind into her tradition.
The encyclical *Divino Afflante Spiritu* has done for the Bible
what Pius X's Decree did for the Eucharist.   There Pius XII
has given an assurance that places are prepared for such conquests.   He appraises the progress of science at its real value
and fearlessly invites it to salvage, along traditional lines, those
riches which were thrown over by Modernism.   He emphasizes
that tradition is not just another method, but a faith and a
Spirit.   Biblical exegesis will inevitably be transformed by contact with technical advances, but it has nothing to fear if it is
inspired by such a faith and such a Spirit.

This open-mindednes is at the very heart of our tradition, as can be seen from the following quotation from St. Augustine. It sums up the encyclical:

> The God-fearing man searches the Scriptures carefully to discover God's will. He must be devout and humble enough to avoid all desire for controversy; he must have a knowledge of languages so that he will not be held up by strange words and expressions; he must be equipped with the necessary knowledge of the nature and properties of the things that he intends to use for comparison; and finally he must have before him a good critical text. Only then will he be ready to discuss and expound the difficult passages of the Scriptures. (*De Doctrina Christiana*, III, ch. 1.)

In this way the constant tradition of the Church invites everyone to eat at this table. All it asks in return is a pledge to study the Bible with care, and to put what is learned into practice.

> To get the full flavour of a herb, it must be pressed between the fingers. It is the same with the Scriptures. The more familiar they become, the more they reveal their hidden treasures and yield their indescribable riches. (St. John Chrysostom, *Homil. 21 in Genesim.*)

CHAPTER II

THE BOOK

I N his *Genie du Christianisme,* Chateaubriand has a wonderful description of the disappointed reader who takes up the Bible for the first time. We see him turning over the pages, rather disconcerted by the variety of books it includes. Here and there he comes on a passage that he remembers from his Bible History, but for the most part he finds this collection incomprehensible. He discovers the existence of the Prophets and of the Sapiental Books for the first time. But what strikes him as strangest of all is to find the " Gospel " and the Pauline Epistles in this volume. He knew them from his Missal, but he is surprised, as are many Catholics, to find that the Bible is not all Old Testament.

Before we approach the Bible itself, then, we need to have some idea of its make-up and of the way it has come down to us.

I

THE BOOKS OF THE BIBLE

Meaning of the word " Bible"; spread of the Book; its two main parts; proto- and deutero-canonical books of the Old Testament; the three Jewish collections; division of the New Testament; apocryphal works.

T H E word " Bible " is the Greek word for " the Book ". The Jews of Greek origin first used it to denote their sacred writings. The Church used it to include all those early Christian writings which she recognized as inspired. Thus the word " Bible " was itself an expression of faith: all these various writings constituted *the* Book.

From a material point of view alone, no other book has enjoyed such fame. Right from the very beginning of Christianity it was copied and translated into every tongue. Where the manuscripts of the great classics can be numbered only in hundreds, the existing manuscripts of the Bible runs into tens of thousands. These are in Hebrew, Greek, Latin, Syriac, Arabic, Armenian, Georgic, Slavonic, Gothic, Coptic, and later in every dialect of the Middle Ages: Low German, Flemish, Saxon, Provençal, Venetian, Tuscan and Catalan. Even now, in the whole mass of printed literature, the Bible has the best sales in every language. This alone justifies its claim to be *the* Book, the witness even in this godless century of the sovereignty of God's Word.

It falls naturally into two main parts, the Old Testament and the New Testament. The word "Testament" is rather ambiguous. It is the translation of a Greek word which can mean not only a last will and testament, but also a covenant. Even for the Greek-speaking Jews it had a complex religious connotation: it meant the divine plan whereby God bound himself to man and made him heir to his estate. Christianity recognizes two manifestations of this plan: the restricted covenant with the people of Israel under Moses, and the new and unrestricted covenant with all mankind under Christ. Our division of the Bible is in accord with these two stages. The Old Testament includes all those books written before the coming of Christ recognized by the Jews as divinely inspired. The New Testament comprises the writings of the chief disciples of Christ which the Church similarly guarantees to be inspired.

THE Old Testament then is the collection of the holy books of Jewish origin. The Catholic Church gives the number as 45, the Protestant Churches as 38. The difference is to be accounted for by the fact that the Jews of the time of Christ were themselves not of one mind over the number. The Jews in Palestine accepted only the 38 books which had been handed down in Hebrew. The Greek-speaking Jews, especially those at Alexandria, added a further seven which had been preserved only in Greek. The Church, which grew up in the hellenistic Jewish communities, accepted the Greek Bible from them. In their anxiety to return to the pristine purity Protestants rejected as "apocryphal" whatever was not in the original Hebrew, namely *Tobit, Judith, Wisdom, Ecclesiasticus, Baruch, 1* and *2 Maccabees* and those portions of *Esther* preserved only in Greek. Catholics usually call these books deutero-canonical, to distinguish them from the proto-canonical books and to indicate that there was some delay about their being received into the Canon of Scripture. The Council of Trent has defined that all are equally inspired.

The Jews divided their Bible into three main sections: the Law, the Prophets and the Writings. We find a mention of this division already in the New Testament (Lk. 24:27, 44); and even 130 years before Christ in the Greek prologue to Ecclesiasticus. This division corresponds more or less to the successive formation of the three main collections.

The *first collection* is called the *Torah* or Law, since it consists mainly of Jewish legislation, although it is set in a historical frame. It is all one work but comprises five books (hence its Greek name *Pentateuch*). *Genesis* is the traditional Israelite account of the origins of the human race (ch. 1-11) and of the Israelite nation under Abraham, Isaac, Jacob and Joseph. *Exodus* tells of the work of Moses, and consequently emphasizes legislation. *Leviticus* is almost exclusively a code of ritual, set in the historical frame of the wanderings of the Israelites in the desert. *Numbers* continues the story of their journey to the promised land and includes further legislation. *Deuteronomy* takes up the story on the eve of their entry into Canaan and is presented as the spiritual testament of Moses. The Lawgiver's final instructions are paraphrased in a burning moral discourse. These are the books of the *Torah.*

The *second collection* has less unity and is known as "the Prophets". One might expect it to be composed of the writings of the Prophets, and indeed it is; but it has a long preface in the *Historical Books.* These are of an entirely different character, although it was in the period covered by these books (from the entry into Canaan to the Exile) that prophetic activity was most marked. Moreover they probably emanated from the literary circles connected with the prophetic movement. The first of these books, *Joshua,* and to some extent also the second, *Judges,* are a continuation of the Pentateuch in both subject matter and literary make-up. Consequently they are sometimes grouped together with the Pentateuch under the name of the

Heptateuch. Nevertheless they are purely historical, telling the story of the conquest and its confused aftermath. In the books of *Samuel* (two books now, originally only one) we see the beginnings of the Israelite monarchy in the stories of Saul and David. The two books of *Kings* similarly form one work and continue the story from Solomon up to the Exile. That is the first part of "The Prophets". The second part contains the four books of the Prophets proper: Isaiah, Jeremiah, Ezekiel and one book comprising the twelve "minor" Prophets, so called because of their brevity.

The *third collection* is even less homogeneous than the second. Its only claim to unity lies in its origin: it did not receive its final form until after the Exile. Some of the books are historical in character *Chronicles* (or *Paralipomenon*) forms one work with *Nehemiah-Ezra,* and gives a résumé of the whole of the past from the creation onwards, to dwell at greater length on the stages of the Restoration after the Exile. The book of *Ruth* (which in our Bible comes before 1 Sam. because it gives the genealogy of David), and the books of *Tobit, Judith* and *Esther* all deal with particular periods of history. *1 Maccabees* is a very important book, being the account of the great national epic of the second century B.C. In this case the second volume (*2 Maccabees*) is a distinct work. It is a précis written in Greek of a much bigger work now lost, and sets out to edify by emphasizing the more moving episodes in the national struggle. The *Sapiental* books form another unit in this third group, and are so called because they are a collection of moral maxims. The oldest is *Proverbs*, which must be dated basically before the Exile. *Job* and *Ecclesiastes* belong approximately to the third century B.C. *Ecclesiasticus*, which comes to us in the Greek rendering of the author's grandson, belongs to the beginning of the second century, just before the time of the Maccabees. *Wisdom* was written in Greek shortly before the birth of Christ.

The *Psalms* belong to this Sapiental group by reason of their content and their form. They acquired a character of their own, however, from their liturgical use in the Temple. This was also true of *Baruch, Lamentations* (attributed to Jeremiah) and the *Song of Songs*. The Apocalypse of *Daniel* is the one remaining book which has not yet been assigned a place.

Catholic Bibles put it among the Prophets, but since its literary make-up is something quite distinct the Jews preferred to place it among the Writings.

Since the thirteenth century Catholics have substituted for this triple Jewish division one of their own devising which is based on the contents of the books. Under the first group, called "historical", are included the *Pentateuch*, *Joshua*, *Judges*, *Ruth*, *Samuel* and *Kings*, *Chronicles*, *Nehemiah-Ezra*, *Tobit*, *Judith* and *1* and *2 Maccabees*. In a second group, called "didactic", come the *Sapiental* books, *Psalms* and the *Song of Songs*. The third group, called "prophetical", comprises the writings of the *Prophets* and includes also the book of *Daniel*. The logic of this division is not altogether evident. It puts the legal writings and works of edification like *Tobit*, *Judith* and *Esther* all together among the historical books; it makes the *Song of Songs* a didactic book; and it puts *Daniel* among the Prophets, where he does not belong. It would seem better to stand by the Jewish method, which takes more account of the actual stages in the formation of the collections.

IT IS much easier to make an inventory of the books of the New Testament. There are the four historical narratives of the life of Christ, called *Gospels*; an account of the early years of the Church in the *Acts of the Apostles*; the 14 *Epistles of St. Paul*; the seven *Catholic Epistles*, so called because many of them were addressed to several communities (two of *St. Peter*, one of *James*, one of *Jude*, and three of *St. John*); and lastly the *Apocalypse* (Revelation). Altogether there are 27 works, some very short, none very long.

The classification of these 27 books is made difficult by reason of their variety. Usually they are divided into historical books (the four *Gospels* and the *Acts*), didactic books (*St. Paul* and the *Catholic Epistles*), and a prophetical book (the *Apocalypse*). Here again the distinction is artificial. A writing as doctrinal as the Fourth Gospel is put under the same heading as the other three; the works of a single author are divided among the three sections; and the *Apocalypse* is given a label which gives no truer idea of its content than the one put on the book of Daniel.

A more pertinent division would be one which first grouped

together the *Synoptic Gospels*, so called because of the similarity of their arrangement; then there would be a *Pauline* group, including the Acts of the Apostles (St. Paul is the central figure even though the book was written by Luke) and the 14 Epistles attributed to St. Paul; thirdly there would be a *Johannine* group including the writings attributed to the beloved disciple: his Gospel, his three Epistles and the Apocalypse; and finally a fourth section would comprise the *Catholic Epistles*. This division preserves individual characteristics and gives a better picture of the main stages in the formation of the New Testament.

T A K E N all round it is easy to see that the Bible is made up of a variety of books, representing every type of literary form and every stage of literary development. Its unity comes from the fact that it is the expression of one religious stream and of one human culture. All these writings, New Testament included, are part of Jewish literature, in fact its main part.

Some books, written at the end of the Old Testament period and at the beginning of the New, have not survived. Others have survived but they were never recognized as inspired. These are known by Catholics as the *apocryphal* books, by Protestants as *pseudo-epigraphical*. Those akin to the Old Testament date from the centuries about the beginning of the Christian era, and are useful guides to the religious thought of the time of Christ and the Apostles. Some of them are noteworthy, like the Apocalypse of *Henoch* and the *Psalms of Solomon*. Others are heavy and turgid. The New Testament apocrypha are generally much later in origin. They have no historical value and are often heretical.

It is clear then that a book was accepted as part of the Bible not simply because it belonged to the Jewish or Christian literary tradition, but because it was seen by the Jews, and later by the Church, to have a religious value. Here we get very close to the problems which concern the Canon of Scripture and the nature of inspiration. We must consider them in their proper place.

II

THE LANGUAGES OF THE BIBLE

*Original texts and translations; the three biblical languages;
the mentality of Semitic languages; their pecularities;
relation between Hebrew and Aramaic; biblical Greek and
the koine.*

HAVING made that rapid survey of the contents of the Bible,
we must now consider the condition in which these books
have come down to us. Can we trust these age-old documents
if we cannot be sure that their accuracy has been preserved?
The Council of Trent has declared that only the original text,
as it came from the author, is inspired. It is not only a concern
for material truth then, but concern for his faith that makes
the Christian examine carefully even these lowly aspects of the
Bible.

Omnis traductor traditor, runs the proverb. It is hard enough
for a translator to preserve the exact shades of meaning of his
original. It is next to impossible to catch its colour and movement. This is true of modern languages where the mental
formation is similar to our own; it is even truer of languages
which have been dead for two thousand years. The very
make-up of the Hebrew language is different from our own, to
say nothing of the Hebrew mentality. There is no real substitute for reading a work in the language in which it was
created.

Unfortunately the people who can read the Bible in the
original are few and far between. It would be a great help,
for the understanding of the New Testament at least, if our
children were brought up on the biblical classics instead of on
the pagan classics. The Bible after all is their heritage. We
are not saying that Homer and Sophocles are not worth bother-
ing about: they have an eternal human value. But is it not
possible to offset the anguished awaiting and enormous pride
of the Greco-Roman civilization with the assurance of St. Paul
and the serenity of St. John? The fact that they are careless
in their use of the optative does not disqualify them from being
two of the greatest minds this world has ever known. This is

true on a purely human level, quite apart from their divine inspiration. How can an education pretend to be Christian when it expounds the pagan mythologies and fails even to mention, except in the stuffy atmosphere of the Christian Doctrine class, the masterpieces of our heritage?

This is in fact the only justification for the effort involved in learning Greek. School-children will never learn it well enough to get the full flavour of Homer, but they could easily become proficient enough to read the New Testament in the original. Hebrew is another thing altogether, but at least an acquaintance with it would help the really earnest reader of the Bible to understand something of its mentality and peculiarities.

THERE are three languages in the Bible: Hebrew, Aramaic and Greek. Most of the Old Testament is in Hebrew. There are only a few chapters in Aramaic: *Ezra* 4:8-6:18; 7:12-26; *Daniel* 2:4b-7:28; *Jeremiah* 10:11; and *Genesis* 31:47. But Aramaic was probably the original language of many texts which we now have only in a Greek translation, the book of *Tobit* for example and *St. Matthew*'s Gospel, and perhaps the Fourth Gospel too. It was also Christ's own language and that of the early Christians. Some of the books in the Old Testament were written in Greek: *Wisdom* and *2 Maccabees*. The whole of the New Testament was written in Greek, with the probable exception of *St. Matthew*. It is also the language in which we now have many books whose originals are lost: *Judith, Ecclesiasticus, 1 Maccabees* (all probably originally in Hebrew: part of the Hebrew Ecclesiasticus was discovered some years ago), *Tobit* and *Matthew* (originally in Aramaic). These "translations" however seem to have been made with some freedom.

Hebrew and Aramaic are related Semitic languages. It is a feature of Semitic languages that they preserve a close affinity to their parent stock. This is not the case with Indo-European languages. Sanscrit, Greek and Latin differ profoundly from their modern derivatives. English and Russian are less obviously related than are modern Arabic and ancient Hebrew.

All the Semitic languages are consistent in the importance they give to consonants in the make-up of words. Nearly all words (nouns and verbs) are basically three consonants. Although there is a wealth of inflection (Hebrew, for instance, has seven modalities to express the action of the verb), the syntax is extremely simple. There is hardly any machinery for making a clause subordinate; there is a dearth of adjectives; there is no range of tenses for the verb. Where we think of an action as past, present or future, the Semite can only regard it as either complete (" perfect ") or incomplete (" imperfect ").

THESE peculiarities of the language are the expressions of a mentality and outlook completely different from our own. Everyone will grant that Greek is a much richer language, but that does not justify some exegetes in blaming the poverty of Hebrew for their own lack of precision. It is materially true to say that a Hebrew mind does not easily lend itself to analysis and abstraction; but this is merely a negative statement, and it does not present the full vigour of the Semitic genius. A true biblical scholar would not compare Isaiah with Plato, because he knows that they represent two worlds so utterly different in outlook that they cannot be compared. It is not possible to summarize the content of these two worlds without seeming to generalize. To get a true picture we would have to go to far greater lengths than are possible here. We can only ask the reader to make the necessary allowances as he goes along.

In general the Greek mentality (it is ours too) is primarily concerned with the world of ideas, where the mind is sovereign. Its method is to reach out perceptively and then to abstract and analyse with great clarity. In its nature it is speculative but it can easily become utilitarian. It easily goes to extremes, from an exaggerated idealism to materialism, from rationalism to scepticism. Its rigorous dialectic is mirrored in its language, which is explicit, exact, precise and capable of expressing the finest shades of meaning. In short it is the incarnation of the civilization of *homo faber*. It could be called the mentality of the rational or *scientific* man. It turned thought into a technique.

The Semitic mentality, on the other hand, reflects the civilization of *homo sapiens*. It is the mentality of the *religious* man, the artist in touch with life. Where the Greek is abstract, this is concrete; where the Greek is perceptive, this is reflective. It owes much to the desert where it was born and bred. It is deeply aware of a sense of values, and though it has great respect for thought (it is essentially contemplative) it does so only to apply that thought to the art of living. It is intuitive rather than logical, passive rather than active. It regards the Greek process of building up a system on a basis of abstraction and analysis as mere mental gymnastics. It prefers to synthesize rather than analyse, to live the truth rather than express it.

It is not surprising to find these characteristics thrown into high relief in the language. The vigorous use of the consonants, for example, shows how closely the idea is tied to the concrete image. The poverty of the syntax reflects a scorn for abstraction, and not as some think a rudeness of thought or a want of light and shade. The appreciation of true values makes the Semite realize that words are only signs; they do not express an idea, they merely evoke it. Without gestures, inflections, pauses and even silences, there can be no real adequation between an idea and its proper expression. To convey the richness of the essential unity of things, the Semite will repeat and imply and symbolize rather than use limping subordinations. Words acquire a host of associations and the right emphasis is governed by an interior rhythm. It is a similar technique to that used by the Impressionists in their painting, and by Péguy in his poetry. The idea attains its fullness by the juxtaposition of separate expressions which individually are hesitant but which together produce a pattern all the more striking because they are not set and rigid. Such a language is not the best medium for expressing abstract speculations, but it is ideal for conveying the pulsations of a living concrete thought. The alleged barbarism of Semitic language is a myth and should be recognized as such.

OF COURSE not all the languages of the Semitic group had the same importance or the same fame. Hebrew is very low in the scale. It was the language of the Israelites from their entry into Canaan up to within a few hundred years of the birth of Christ. We know very little about its origins because apart from the Old Testament we have little else to judge it by. Probably it was the language of the Canaanites, and the Israelites may have adopted it when they first entered Canaan under the Patriarchs, or, more likely, after their conquest of Canaan under Joshua. It invariably happens that the military conqueror is himself conquered by the higher civilization of his enemy. Hebrew had its golden age in the time of Isaiah. From the time of the Exile it began to be tainted with traces of Aramaic. Round about the fourth and third centuries B.C., Aramaic began to take its place as the language of the people. Hebrew gradually became a dead language and was used exclusively for religious purposes. This was its only use at the time of Christ's birth.

It must not however be supposed that Aramaic was a derivative of Hebrew, as French is a derivative of Latin. Hebrew and Aramaic sprang from the same source but they are independent of each other. In fact Aramaic is older than Hebrew and enjoyed a much more brilliant fortune. Abraham was an Aramaean. His clan came from that important group of semi-nomadic tribes which wandered along the edges of the desert, from Mesopotamia to Palestine, and ever since the third millennium had made constant short-lived attempts to settle in these countries. Their very mobility, the wide range of their settlements, and their participation in international commerce, all conspired to make their expressive language the *lingua franca* of the whole Semitic world until the time of the Arab domination.

There is no doubt that the Patriarchs spoke Aramaic. It was during the Exile and after, when the Jews had to mix with these peoples again, that they began to use Aramaic freely and lost their Hebrew. There were many dialects: by the time of Christ a Judean could be distinguished from a Galilean by the way he spoke. But we do not need to imagine that the differences between these dialects were very pronounced. There is not even a great difference between Hebrew and Aramaic, and there is no difficulty in recognizing their common source.

IT REMAINS to say something about biblical Greek, the name given to the language of the New Testament and of the

Septuagint version of the Old. It used to be thought that many of the unclassical elements in this language were the legacy of the original Hebrew, and there is some truth in this. But the discovery of many Greek papyri of the same period has shown that Greek itself suffered a change when it became the common (or *koine*) language after the conquests of Alexander. A popular form of this Greek is used throughout the New Testament except in the Epistle to the Hebrews and in St. Luke (Gospel and Acts). These are written in a more polished *koine*.

The grammar and syntax of *koine* are extremely simple. Only the ordinary moods of the verb are used (there is no optative) and the irregular forms are almost non-existent. In this it shows the influence of the Semitic languages.

It would be wrong however to explain all the peculiarities of biblical Greek in terms of the *koine*, as some exegetes have tried to do. A more reasonable explanation is one which takes account of the fact that the writers of the New Testament were all profoundly conditioned by their Hebrew outlook and influenced by its literature. Even when they set out to write in Greek style they very soon slipped back into the Semitic rhythm. We have only to read St. Paul and St. John to discover that. The language of St. John's Gospel is good *koine* but everything else about it is Semitic; in fact it is the most perfect example we have of the Semitic mind. We must remind ourselves again of the importance of getting inside this mentality if we are to understand even the New Testament. From this angle alone the Old Testament is indispensable as an introduction to the New.

III

WRITING AND MANUSCRIPTS

"Publication" in antiquity; origin and forms of writing; types of Hebrew and Greek writing; papyri and parchment; private copies and scholarly editions.

WE MUST now examine the methods of "publishing" books before the invention of the printing press. It will explain how our texts have come down to us.

The circumstances in which books were then published left much to chance. To begin with, every book had to be written by hand. A single short text dictated to ten people will often result in ten different versions. We can well imagine the final result of a long text copied from a copy of a copy. In this way some passages from ancient authors have become unrecognizable by the time they have reached us. There are other things to be considered too: the difficulty of working with poor materials, the complicated lettering itself, the quality of the parchment and so on. A book was no sooner "out" than it bristled with variant readings.

A word first about the different types of writing. It is well known that the alphabet is a comparatively recent invention. It evolved from pictures drawn to illustrate a given thought. Many elementary ideas became stylized in easily recognizable signs, or *ideographs*. Egyptian hieroglyphic writing developed from these. Such writing demanded great skill and was confined of necessity to a professional class of scribes. When it was found that a single syllable could be represented by a single sign, the science of writing had gone a long way forward. The Assyro-Babylonian cuneiform is of this *syllabic* type of writing. The many signs and shapes required made this a clumsy method of writing, and a further step forward was made by the Semitic peoples of Palestine (reputedly incapable of abstract thought), who first perceived that a syllable is composed of consonants and vowels. They first invented the letter as such. It is likely that they were helped in this by the consonantal character of their language; in fact their first alphabets were devoid of vowels.

The ancient Hebrew alphabet bears a marked resemblance to the Phoenician alphabet which is at the base of the Greek and Latin ones. It is what we should expect, because the Phoenicians and the people living in Canaan were bound by many ties. Until recently the discovery of the alphabet used to be dated about the twelfth or eleventh century B.C. and biblical writings were consequently dated after that time. But the discoveries made near Mount Sinai, at Byblos, and more recently still at Ras Shamra (all three in the same Crescent) have brought to light three alphabets which date from the middle of the second millennium, well before Moses.

D

T H E massive square characters of the present Hebrew alphabet are familiar to anyone who has seen the front of a kosher butcher shop. They are the stereotyped result of older characters, and date only from the first few centuries A.D., as do the points which mark the vowels. Before this there were no vowels in the alphabet. The Greek script is more familiar, and has remained almost unchanged except that originally words were strung together continuously without break or punctuation. Sometimes it was written cursively, the letters being joined as in our modern handwriting. Easier to read was the more formal or copybook script used chiefly by professional scribes.

Fairly important documents were written on papyrus or parchment. Papyrus is a kind of paper made by gluing together the fibres of a plant which is common in the Nile valley. For the "de luxe" editions and for longer works parchment was used. From the fourth century onwards this became more common, and so it remained throughout the Middle Ages until the discovery of the printing press brought in the use of paper. Originally the leaves were bound by being stuck end to end to form a scroll. It was not until the second century A.D. that the leaves were stitched together in fours. These "quaternions", as they were called, were then bound together to make a volume. The early Christians seem to have been instrumental in popularizing this method, which to all intents and purposes is the one we still use.

B O O K making was not exclusively a private enterprise; there were also the big "publishing houses". Here a publisher would have a number of professional copyists working together in a scriptorium. The work would be dictated to them all by a single reader. Then the scripts would be revised to eliminate mistakes; the methods used were surprisingly efficient. When it was a question of re-issuing a work that already had a wide circulation (and was therefore probably faulty) they gave it a thorough searching to try and restore the original text. These critical editions go by the name of "recensions". In the Middle Ages this work of copying and correcting was confined almost exclusively to monasteries and religious houses.

Books of this sort were obviously expensive things to buy and for the most part beyond the reach of the poor and persecuted Christians. They had to be content with privately made copies and cheap editions which were not nearly so carefully purged of mistakes. It is in this form that Christian writings were published during the first two or three centuries, and we do not possess any other type of book older than the fourth century. It is only after that time that the sacred texts were copied with greater elegance and beauty, sometimes even in gold or silver lettering on purple parchment.

IV

ORIGINAL TEXTS AND VERSIONS

Direct and indirect witnesses; Hebrew manuscripts and the work of the Massoretes; different types of Greek manuscripts of the New Testament; the famous codices; Greek version of the Septuagint; old Latin versions; work of St. Jerome and St. Augustine.

SINCE we do not possess any autograph texts of the Bible, we must reconstruct the original from copies which have come down to us. In doing this we employ two sorts of evidence: the direct evidence provided by copies of the original, and the indirect evidence provided by translations of the original and by quotations of it in ancient writers.

The actual manuscripts are numbered in thousands but they are not all of the same value. None of the existing Hebrew manuscripts of the Old Testament is older than the ninth century A.D., and all of them are exasperatingly uniform. It is true that a recent discovery in a cave near the Dead Sea brought to light some fragmentary copies of Isaiah and other writings made well before the Christian era; but the text of Isaiah still bears a close resemblance to the other manuscripts already existing. This confirms the great age of the text represented by these manuscripts and enhances their value, but the discovery has offered no explanation of the considerable difference between this uniform Hebrew text and the Greek Septuagint version. All it has told us is that the regulative

measure which resulted in the uniformity of all existing manuscripts must have been begun earlier than we once thought.
From the early Middle Ages, generation after generation of
Rabbinic scholars had worked with meticulous care to produce
the definitive text now known as the *Massorah* (hence the name
Massoretes). It was part of their policy to destroy all manuscripts which were prior to their reform. They must have
started very early, because the text underlying both Origen's
Hexapla and St. Jerome's Latin version cannot have differed
much from other existing texts. By the ninth century the
Massoretes had achieved their aim, as is clear from the fact
that, apart from a few fragments, we possess no manuscripts
older than the ninth century.

When we come to the New Testament originals we are faced
with a very different state of affairs. Here we are overwhelmed
by a great mass of copies, from every age and with numerous
variants. These Greek manuscripts fall into three main classes:
minuscules, uncials and papyri. The *minuscules* are later than
the ninth century, and for the most part give the standardized
text known as the Received Text. Even so it would be possible
to subdivide them further, and a closer study of these relatively
late manuscripts would be well worth while. Perhaps too much
emphasis has been given to the great *uncial* manuscripts, with
their fine bold capitals, written between the fourth and the ninth
centuries. Some of them are very well known: the *Codex
Vaticanus* of the fourth century; the *Codex Sinaiticus*, also of
the fourth century, found by Tischendorf in a waste-paper
basket at Sinai and sent to St. Petersburg, whence it was sold
by Russia to the British Museum; and the *Codex Bezae* of the
fifth century, a Greek and Latin manuscript which was stolen
from Lyons by the Huguenots in 1562, and given in 1581 by
Theodore de Beza to the University of Cambridge, where it is
still kept. Nearly all of these manuscripts are elegant and show
evidence of careful recension.

This cannot be said of the *papyri*. These have come to light
only within the last fifty years, in Egypt, and are the oldest
copies in our possession. The fact that such fragile material
has been preserved at all is due to the dry climate of the Nile
valley. It is not known how these precious fragments reached
the shops of Cairo, but that is where they were found by

Western scholars, who paid dearly for them. Perhaps the most remarkable among them are the *Chester Beatty* papyri and those acquired by the University of Michigan. Together these give us three codices of the third century, and one of them supplies almost the complete text of St. Paul. We have only fragments of anything written prior to this date. The oldest would seem to be part of the Gospel of St. John found in 1935, and assigned by the experts to the first half of the second century. Written less than fifty years after the original, it was enough to destroy Loisy's theory that the Fourth Gospel could not date from before the middle of the second century.

OBVIOUSLY such close proximity to the autograph text is exceptional. Despite the vast number and the worth of the manuscripts that we possess, there is usually a gap of centuries between them and their originals. For the New Testament it is a mere two hundred years, but for the Old Testament it varies from a thousand to as much as eighteen hundred years. It is indeed fortunate that we have the means to check them. The method is admittedly an indirect one, but it is not less important for that. The various original works very soon came to be translated. It is these translations that help us to reconstruct a text very close to the original, based as they are on manuscripts far older than those now existing.

The most important translation of the Old Testament is the Greek version known as the *Septuagint*. It was made in Egypt during the third and second centuries B.C. As a witness it is of the highest value because the translation was done with great care, and because it takes us some ten or twelve centuries nearer to the original than our Hebrew manuscripts. It is quoted frequently in the New Testament and was in wide use among the early Christians. So highly was it esteemed that St. Augustine and many others considered it inspired in its own right, and on a par with the original Hebrew. There were other Greek versions such as those of Theodotion and Aquila, but we know nothing of them apart from the few fragments preserved in the Hexapla of Origen.

In addition to the Greek versions of the Old Testament, many other translations of the entire Bible were made into the chief languages of early Christian times. As far as the Old Testament is concerned, only one was made directly from the Hebrew. All the others were made from the Greek Septuagint, and although they are most important, they are translations at second-hand, and their only use is to establish the text of the Septuagint. The translations of the New Testament are more important, especially the Latin and Syriac versions, which were made less than a hundred years after the originals, towards the middle of the second century, and so are two hundred years older than the oldest of our Greek manuscripts. This is true at least of the earliest of them. Many of the Syriac versions are much later; the most famous of them,.the *Peshitta*, dates from the fifth century.

THE Latin versions deserve special consideration, not only because of their vast number and age, but because we ought to know something about the origin of the texts with which the liturgy has made us familiar. In dealing with them a distinction should be made between St. Jerome's work, known as the *Vulgate* or popular version because it eventually won the field, and the older versions which preceded it.

We will deal with the Vulgate below. From a critical viewpoint the older versions are more important. To judge from the copies we now possess, these must have been very widespread. They offer a variety of readings which makes it impossible to tell with any certainty whether they derive from a single primitive version or from several. Unfortunately they are rare, because the Vulgate soon replaced them. The Gospels are best represented, although only about fifteen manuscripts exist. These are very old. Some, like the one which belonged to Eusebius (Bishop of Vercelli, +371) and the *Palatinus* from Trent, date from the fourth century, and so are as old as our most ancient Greek manuscripts. The care and beauty with which some of these have been produced bears witness to the veneration for the Word of God in this glorious period. Their text can still be found in parts of our liturgy, and they formed the basis for numerous further translations into Arabic, Gothic, old Dutch and Provençal.

These had their faults. They were not very accurate and they varied among themselves a great deal. This may be

accounted for by the popular background in which they were
made in Africa about the middle of the second century. By
the fourth century they had become so corrupt that there was
obvious need for a revision based on the originals, and it was
St. Jerome who answered the need. He was born some time
between the years 347 and 349. He became a monk and lived
in Rome and Bethlehem, where he died in 420. By nature
he was impetuous, lively and obstinate. In spite of his asceti-
cism he had a great love of literature. He knew Greek well
and mastered Hebrew. It was his friend Pope Damasus
who encouraged him, as a private venture, to undertake
his great biblical work which was to leave such a mark on
the Latin Middle Ages and on western civilization as a
whole.

His original intention was simply to revise the old Latin
version in the light of the Greek Septuagint. In this way he
twice revised the Psalter. It is often thought that the *Roman
Psalter* was the result of his first revision, but this is in fact
an unrevised old Latin version. His second revision met with
great success in spite of its many imperfections, and it is this
that was until recently universally used in the Latin Church.
Its wide acceptance throughout the whole of Gaul gave it the
name of the *Gallican Psalter*. St. Jerome treated the Gospels
in the same way, revising an old Latin text in the light of the
Greek. It would seem that he went no further with the New
Testament, for in 382 he started an arduous new work
which by itself justifies his fame. This was not a mere work
of revision, but an entirely new translation from the
orginal Hebrew of all the proto-canonical books of the Old
Testament.

It is Jerome's translation of the Hebrew Old Testament, and
his New Testament revision of the Gospels, that are to be
found in our Latin Vulgate. To these he added the deutero-
canonical books in an already existing Latin translation. The
Acts of the Apostles, St. Paul, the Catholic Epistles and the
Apocalypse, as we now have them, were probably not his work.
They did not appear in the Vulgate until after the time of
Cassiodorus (+ *c.* 583).

All the old texts bear traces of different revisions of this sort,
and it would be wrong to imagine that St. Jerome was alone in

this field. St. Augustine is a case in point. His genius has always been thought of as a purely speculative one, but an important recent discovery shows that he had a rare mind for critical studies too. He revised nearly all the books of the Bible, and at times his version is better than the Vulgate. This is especially true when he deals with St. Paul. There is no doubt that his modesty had much to do with his own work being suppressed in favour of the Vulgate. But the chief reason was that Jerome's recourse to the Hebrew gave the Vulgate Old Testament an incontestable superiority.

IN ADDITION to all these documents, there are the innumerable quotations from the Bible to be found in all the Christian writers from the second century onwards. These are often long verbatim extracts, and are valuable because they help us to put the history of this material into some sort of order. By using them we can often fix the place of origin and the approximate dates of the different kinds of texts.

V

TEXTUAL CRITICISM

Its importance; external criticism and the main types of text for the New Testament; internal criticism; conclusions.

THE reader will want to know how all these documents are used to reconstruct the original text. He will also want some reassurance about the practical value of the knowledge that has been gained in this field—the knowledge for example that the number of variants is enormous, that there are some two or three thousand for the New Testament alone, that hardly a single verse finds unanimous approval, that the book of Jeremiah is one-sixth shorter in the Greek than in the Hebrew, that in some manuscripts of the Acts there are different and often longer readings of the same phrase so that almost every line gives changes of details. . . .

What have we to guide us in making a considered choice among these variants? How do we distinguish between the reading which is a true reflection of the inspired writer and all the other readings which are the accumulated result of careless copyists and clumsy revisers? In reply to these questions, textual criticism offers two guides which, although they are distinct in themselves, must of necessity always be combined and applied together. These two guides are *external* and *internal* criticism.

External criticism tries to assess the value of every reading, whether it comes from a manuscript or from other sources. In this respect a number of widely held prejudices must be set aside. It is often taken for granted that the oldest and most frequently found reading is invariably the right one, and that the reading which is in the original language is to be preferred. This is not so. The antiquity of a manuscript proves nothing. For example, a manuscript of the fifth century may be only a copy of another contemporary manuscript, whereas one of the ninth century could be a copy of a fourth century manuscript. In this case the text of the later document is closer in date to the original than the older manuscript. We must be equally careful when dealing with numbers. A hundred copies taken from a single manuscript gives us only one witness, whereas three copies taken from independent manuscripts will give us three witnesses. The prejudice which favours manuscripts in the original language must be dealt with more carefully, but it is true to say that a Hebrew reading from a manuscript of the ninth century A.D. is not necessarily to be preferred to a variation in a manuscript of the Septuagint, since the Septuagint is nearer to the original by thirteen centuries.

One of the most important functions of external criticism is to reconstruct, as far as possible, the different stages of the text, by grouping all the documents historically to discover the reasons for the variations. This work is still in its infancy, since the pertinent material has not yet been conveniently collected. Many of the quotations from the Fathers, for instance, are available only in old and faulty editions. As far as the Old Testament is concerned, we need to know more about the history of the Septuagint and improve the present state of its text. On the New Testament more work has been done, and we are able now to discern three or four stages in the history of its text.

The first stage takes us from the beginning to the third century. In this period the work of copying was done without a great deal of care, but at least there were no synthetic revisions. In spite of their antiquity these texts are more corrupt than any. All the same they are valuable because it is possible to find grain among the chaff. The present tendency is to lay more and more stress on the papyri and the ancient Syriac and Latin versions which bear traces of these popular copies. For no good reason, this text has been called the *Western Text*.

The second stage stretches from the third to the ninth century and comprises those scholarly revisions which go by the name of *Eastern Text*. These have purged much of the dross which was in the popular texts but unfortunately have also got rid of much that was good. In this stage we usually distinguish three revisions. The *Alexandrian* was made in Egypt at the beginning of the third century, and it is from this that our best uncials stem. The *Caesarean* was made in Palestine, and the *Lucianic* at Antioch. From the ninth century this Lucianic revision, which is the most elegant and the most unfaithful, was the one that prevailed among the Byzantine texts. It dominated the third stage, that of the *Received Text*. The fourth and final stage was inaugurated by the critical and textual studies of the nineteenth century.

EXTERNAL criticism, by itself, cannot always be decisive in its judgments. Even the classification of manuscripts which it demands is only made possible by the use of *internal criticism*. This method assesses the value of readings by their content. It is not difficult to correct some of the more obvious errors even when they have the support of all manuscripts. The reading in Luke 15:8, *evertit domum* (she turned the house upside down), represented in all the Vulgate manuscripts, is a mistake for *everrit* (she swept). But there are cases where there is nothing to choose between the variants, as in the Prologue of John 1:13, where the singular reading "who was born" is just as acceptable as the more usual "who were born". In such cases only external criticism can give a final judgment (in the example given it seems to decide for the singular, despite the rarity of such a reading). There are other cases which cannot so easily be decided until a more thorough internal examination has been made.

To achieve this, the critics have drawn up a number of rules which for our purpose can be reduced to two. The first is that of context: the reading which fits most happily into the particular mode of the writer's thought, and especially into the particular mode of the pertinent passage, is more likely to be the right one. Thus the attribution of the *Magnificat* to Elizabeth is contrary to the whole plan of St. Luke, and is certainly to be rejected in spite of the value of the documents in its favour and in spite of some lack of cohesion in the details of the text which attributes it to Mary. The second rule is more positive: the reading which explains the origin of the variants, and is not itself explained by them, is to be preferred. An example may be taken from Mark 1 : 41. " Jesus was angry with him " cannot evolve from " Jesus was moved with pity for him ". Nobody would have thought up such a reading so contrary to the usual pious instincts of a Christian. " Moved with pity " however can easily be seen as the correction of a startled copyiest, who knew that the parallel message in both Matthew and Luke read " moved with pity ".

These few examples are enough to demonstrate the limitations of textual criticism, dealing as it does with imponderables. Often its conclusions can be no more than probabilities based on cumulative arguments which, if they were taken separately, would be tenuous. What is quite certain is that external and internal criticism must go hand in hand all the time.

W E D O not wish to finish this chapter on a note of exaggerated scepticism. Whilst the examples quoted ought to demonstrate the practical use and importance of this critical work, the reader must not be afraid that it will in any way endanger the foundations of his faith. The vast proportion of these variants carry no doctrinal import whatsoever. By and large we possess a text which gives not only the thought of the sacred author but also his actual manner of expression. We must be careful not to go to the other extreme and say that critical research has no practical value. It should be given a just appraisal. No variant in a manuscript will ever imperil any point of dogma. All that critical research seeks to do is to throw more light on the nuances of the writer's thought by trying to find out exactly what he wrote. Like any other biblical science it is concerned not with the foundations of the faith, but with its appreciation.

CHAPTER III

THE BACKGROUND

I

THE GEOGRAPHICAL BACKGROUND

Effects of Palestine's geography on its history; its situation in the centre of the Egyptian-Babylonian Crescent; its lack of unity; variability of the soil; importance of rainfall; permanent menace of the desert; rival attractions of nomadic and sedentary life.

THERE is hardly a page of the Bible without some reference to a place or village in Palestine. To understand the Bible properly, we shall need to have some idea of the land where it was born and to know its relationship to neighbouring countries. There is nothing that so moulds a nation as the soil to which it belongs.

Palestine takes its name from the Philistines, a race whom the Israelites always regarded as intruders. Such a paradox is not uncommon in history. The name is of Greek origin and did not become official until the time of the Roman occupation. The Israelites themselves, and Christ too (Mt. 5:4) called it simply "The Land". Immediate neighbours knew it as the "Land of Israel". In older times the Bible uses the name *Canaan*, a title to be found already in the Amarna tablets (the Egyptian diplomatic documents of the fourteenth century B.C.), and later in Assyrian documents.

A glance at an atlas will show that the land of the Bible is not isolated, but is part of a great land-mass. This is of prime importance because it is the key to the history of Israel. To the north there is no clear line of demarcation between Israel and what we now call Lebanon and Syria. Geographically it is all one country, united by the same mountain formation, boarded on the west by the same Mediterranean Sea and on the east

by the same almost impassable Arabian desert. The whole
forms one narrow corridor. At each end it opens on to vast
regions whose very names are an index of their importance. To
the north lies the valley of the upper Euphrates giving on to the
immense plain of Mesopotamia; to the south lies the valley of
the Nile.

Palestine, then, lies at the centre of a vast crescent which
sweeps from the Persian Gulf to Ethiopia. The importance of
its position will be obvious to anyone who reflects on the might
of the two great powers which it unites and divides. Until the
advent of Greek civilization these two, Egypt and Assyria,
were the principal contestants for power in the Middle East,
and their history is the rise and fall of their mutual struggle.
There were some others, like the Hittite Empire in Asia Minor
and Mitanni in Syria, but they were not of the same importance.
For trade and for war there was only one line of communication between the desert and the sea, and that line ran through
the corridor of Palestine. Palestine was the cockpit of the East,
playing the rôle that Belgium played in the Great War. Centre
for trade, crucible of the nations, and bone of contention, that
was her fate. Until the fifth century B.C., the master of Canaan
was virtual master of the Middle East.

Such a tenuous position might have been counterbalanced
by some physical unity within the land, but such is not the case.
At its northern and wider end the corridor, with its two enormous Syrian mountain ranges of Lebanon and Anti-Lebanon,
is vastly different from the southern end. And even this
southern end, which corresponds to the old land of Israel, is
anything but homogeneous. Its area is only a little larger than
that of Wales, some 10,000 square miles. From furthest north
to south it measures only 175 miles, from east to west 150.
Yet in spite of its small size it is geographically split up and
divided, and this had such an effect on its political life that all
attempts at unification were to prove fruitless.

This lack of unity is the result of a physical configuration
which is without parallel anywhere, the phenomenon of the
Jordan valley which runs the length of Palestine. Unlike other
rivers such as the Nile and Euphrates, the Jordan has no fertile
hinterland: it is a sterile ditch. This enormous rift, which starts
some 1,700 feet above sea level and falls to 1,200 feet below,

bisects the plateau which rises to a height of 3,000 feet on either side. It is not the river itself which has worn such a deep gorge. The river is a prisoner until it empties itself into the desolation of the Dead Sea. The cleft is a geological fault which has split one-sixth of the earth's crust. The Jordan valley is only one section of what geologists call the Syro-African Rift. It begins in Syria between Lebanon and Anti-Lebanon, and continues south of the Dead Sea, through the arid valley of the Araba, across the Aqaba Gulf and the Red Sea to finish in the Lakes of Central Africa.

This Rift has cut Palestine into three well-defined strips. To the east there is the elevated plateau which terminates abruptly at the Dead Sea. To the west are the rolling mountains of Judah and Samaria which drop sharply on the one side to the Jordan and on the other slope gently towards the Mediterranean to form the large coastal strip of the Sharon plain and the Shephelah.

That is not all. Beside these three vertical strips (the coastal plain, the mountains of Cisjordania and the Transjordanian plateau) there are horizontal demarcations as well. In the far north there is the natural frontier of the furrow cut by the Nahr-el-Qasimiyeh from Hermon to the sea. In the extreme south a similar frontier is provided by the " River of Egypt " and the mountains of the Negeb. In between, the rivers and wadis that empty into the Mediterranean on the west, or the Jordan and Dead Sea on the east, carve out another series of parallel divisions. Two of these have a special importance. In the north the vale of Esdraelon (or Jezreel) divides the hills of Galilee from Mount Ephraim, and thus affords access from the coast to the Jordan valley, over the passes of Gilboa to Bethshan. It forms the basin for the river Kishon (Judges 4-5, 3 Kings 18:40) and has made possible the great international route from Egypt, along the coast, over the shoulder of Bethshan, and by the upper Jordan valley through to Damascus and Mesopotamia. There is a division further south caused this time, not by a river, but by the mountain massif of Samaria on the one side and of Judah on the other. It was around these two central groups of mountains that the two rival peoples settled who were to live out the history of Israel. Less exposed than Galilee, Samaria has not the protected position of Judaea

It was this isolation between the Dead Sea and the desert that was to make Judaea the bulwark of Judaism after the fall of the Northern Kingdom.

Thus the configuration of the land of Israel makes of it a chess-board whose lines are the inter-crossings of natural obstacles. There is very little plain land. It is nearly all mountain massifs deeply scarred by numerous ravines, and cut into two from north to south by the Jordan Rift.

THERE is no compensating richness of soil to make up for the difficult terrain. To the Hebrew nomads who roamed the wastes of Sinai this land of Canaan seemed from afar a veritable paradise with promise of milk and honey. But although there are some fertile parts the modern traveller will be surprised to find it for the most part a barren land, poor and badly watered. One must obviously make allowance for the changes that have taken place throughout Palestine since ancient times. Successive invasions have denuded the woodlands, and deportations of the people have impoverished the soil. Even so it does seem that the biblical descriptions of the land were greatly exaggerated.

The very quality of the soil is to some extent due to the geographical configuration. The coastal area, the plain of Esdraelon and some parts of the Jordan valley are fertile enough. Galilee, too, is well wooded and fruitful. But the central hills of Samaria are barren, and they get worse as they continue south to Judaea, to become almost a desert at their eastern end (the desert of Judah). The Negeb is mere steppe country and becomes more and more arid as it approaches the real desert of the Sinaitic peninsula. Similarly, Transjordania deteriorates towards the south. In Gilead it offers rich pasture land, but near the Dead Sea there is nothing but dry plateau.

None the less it is not the nature of the soil that has determined the standards of life in Palestine. The plains can produce a good yield of wheat and the hills have their vineyards. The prime factors which determine everything are the climate and the water-supply—vital problems for Palestine. The climate is sub-tropical and has only two seasons, the rainy season from October to May and the dry season from June to September. The temperature varies according to the distance from the sea but is, on the whole, fairly temperate. Frost is rare although the variation of temperature between day and night is very marked. A far more important part is played by the winds, which determine the rainfall.

In Palestine, more than anywhere else perhaps, water is life itself because it is rare. There are very few good rivers. The Jordan is imprisoned in its cleft and can never over-reach its high banks. Streams are plentiful but they are too steep to hold the water. Rapid evaporation also helps to keep them dry for most of the year. Springs are few, and the soil is porous, and in the mountains at least it holds no volume of water. The Palestinian looks to heaven for the water to feed his land, and that is why he respects it in the Bible as one of the most precious of God's gifts. There are three stages in the winter rainy season: the first or autumn rains, the more plentiful January and February rains when even short-lived snow may fall, and the late or spring rains. The rain is usually brought by the west wind which comes in over the sea, a wind which is also responsible for the heavy summer night dews. The sultry south wind brings only winter storms and destructive hail. The total mean rainfall is low and much of it is lost through evaporation and drainage. It must be conserved as far as possible. The wells and cisterns along with the springs are the nerve centres of the whole country and on their maintenance depend the lives of all. It is not surprising that they have such a unique place in the Bible literature.

To sum up, then, the land of Israel will be fertile only at the price of unceasing husbandry. It is surrounded on all sides by the desert which will encroach at the smallest sign of negligence. To the east there is the immense waste of burning sand and stones; to the south Sinai creeps up in the arid steppes of the Negeb (the name means " dry land "), and into the heart of the land itself in the desert of Judah, on the edge of the Dead Sea. This abiding presence of the desert is one of the features which has exercised a profound influence on the lives and thought of the people of Israel. It has a double fascination which attracts and at the same time repels and makes them sigh for an easy settled life. The subconscious ideal of the Israelite, the noblest part of him, will always thrill to the life of a nomad. It was the desert which gave rise to every national and religious move-

E

ment, from Moses, David, the Prophets and the Maccabees down to Christ. By the contrast which is to be found in the very geographical formation of the land itself, this austerity of the nomad highlights the attractions of a settled agricultural way of life and minimizes its drawbacks. Even when he has settled, the Israelite is always a nomad at heart, lured on like the bedouin by the next oasis, and haunted by the freedom of an endless solitude.

THIS two-fold attraction can be found in every walk of Palestinian life. By necessity the Palestinian must till the soil, but he is nearly always a shepherd too, in fact a small farmer. Except in the plains where Israel was never master, the land is uneven and lacks sufficient water for the large scale wheat farming of the Nile Valley. Even the vine cannot be widely cultivated, because of the labour involved. The beast of burden is not the horse, which is of recent introduction, but the ass, that tough, docile and long-staying animal which is more suited to hilly country even though its scope is limited.

Under fair conditions, this type of small-farming affords a reasonable living. To augment it the farmer has his live stock, which can easily survive on the badly watered semi-desert steppes. Even here cattle are rare, and only the complete nomad will rear camels. The Palestinian must be content with sheep and goats which can wander over the steppes, with fierce dogs to ward off wolves and jackals (the lion has long since disappeared).

Thus the Palestinian becomes a "settled nomad", rooted in the soil without ceasing to be a shepherd. There is a continuous coming and going between the desert and the farm-lands, a constant barter between the settlers, the semi-nomads and the nomads, and this interflow between people and things is at the root of another and deeper exchange. This interchange goes to form the soul, the culture, the religion and the mentality of the inhabitants. This is just as true of the modern Arab as it was of his Jewish counterpart in the land of Israel. He is moulded by a double influence. Nomad or settler, the wide open spaces and the easy pleasures, he hears the call of both.

WE OUGHT to try to describe what it means to live in the desert, because anyone who reads the Bible without making an effort to appreciate its hardships and its sublimity will miss many of the nuances of the sacred text. To this end we would recommend the reading of some book on eastern travel, such as Lawrence's *Seven Pillars of Wisdom*. This story of the author's experiences during the Great War catches the vivid contrast between our western outlook and the outlook of the desert-dwellers, whose very manner of life has not changed over the thousands of years.

The life of the nomad is set in a rigid frame, where material comforts are cut to a minimum. In these desolate wastes a settled home is impossible. The nomad's home is his tent, and he carries it about with him wherever he goes. Around it is centred that solidarity of family and clan, which for him is an all-important, fixed and absolute bond. The desert develops his personality and his individualism since it demands of him great powers of resistance, courage and composure. At the same time it makes him a slave to his people in the sense that their actions are his responsibility, for he knows that left to himself in the desert he is lost. The social group is small, and can never exist on a grand scale. Everything is held together by ties of blood and family. Authority is absolute, and yet the tribesmen feel themselves to be on equal footing with their sheik. Money does not count here; the poor man, among his own people, is a free man.

Merely to exist in the desert is hard. If a man lives on the desert fringe, his only means of livelihood are his flocks and his camels. These are happy enough with the poor pastures of the steppes, and when they have exhausted one particular area they move to another, and the whole clan moves with them. The only fixed landmark for these journeys is necessarily the next water-hole. If he lives in the interior he becomes either a caravan guide or a robber. This land of surprises teaches him to watch for his opportunity.

From this life of adventure the nomad learns what it means to fight for existence, to be disciplined and temperate. He learns the habit of silence and reflection, and an appreciation of lasting values. He has a profound scorn for the comfort and slavery of civilization, and yet at times his repressed sensuality runs to excess: the imagined comforts of a sedentary life fascinate him almost beyond endurance. He is proud, but weak, individualistic and yet submissive to his clan, deeply religious and yet often fanatical, violent but loving and warmhearted. Perhaps the strongest trait in his character is his pride: pride in his independence, in his blood, in his sense of liberty, pride even in his poverty. He is not easily bent to a yoke not of his own choosing. Even if he settles down he never loses the imprint stamped on him through generations by this terrifying but compelling background which is his birthright. Even after centuries his descendants, in the decadence of their sedentary life, will still be haunted by the memory of it, and deep down in their hearts they will yearn for the life of the wanderer.

SUCH then is the complex character of the people and the land of Palestine. Its lack of cohesion, which amounts almost to a disjointedness, is reflected in the disposition of the population. Whether he is a peasant or a semi-nomad, the Palestinian knows only small villages thrown up on some ancient site offering strategic advantage. The important towns, like Jerusalem and Samaria, are political centres and owe their importance to their key positions. The ports are only second-rate, because this coast is rocky and offers no safe anchorage or shelter. The life of the city will never conquer the individualistic family spirit, which is the heritage of the nomad and is perpetuated by nature's own division of the land. It was not in Palestine that the Jew learnt to become a shrewd and hardheaded business man, but in the land of his exile. There was no room in the land of Israel for big business, only for crofting and farming. This is so true that the sacred writers quite naturally projected this state of affairs on to the beginnings of the human race, and asked us to recognize in Cain the peasant and Abel the shepherd the two prototypes of the land of Israel, and to detect in the psychological picture of their religion that nostalgic yearning for the desert which always haunted the nation's most fervent minds.

II

THE HISTORICAL SOURCES

Historical ties between Israel and the Ancient East; the Bible as a record of history; errors of concordism; fruitfulness of the comparative method; documents and archæological discoveries.

THE land is the cradle for the people: the stage is the setting for the play. This particular corner of the world seems hardly fitted by nature for the great drama which was to be played out there. By rights it should have been no more than a land of transit. Instead we find here a nation which was to be so closely knit together that nothing has since been able to break it to pieces, and a religion so strong that it withstood all repeated attempts to supplant it.

Judged by human standards Israel's history has no significance. In the eyes of its powerful neighbours it passed almost unnoticed. The great powers of Egypt and Mesopotamia looked on Israel as just another of those countless little peoples who lived in their great shadows and whose very names have now been forgotten. The extraordinary thing is that it is precisely Israel's history that has come down to us. It is of the great Empires that we know nothing, or did not until the chance discoveries of modern science restored a little of their former glory. What is more, even if all the annals of these nations were found, they could never be brought back to life, for all the power they wielded over so many years. Yet the literary and historical heritage of the Jews has not only been preserved, it has been read and known in its smallest details all over the world for hundreds of years. The nation itself continues to exist, however much it has been cut about, and its dynamic spirit still lives on, transformed now into the most powerful religious movement that the world has known.

THE sources of this history are varied. In the first place there is the Bible itself. Many of its books describe the growth and development of the nation of Israel. They were, of course, written from an essentially religious and subjective viewpoint, and consequently others aspects are neglected. They deal only with certain sections of their history and so leave our curiosity unsatisfied, and they ignore others which we would have considered essential. Again there is no indication of those indeterminable elements which go to make up a historical milieu, and they presuppose a knowledge of situations and conditions which time has changed beyond recognition. It is not surprising then that modern criticism has questioned the value of these records, for example with regard to the history of the Patriarchs and the Conquest. There are other parts whose historical value has been admitted more freely, such as the chronicles of the reign of David, the book of Kings, the memoirs of Nehemiah and the first book of Maccabees. More of this later. By and large these documents, taken for what they are, provide us with enough material to sketch a fairly general picture of the main stages of Israelite history, if we supplement them with the data provided by sources outside the Bible.

In addition to the Bible, secular history provides us with further information.

So closely was the history of Israel bound up with the other peoples in the Fertile Crescent that we are able to shed light on the Bible simply by restoring it to its historical context. When we apply the results of modern discoveries, our picture of the background becomes even clearer and more detailed. It is true, as we have already said, that hardly any of the Egyptian, Assyrian or Babylonian documents make any explicit mention of Israel. The stele of Menephtah (1226 B.C.) gives no more than a mention of her name among a list of conquered peoples. The expeditions of the eighth and seventh centuries are recorded in only a few of the Assyrian inscriptions. It would be pointless therefore to look to these parallels for a concordism with the Bible which is not really there. At the same time a better informed knowledge and appreciation of the movements and customs of peoples in the ancient East, and a study of their monuments and literature, cannot fail to give us a deeper insight into the whole background of biblical events. With their help we shall more easily get into the minds of those far-off people, and began to appreciate the feelings, friendly or otherwise, which the great powers aroused in the hearts of their small neighbours.

WE BASE our knowledge of the peoples of the ancient East on two kinds of sources, literary and archaeological.

From the excavations made in Egypt and Mesopotamia within the last hundred years, we have acquired a vast number of written records. Thanks to Champollion's discovery of an inscription written in three kinds of script, we have since 1823 been able to understand the Egyptian hieroglyphic texts. The middle of the century saw us able to read the Babylonian and Assyrian cuneiform. The Mesopotamians kept their records on tablets of baked clay, and this has preserved for us whole libraries, like the one of Asshurbanapal (+626 B.C.). These libraries have preserved precious texts which take us back some thousands of years and show that man has committed his mind to writing from earliest times. Recently finds have been deciphered which show the existence of a civilization where it was not even suspected. The discoveries in Bogasköi in Asia Minor have brought to life again the once powerful Hittites, who had previously been just a name in the Bible. The finds at Byblos and Ras Shamra reveal the existence in the fifteenth century B.C. of an intense literary activity, close to the land which was later to become Israel. The texts are a mixed collection of religious poems, trade agreements, diplomatic reports, rituals of magic, and legendary and historical narratives.

These archaeological excavations do not merely unearth texts; they restore to us the actual material trappings of a lost civilization. For a hundred years now, improved methods have been used in excavating the *tells* or artificial mounds which cover ancient sites of the Middle East. These mounds have been formed by the accumulated remains of towns built over the ruins of older towns. A trench cut through the *tell* will reveal the successive layers, with the oldest at the bottom and the most recent at the top. In removing each layer the diggers bring to life a lost civilization. They yield not only countless objects of every kind, but also the remnants of buildings, temples, palaces and private houses, with the works of art that decorated them. All these things help us to understand more about these forgotten peoples.

Sometimes the results are sensational. At Ur in Chaldea, the town of Abraham, the unbroken tomb of a king was found with all his panoply of wives, soldiers and dancing girls. All were shrouded in gold and stood there exactly as they had been buried 4,000 years ago. Apparently it was the custom for them to be buried alive, so that they could continue to minister to the needs of their lord in after-life. Similarly, not far from the old site of Babylon are the ruins of a temple with its tremendous tower. Seemingly, it was this and similar ones found in Mesopotamia which occasioned the popular account in the Bible of the Tower of Babel. Many of the things unearthed in the course of these excavations have found their way into our western museums. A visit to the Egyptian and Assyrian Rooms of the British Museum would provide an admirable introduction to this aspect of biblical understanding.

The sites which have been excavated in Palestine itself cannot compare with these. In spite of their number they have been only partially excavated. All the same it is possible, as at Jericho, to read the various stages of Israel's history in the very soil of Israel. We can often learn of the beliefs and way of life of the people who inhabited the land before the Israelites, as at Gezer. Gradually, then, the discoveries are throwing more and more light on the picture of the origins of the Jewish people in general, and on the period of the Patriarchs in particular. Slowly the story emerges from the twilight of legend as it makes contact with the history of Mesopotamia, Egypt and Canaan, but always that story keeps the flavour which it acquired through being handed down by word of mouth from generation to generation.

III

THE BEGINNINGS

Witness of the Bible; Sumerians and Semites; from Ur of the Chaldeans to Haran of the Arameans; migrations in the time of Abraham; partial sedentarization of Abraham's clan in Canaan; migration to Egypt in the time of the Hyksos.

THE people of Israel began where our own civilization began, at Ur. With that strong feeling for the past which is characteristic of the East, the Bible has kept the memory of it fresh in the old text of Genesis addressed to Abraham: "I am Yahweh, who brought you from Ur of the Chaldeans" (Gen. 15:7; cf. also 11:28-32, Nehem. 9:7). The story of the rest of the journey is continued in Deuteronomy, where the Israelite descendant of Jacob is commanded to say: "My father was a wandering Aramean. He went down into Egypt with his people. They were few in number and lived there as strangers; but they became a nation there, great, mighty and numerous. The Egyptians afflicted us, oppressed us, and laid upon us a bitter yoke. Then we cried to Yahweh, the God of our fathers; and Yahweh heard our cry and saw our affliction, our toil and our oppression. And Yahweh brought us out of Egypt with a mighty hand and an outstretched arm, terrifying them with miracles and wonders. And he brought us into this land, and gave us this land, a land flowing with milk and honey". (Deut. 26:5-9). The text is stylized, but it is a striking summary of the chief stages in the formation of Israel.

UR IN Chaldea, the birthplace of the Israelite nation, is one of the most ancient towns of lower Mesopotamia. Excavations have shown that its flourishing civilization goes back to the very dawn of history, in the fourth millennium B.C. It lies on the banks of the Euphrates, in the southernmost part of the segment of land between the two rivers.

From earliest times this land seems to have been divided into two parts, Accad in the north and Sumer in the south. Two peoples, distinct in origin and language, shared its principal towns and disputed its sovereignty. Yet despite their racial and ethnological differences, they shared a common culture, way of life and religion. This culture was already flourishing at the beginning of history, and it becomes increasingly more certain that it was founded by the Sumerians, a race whose beginnings are shrouded in mystery. It was the Semitic Accadians who were the invaders, and they came from the north-west in successive waves. About 2700 B.C. their king Sargon united the two peoples under his sole rule, and the Accadians gradually came to adopt the Sumerian culture. Ur was one of the oldest centres of this Sumerian culture, although from very early times there had been considerable numbers of Semites living in and around it.

Where the Semites came from originally is a matter for debate. Inscriptions refer to their main centre as Amurru, a land lying between the Mediterranean and the Euphrates, in what is now Syria. From the third millennium B.C. groups of these Semites began to migrate from these settlements towards southern Mesopotamia, wandering as nomads or semi-nomads the whole length of the Euphrates, on the fringe of the Arabo-Syrian desert. They tried to settle or at least gravitate around the important urban centres, which served the double purpose of a religious focal point and a commercial market for their flocks. According to later documents these people acquired the name of Arameans, and then of Chaldeans.

Terah, the father of Abraham, is supposed to have been the head of one of these groups that lived in and around Ur. This supposition has the merit of fitting well with the biblical record, and certainly it seems more likely than the opinion which fixes his original home further north, near Haran. It is true that the Bible has an even stronger tradition of the clan's settlement at Haran, and recent discoveries in that part of Upper Mesopotamia confirm the existence there of names identical with those borne by members of the clan of Terah. But Genesis makes the entire clan come to Haran from Ur (Gen. 11:31), and this statement has not been proved to be simply an attempt by the author to reconcile two parallel traditions. It is also true that Ur could not have been called " of the Chaldeans " until much later, and that no document outside the Bible gives any confirmation of this primitive migration. But it is certain that from the beginning of the second millennium B.C. the history of Ur was closely linked with that of Haran. Both were dedicated to the god Sin, the moon god who ruled life in the desert, and in the texts Haran is spoken of as the first of Sin's sanctuaries after Ur.

This religious tie is significant, and argues to other contacts between these peoples of common ancestry. For one thing there were, as we have seen, the constant comings and goings along the river belt. At the beginning of the second millennium B.C. Mesopotamia was invaded by another branch of Semites, the Amorites, who swept in from the west and tried to settle in the Fertile Crescent. Some of them went south towards Syria and Palestine, and it is there that we find them, a thousand years later, absorbed into the urban civilization of Canaan. The greater proportion made for Mesopotamia, where they settled in the central Euphrates valley. These later set up the powerful kingdom of Mari, where some 20,000 texts covering this period have been found. Some of them went even further south, and set up states which under the powerful king Hammurabi (1728-1686) finally absorbed the kingdom of Babylon. Hammurabi's code of law, now in the Louvre, bears eloquent testimony to his fame. The Third Dynasty of Ur crumbled under the weight of these successive invasions about 1940 B.C. In the light of all this, it is not unreasonable to suppose that some of the Semitic clans that had settled around Ur were forced to go back to their wandering life, eventually to return to their former homes and kinsmen at Haran in the north.

WHATEVER the truth about this first migration, the settlement of the clan of Terah at Haran and their subsequent migration from Haran to Palestine is based on much more solid historical evidence. It is here that we come to the beginnings of Bible history proper. It was Abraham the son of Terah who revolutionized the material and spiritual life of his people.

We may wonder at the reasons for such a decision, and ask whether it is possible to give it an approximate date. The Bible explains it as a new religious experience which uprooted Abraham from his social background. This religious explanation fits in well with the psychology of the nomad, and with the desert life, where there is nothing to stifle the inner voice. In the desert, religion and life are one. If a man turns away to serve a new God, he automatically cuts himself off from his people: he must found a new clan in a new land. At the same time, God works through human agents, and it has been suggested that this decision of Abraham's coincided with the western expansion of Hammurabi, king of Babylon, whom we have just described as the leader of the Amorite invasion. In the famous expedition of the four kings against Palestine in Genesis 14, Amraphel, King of Shinar, would be none other than Hammurabi, King of Babylon. The identification has been rejected by recent studies, but this strange chapter of the Bible has provided a strong basis for another theory, put forward by Pere de Vaux in the *Revue Biblique* of 1947 and 1949.

His theory stresses the value of the ancient place-names in Genesis, confirmed as they so often are by recent excavations. It may not be possible to identify the four kings absolutely, but their lands were certainly Syria, Upper Mesopotamia and Elam. Without any doubt, the route they chose for their military expedition was designed to give them control over the great High Road that runs through Transjordan, from Syria to the Persian Gulf.   Modern excavations have confirmed that there is no evidence of urban life throughout the length of the route for the period between the nineteenth and thirteenth centuries. This can only mean that the whole country was invaded and overrun by nomadic hordes.   These conditions do not fit the expansion of the first Babylonian Empire, but they tally well with the Horite invasion from the north a hundred years earlier.

The warlike Horites were not a Semitic people.   They came down from their mountain country on the borders of Mesopotamia at the same time as the Amorites invaded the Crescent, and settled in upper Syria.   It was here, as we have said, that the clan of Terah was established.   Stronger elements of the Horites penetrated further south and turned chiefly to the towns.   In their wake followed numerous contingents of nomads, who settled throughout the length of the country in the places devastated by the military invader.   It is this exact situation whose memory has been preserved in Genesis 14, which seems to be based on some contemporary document. The migration of Abraham is presented as part of the Horite expansion, in which case he must have left Haran about the year 1850 B.C.

The theory is confirmed to some extent by the use of the word *Hebrew* to describe Abraham in this passage of Genesis. The word is rare in the Bible and is invariably a non-Israelite expression.   It no doubt has an affinity with the word *Habiru* which recurs constantly in documents recently brought to light. During the second millennium B.C., from upper Mesopotamia to Egypt, *Habiru* meant strangers employed as mercenaries or slaves.   It had a social connotation, but would easily be applied to those restless and stormy elements, later to be called Arameans, who wandered the length of the Arabo-Syrian desert. Once again then, non-biblical testimony enables us to pinpoint Abraham with more historical precision than was once thought possible. We can only conclude that the old biblical accounts give an extremely faithful picture of the period under the Patriarchs, in spite of the fact that their way of life was later to disappear.

The land of Canaan was indeed a land of many attractions for the nomads who came from the desert. With its good and varied soil, it combined the advantages of a settled life with a wide scope for grazing. When Abraham came there, it had already been inhabited for more than a thousand years by a people who were Semites like himself, but whose settled ways had encouraged a high measure of civilization. The Canaanites lived chiefly in the plains. The Amorites, who came later, and who were cousins of the invaders of Babylonia, kept to the hills and Transjordan. These peoples were all subdivided into numerous little principalities by the very contours of the land. They built strongly fortified towns, and their chiefs pompously called themselves kings.

Such a state of affairs could result only in perpetual intrigue and rivalry, with the two big neighbouring powers doing their best to exploit the situation. The nomad who could keep in with his neighbours was in a sound position. It was this spacious land that Abraham chose for his wanderings. He roamed here and there with his small tribe of some 300 men (Gen. 14:14), feeding his flocks from pasture to pasture, from the hills of Samaria to the borders of Egypt. Through his own industry, integrity and wealth he soon came to be a strong and powerful sheik.

SO TOO his descendants stayed, where the mien and power of their Patriarch was respected. The situation was not without its difficulties. We see Isaac, and later his son Jacob, having to insist on the rights that they had acquired. They did not lose all contact with their people at Haran. Obeying the custom of the desert, Isaac and Jacob both went back there to take a wife from among their own folk. Nor did they allow themselves to become absorbed by the people among whom they moved: in fact they despised them. Gradually their small numbers increased, especially after the birth of Jacob's twelve sons, and their self-assurance grew.

One big factor which saved the clan from being absorbed by

the people of Canaan was a series of droughts. We have already seen the importance of rain in Palestine. A prolonged drought spelt ruin because the annual yield of crops was not large enough to allow of stock-piling. The flocks of a semi-nomad must have water or die. There was only one solution to the drought—a journey to Egypt. We have vivid Egyptian paintings which show row upon row of these Semites from Asia, seeking permission to stay with their flocks and possessions in the wonderfully fertile valley, even though it meant the loss of their freedom.

The acceptance of Jacob's people in Egypt was made easier by Joseph's rise to power. Egyptologists have long recognized the remarkable accuracy in the Bible's detailed account of his life in Egypt, although they can find no trace of Joseph's name among the Grand Viziers.

This might well be explained by the fact that the event would have taken place in the middle of the *Hyksos* or "Foreign King" Period, about the year 1600 B.C. *Hyksos* was the name used to designate those Semitic invaders who ruled Egypt under two dynasties from 1750 to 1550. These foreigners would have showed preference for their fellows who had immigrated into Egypt, by appointing them to key positions in the realm. The Egyptians had such bitter memories of this domination that after their expulsion they systematically destroyed every shred of evidence for the period. This would explain both the plausibility of the story of Joseph and the silence of existing documents.

So we find the clan of Jacob, still "few in number" (Gen. 34 : 30), living a semi-settled life in the land of Goshen, between the Nile Delta and the eastern desert. It was a land that offered wide pasturage, not rich like the Nile Valley, but still not desert either. Its relative isolation helped them keep their identity, and its soil their pastoral customs. They had journeyed from one end of the Fertile Crescent to the other, and they had lost neither the purity of their race nor their pride in their semi-nomadic way of life.

IV

EVENTS IN THE CORRIDOR

1. The Exodus after the defeat of the Hyksos; Moses, seer and leader; the desert, crucible of Israel; the attempts to penetrate the land of Canaan.

2. The Conquest in two phases; Joshua destroys the Canaanite principalities slowly but incompletely; national and religious crisis under the Judges.

3. The Monarchy encouraged by the Philistine danger; David overcomes the reluctance of his people; the Schism and religious decadence compromise his work; fall of Samaria in 721; fall of Jerusalem in 597.

4. Judaism; the exiles regroup and return as a religious community; the Maccabee revolution and Roman occupation; historical reasons for Good Friday; the year 70.

The Exodus

"Now there arose a new king over Egypt who did not know Joseph" (Ex. 1 : 8). This terse statement summarizes a period of two or three hundred years; for a further record of that time we must return to the documents of Egypt. The memory of Joseph was forgotten not so much because of the passage of time, but because of the change of fortune resulting from the overthrow of the Hyksos by the XVIIIth Dynasty. The upheaval took place about 1550 B.C., soon after the Israelites had settled in Egypt, and it was typical of the strong and proud nationalism of the Pharaohs of the time. There is no reason to suppose that the clan of Jacob was singled out immediately. They lived on the desert fringe, far removed from the main stream of Egyptian life, and it was not until their numbers and solidarity had become marked that they were noticed at all. But their standing did begin to go down, and along with other groups of Semitic settlers they came to be regarded as pariahs, fit only to dig and sweat on the great new public buildings. The actual Exodus cannot be dated with certainty: historians hesitate between the fifteenth and thirteenth century B.C.

General opinion favours the thirteenth, in which case the last great oppressor of Israel was Rameses II, whose long reign was marked by intensive building activity and imperialistic aims. The Bible gives his name to one of the towns on the Delta which the Israelites were forced to build (Ex. 1 : 11).

Three hundred years had gone by since Jacob's small clan had first come to Egypt. By now it was, in the words of the Bible, " a numerous and formidable people ". In assessing their numbers we must make allowance for the usual oriental hyperbole, and we do not have to imagine a homogeneous group of several hundred thousands. All the same, there was always the latent danger that they would unite with their kinsmen in the desert to form a real threat to the safety of Egypt's borders. Pharaoh determined to suppress the danger by reducing them to abject slavery, and he seemed to have succeeded in crushing their spirit altogether. But the nomadic pride was not entirely quenched. It burst into flames again, unexpectedly enough, in an Israelite who had escaped the oppression and had been brought up as an Egyptian. From the very beginning, Moses displayed the high qualities, the pride, the imperiousness and the self-sufficiency of a born leader. The indignity of his people's enslavement galled him bitterly. It was the mental rather than the physical slavery that appalled him and made him into a fervent nationalist. He found himself forced to seek refuge in the desert, and it was there that he recaptured the old nomadic spirit of his ancestors. He discovered anew the God of his Fathers, and the experience changed him. Now he had only one aim: to rescue his people from their nothingness, to bring them to the desert, and to give them back their self-respect and their God.

It was no easy task. The Egyptians would not surrender their profitable labour-force without a protest. The Israelites themselves were not over-eager to exchange the flesh-pots of Egypt for the hard fare of the desert. It was only his own personal dynamism that enabled Moses to weld them together, and only his influence at court that won the unwilling consent of Pharaoh. Early efforts came to nothing. It was the unexpected that finally helped him to prevail. He outwitted the suspicious Egyptians and managed to shatter the apathy in the hearts of his kinsmen. His religious prestige was heightened by a succession of God-sent catastrophes that captured the imagination of Egyptian and Israelite alike. Once they had journeyed beyond the chain of lakes north of the Red Sea, the fugitives found sanctuary in the desert.

THE desert of Sinai was to be the crucible for the tempering of Israel. The various elements which Moses had led out were there forged into a single unit with a common destiny. Up to this, they had only the scorn of Egypt to remind them of their common stock and unique heritage. Their already feeble unity was further endangered when other groups of wandering Semites joined them. Under the influence of the hard desert life, the isolation, and the authority of a chief, they were gradually moulded into a homogeneous unit. It was for Yahweh alone to make of them a real people.

In the East it is religious unity that sets the seal on national unity, and only service to a common deity can make a real nation. It was precisely in order to consecrate them to Yahweh that Moses made use of the hardships of his people and brought them back to the desert. In rescuing them from the sedentary life which would surely have absorbed them, and in restoring them to the ways of their Fathers, his only aim was to put their national consciousness on a firm foundation—a solemn consecration to the God of their Fathers. That is the true meaning of the Covenant at Sinai, and of the religious, social and juridical code which Moses established there. The ensuing years of wandering around the religious centre of Kadesh gave the tribes of Israel the opportunity to make this constitution part of themselves.

For the time being, lest they lose heart, Moses conjured up for them pictures of the delights of Canaan, their proper homeland. It was not unknown to many of them, since some of the clans had stayed on there, or had left for there, before the general Exodus. It was not enough, if he was to fashion a real people, to make them realize their unity through ties of blood and common worship. They must also possess a land, where their God could find a dwelling place.

This in itself was no easy matter, as the badly armed and undisciplined group found when they tried to force an entry into Canaan from the south. For a long time the natives had

F

been practised against the periodic raids of gangs from the desert. Their civilization had taught them how to meet the ragged attacks of the nomad bedouins with armed strength. The difficult terrain and a chain of fortifications effectively barred all the main approaches from the Negeb. The Israelites were utterly routed at Hormah (Numbers 14:45) and were forced to withdraw back into the desert.

Moses tried a new tactic. Some of the clans living on the borders of the coveted land were related to the Israelites. They had not followed Jacob all the way into Egypt, but had settled here, and had reached a high degree of civilization. Edom and Moab, for instance, had by this time already established a monarchical system of government. Moses tried to form an alliance with these, but failed. Edom would not even grant him free passage for his people, and Israel could do nothing but go back and for many years continue to wander. But there came a time when the tribes felt that they were strong enough to try again. Moab protected Canaan along the right flank; if the Israelites could only get over Moab, they would be almost in the heart of the "promised land", where an element of surprise would give them the upper hand. The first step was to put no trust in the false Moabites, and to overcome the Amorites living with them in Transjordan. One success after another brought them through to the banks of the Jordan, opposite Jericho, in sight of the hills of Palestine. They were now on the open flank of the unsuspecting Canaanites.

The Conquest

FOR forty years, the life span of a single generation, Israel wandered in the desert. Moses had died shortly before they were ended, and it was for his lieutenant Joshua to launch the entry into Canaan. His plan was deceptively simple. Once over the Jordan he concentrated all his forces together in one immense camp on the bank. From there he planned a series of raids into the interior. Jericho was unprepared and fell at a single blow, and the gateway to the hill country was open. He quickly marched up the valley behind Jericho, and assaulted the two citadels Ai and Gibeon in the very centre of the mountain range. This daring manoeuvre cut in two the numerous small Canaanite principalities of the hill country before they had a chance to sink their personal rivalries and unite against a common enemy. Later they did rally, and the southern princes formed a coalition under the leadership of the powerful key city of Jerusalem. Joshua attacked, and with great difficulty defeated them at Gibeon. He then wheeled against the northern princes, who were already demoralized by the news of the victory in the south. His chief tactic was again speed of movement, and he caught them unprepared near Lake Merom, and cut them to pieces.

A casual reading of the book of Joshua might give the impression that these swift sallies had subjugated the whole land of Canaan and forced it to yield its riches to the conqueror almost overnight. A closer study shows that it was not so. These were only the preliminary skirmishes. The enemy's lack of unity made him hard to pin down; he quickly retreated and took refuge in his impregnable strongholds. The most that can be claimed for these victories is that they gave Israel a foothold and opened up the country. The whole work of occupation had still to be achieved. This was a slow and difficult business, and was not carried through in a single campaign. It was not completed in the lifetime of Joshua, who never had a more permanent home than the camp at Gilgal. Right through the period after his death, down to the time of the Kings even, Israel was engaged in subjugating the land she had taken. In fact the operation can best be described as a gradual penetration, where each tribe on its own initiative carved out territory for itself as best it could. Their efforts met with varying success. In the south, Judah and the clans allied to it managed to established themselves so strongly that the Canaanites virtually disappeared. In most other places it was a case of compromising with the enemy. Sometimes it was Israel who prevailed, and the enemy had to bide his time to strike again. Sometimes there was a tacit agreement to equal shares of land. Sometimes Israel was the underdog, being no more than tolerated by the proud Canaanites.

THE outcome of this all but abortive conquest was the dark period named after the Judges. The invading tribes, whom Moses had so dearly welded into a unity, were now dispersed, sometimes existing merely as isolated colonies in the labyrinth of Canaanite principalities. This dissipation of their strength was danger enough; more dangerous still was their cultural inferiority. These nomad bedouins had no knowledge of how to till the soil. In having to learn from the men they had conquered, whether they liked it or not they came under the influence of the culture, and what was worse the religion, of Canaan. The only real bond that held the nation together was the common belief in Yahweh, and this itself was now being undermined by the sensual cults of the Canaanites. The Baals of the settled farmer were far less demanding than the austere God of the nomad warrior.

It is difficult to imagine how the work of Moses was able to survive such attractions. But the old ideals were preserved in those clans which were more faithful to the old ways, especially where the hand of the Canaanites bore down heavily on them or where they were near to the desert. It was from these strongholds of Yahweh that the " Judges " came. The name gives a poor idea of their function, since it involved no permanent juridical status. Their authority was temporary and circumstantial, and more often than not martial in character, after the fashion of a *dictator* of the Roman Republic. The Judge was generally an outstanding sheik who had risen to the occasion to free his clan or tribe from the oppression of the natives. Usually his action was limited to his own immediate neighbourhood, although occasionally he assumed the leadership of several tribes who were threatened by the Canaanites from the plains or by the nomads from across the Jordan.

There was, then, no concerted action or fixed authority. Faced by a people whose constitution was already monarchical, the people of Israel clung tenaciously to their patriarchial and nomadic way of life. They even emphasized their individualism by internal rivalry, and the mistrust of one tribe for another amounted to something like a desire for supremacy. The tribes from the north first played a dominant part under Deborah. The tribe of Benjamin made a similar attempt. But it was Ephraim, the most central of the tribes in their hill-country of Samaria, that finally turned all these feuds to its own profit by sheer brute force.

All this time, Judah seems to have lived a life apart. Isolated in the hills, it merged closely with neighbouring clans, biding its time. Towards the end of the period of the Judges, a new danger made Judah's mission clear. The threat of the Philistines, which was already hanging over the whole of Israel, was to make Judah the defender of the whole nation. The Philistines were newcomers on the scene. They were not Semites, but belonged to the pre-Hellenic groups that were known as "The Peoples from the Sea". They were an Indo-European race, closely related to the Mycenaeans or Cretans, whose civilization has been brought to light by excavations. Their migration was part of that general dispersal throughout the Aegean that followed the arrival of a kindred race, the Dorians. The Trojan war, immortalized by Homer, was part of the same upheaval. By land and sea they made for Egypt, only to be repulsed and thrown back to the coast of Palestine about the time that Israel was herself engaged in taking over the country. They quickly merged with the Canaanites and adopted their civilization. But they brought their own contribution, too, iron chariots, the use of the horse, and the Greek armour which makes the description of Goliath so reminiscent of a hoplite. With such weapons they soon became masters of the plains. They firmly established themselves in five principalities on the southern seaboard, and from there they set out on a methodical conquest of the interior.

The Monarchy

THE gravity of the impending danger was not at first appreciated. There were some preliminary skirmishes like those which popular imagination built around the near legendary figure of Samson. But it became increasingly obvious that something more than mere provocation was needed. The Philistines were slowly beginning to penetrate the hill country of Ephraim, with the obvious intention of cutting the country into two and dealing with Israel piecemeal. Israel realized the danger too late; her attempt to halt the enemy at Aphek met with failure. The tribes were greatly alarmed, and they determined to come together for a supreme effort. They brought the

Ark of the Covenant from Shiloh and, as was their custom during the time of the conquest, they followed it into battle. But this time Yahweh had decided to abandon his people. Their losses were disastrous—the Ark of the Covenant was lost and the Israelites of the hill country were reduced to slavery.

This unprecedented catastrophe was the prelude to a profound change in the social constitution of Israel. On the one hand the Yahwistic faith was raised from its torpor to become a religious movement which was fiercely reformatory and nationalistic. This "Prophetism" was destined to play a decisive rôle in the future. Sometimes it took the form of communities grouped around an outstanding personality—the "sons of the prophets" in the beginning of the book of Samuel are a typical example. But there were others, more realistic in outlook, who knew well enough that religious fervour does not dispense with human endeavour. It was clear that Israel's defeat was due in large measure to its nomadic character. They were unable to cope with the present situation and were no match for their more sophisticated neighbours. Even in the period of the Judges, these enlightened men had advocated a closer coalition of all the tribes under a stronger and more stable authority. Gideon had been approached with this in mind, but although he liked to play the oriental potentate he still kept to the old nomadic and theocratic idea that Israel must have no king other than Yahweh (cf. Judges 8 : 22-23). The moment was not yet opportune, and it was not to be until Samuel's time that the urgency of the situation began to weaken the traditionalist opposition which lived on in prophetic circles. From this time dates the open breach between the prophetic and royalist camps. It is here that the struggle for the leadership of the nation has its beginnings.

Samuel did in fact yield, but not without misgivings. He took the precaution of defining the exact place that this innovation was to occupy in the life of God's people by stressing the absolute primacy of religion. Israel's monarchy must always be secondary to Yahweh. In no way could it be compared with the absolute and tyrannical monarchy of other peoples. The Israelites must always stay faithful to their nomadic ancestors, free men of their clans and subject to no one but

Yahweh. The king of Israel was to be no more than Yahweh's representative, to wage Yahweh's wars and to protect Yahweh's people. This was the yardstick by which the religious elite of Israel—the prophetic groups—were to measure the worth of kings on the throne of Israel. In short, the royal power would always be regarded as limited, subordinate, and in almost inevitable opposition to the prophets, who had their authority direct from God.

From the outset Israel's monarchy gave promise of future discord. The very beginning was unpropitious. Saul, of the tribe of Benjamin, was Samuel's own choice, and although he was entirely obedient to the prophet's orders at first, he became drunk with his early success against the Philistines and was soon asserting his independence. His fiery and unbalanced temperament brought him into conflict with Samuel, who was bitterly hurt. Saul was in fact his own worst enemy, and himself paved the way for the triumph of his successor David.

I F W E can credit the old popular accounts, David was no more than a boy when a strange twist of fortune turned him into a hero. This frank and vigorous youth was too young to bear arms, and so had been left to tend his father's flocks. All the same he took up the challenge of Goliath the Philistine, and his totally unforeseen victory gave evidence not only of his skill and adaptability, but also of his deep devotion to Yahweh. He became attached to the king's retinue and won the love of the royal daughter. It was not long before the whole of Israel was talking about the exploits of this young captain in the war against the Philistines. Such fame could only anger the neurotic and lonely king, and David's fall from favour was inevitable. He was forced to seek refuge in the desert, and there he found himself surrounded by a group of malcontents. With their aid he ruled the Negeb, and enhanced his reputation and social status. He was hunted by Saul, but he had enough sense not to compromise his own future by laying a hand on Yahweh's anointed. When the chase became too hot, he enlisted with the Philistines, but refrained from any action that would harm Israel.

Such a delicate situation was happily and dramatically resolved at Gilboa. Saul was killed in an encounter which opened to the enemy the approaches to the Jordan and gave them the key to the north. David immediately returned to his people, and at Hebron his own tribe Judah proclaimed him king. The Schism had already begun. The tribes of the north remained faithful to Ishbaal, the colourless successor of Saul, although he was on the throne only because the Philistines permitted it. David himself made a temporary settlement with the enemies of the nation, and trusting implicitly in Yahweh he bided his time. He had to wait seven years. Ishbaal was the victim of court intrigue, and envoys came down from the north to offer the crown to David. He had shown his ability to rule by doing no more than take the gifts of Yahweh as they fell into his lap.

By the sheer grace of God and under his care alone, this one-time shepherd had within the space of fifteen years become king of all Israel. Now for the first time since the days of the desert the followers of Moses were a single people. Single, that is, to the outward eye. They were far from being single-minded. It was to achieve this that David applied himself. His first concern was to find a city for his capital that would not tie him to any one tribe. He decided on Jerusalem, a city in the very heart of the country still held by the Jebusites. He captured it by a tactic which brought his men to the centre of the stronghold by means of an underground passage which joins the citadel to a spring outside the walls and can be seen to this day. Having established himself in Jerusalem, his prime concern was to install the Ark of Yahweh, so that henceforth Israel's God, King and capital would be indissolubly bound together. It still remained to overthrow the Philistines once and for all. By a series of successful campaigns he threw them back to the plain, and reduced them to a state of bondage. He was even able to establish the might of Israel throughout the whole of Canaan, and into Edom, Moab and Ammon. By the middle of David's reign Israel was more or less free from her enemies.

It was now that internal weaknesses began to show. The king's sons disputed the right of succession, and did not hesitate to stir up those strong feelings for independence which were part of the tribal birthright. Absalom openly revolted and was very nearly successful. The later years of the aging king were saddened by intrigue, and it was such intrigue that enabled

Solomon, a son of the king's favourite wife, to supersede his eldest brother Adoniah.

DAVID'S success was mainly due to his personality. His nobility of outlook, his independent spirit, his frank and generous love, equalled only by his cunning: these made it easy for him to impose his will on others. Above all he had utter confidence in Yahweh, his God. All the same, he would never have enjoyed such success within the country if the international situation had been otherwise. Egypt and Assyria would not have been spectators to his policy of solidarity and unification in the Corridor if they had not themselves been almost eclipsed by internal strife.

Solomon tried to take full advantage of their plight to build Israel into a first-rate power. For a short while he achieved his purpose, but he had not his father's lofty character to carry him through. He abandoned the paternal approach to the tribes, in favour of a harsh centralized administration. But we must not underrate the importance of his achievements. The Temple, the palace and his harem, which included a daughter of Pharaoh, all these gave him a lustre which compared favourably with the magnificence of his great neighbours, and was in fact a conscious imitation of them.

Unfortunately he was not able to maintain these standards for long. In order to achieve them in the first place, Solomon had to reduce his freedom-loving people to the level of slaves. Worse still, he had abandoned the theocratic ideal of the monarchy, and had become an arbitrary tyrant. On his death, the spirit of rebellion, which had always smouldered under the eager encouragement of Egypt, burst into flames, and the tribes instinctively went their individual ways. The Schism was complete. North and south separated into two distinct kingdoms, under the rival tribes of Ephraim and Judah.

The northern kingdom centred on Samaria, the capital of Ephraim. Its history was nothing other than a sequence of short-lived prosperity and bloody revolution. Dynasties followed each other in rapid succession, and were nearly all marked by an increasing abandonment of the theocratic ideal and faith in Yahweh. Elijah, Elisha, Amos and Hosea, the first of the great prophets, had only disaster to preach to the people. Assyria began to regain power, and her harsh rule was soon to be felt in the political life of the Corridor. The kings of Samaria, trusting too readily in Egypt, offered resistance, but in the year 721 Sargon II took the city, and deported the élite of the northern tribes to Mesopotamia. It was the beginning of the end for this, the larger half of the chosen people. Those who were allowed to remain intermarried with the imported foreigners, to form the mongrel people known as the Samaritans.

Meanwhile the kingdom of Judah lived through her crises, and remained loyal to her dynasty and her God. Her isolated position helped to preserve her even after Samaria had fallen. She was helped too by the great reforming prophets, Isaiah under Hezekiah, and Jeremiah under Josiah. They counterbalanced the evil influence of the pro-Egyptian party and their attempt to reject the Assyrian protectorate. After the sudden fall of Assyria's capital Nineveh in 612, the policy of this party seemed to prevail but, under her king Nebuchadnezzar, Babylon proved to be another Assyria. Jerusalem was put under siege, and finally taken in 597. The last elements of resistance were stamped out by the mass deportations to lower Mesopotamia. Those who were left fled to Egypt, and by the year 586 the destruction was complete.

Judaism

IT IS difficult to measure the profound despair of the deportees. It would have been bad enough if it was only political sovereignty that had been taken from them, as it had been from so many others. But they were deeply convinced that the universal triumph of their God, the one true God, was inextricably bound up with their own national survival. Israel's disappearance as a nation meant that her faith itself was at stake.

How she ever managed to survive is one of the most astounding facts in her history. At every stage of her development, she emerged unscathed from crises which engulfed the great powers. Under the stimulus of Ezekiel's preaching, the captive exiles gradually came back to life. Ezekiel showed them the providential design behind the disaster and they started off again on a new footing. This time there was no question of national autonomy—they were only cogs in the great machinery of the Babylonian Empire. But they still had religious and social freedom, and took advantage of it to form fervent cells which fostered the hope of return, and they prepared for it by a life of strict fidelity to the religious ideals of the past.

The only authority they had left was that of the priests. Their overwhelming influence encouraged this new spirit to grow into a national consciousness which was on a plane altogether different from that of the pre-exilic Israel. The emphasis now was on worship and obedience to the Law. It was from the ashes of the Israelite nation that the Jewish community was born.

About the year 536, the seed that had been sown during the Exile blossomed forth. The predictions of the writer of the second part of the book of Isaiah became fact. The Babylonian Empire was crushed by the Persian Cyrus, who showed considerable religious toleration towards his subjects and even allowed the re-establishment of the peoples his enemies had oppressed. This does not mean that all the exiles took to the road immediately. Many of them had prospered in exile and had settled down. The first contingent set out for Jerusalem under the Davidic prince Zerubbabel (it would seem that he must not be confused with Sheshbazzar). Their first concern was to rebuild the Temple, a task which dragged on laboriously until it was finally completed about 526, at the instigation of the prophets Haggai and Zechariah. This achievement so aroused the jealousy of the people who had been brought in to populate the plains that they opposed the reconstruction of the city walls, and for half a century the little colony was unable to develop further.

Fortunately, in the year 445, Nehemiah appeared on the scene. He had been cupbearer to the Persian king Artaxerxes II, who granted him privileges even greater than those granted by Cyrus. His faith, worthy of David himself, overcame all difficulties, and gradually the walls of the city were rebuilt. The work of Nehemiah was consolidated by another group, some forty years later, under Ezra the priest. His particular achievement was the detailed organization of the life of what was now a religious community. Political autonomy was out of the question, for Judaea was no more than a Persian satrapy. The advent of Alexander in 333 meant only a change of overlord, and the country came under the jurisdiction of the Lagidae of Egypt. This was certainly the most fruitful and peaceful period in the whole history of the Jewish community.

THE year 198 saw a sudden change. Palestine passed out of the control of the Lagidae, and fell into the hands of the Syrian Seleucids. Their plan was to absorb their new acquisition into the hellenistic culture of their kingdom, and thus ensure the religious, moral and social unity of the old Empire of Alexander. The plan had the backing of an important section of the ruling class within Palestine. Even some of the priests adopted the Greek customs and ideas. Greek schools and baths were opened in Jerusalem, and circumcision became a thing to hide. Antiochus Epiphanes went so far as to impose the Greek religion, and had Jewish priests offering sacrifice to Greek gods in the Temple.

The situation was grave. The protest came, unexpectedly, from a little country town near Jerusalem called Modein. It was here that the movement was born which was to restore to the Jews their national independence for a whole century. A zealous priest named Mattathias refused to offer sacrifice to the gods. He fled to the desert, the constant refuge from persecution and crucible of religious purification. A band of rebels gathered around his sons, prepared to do anything to safeguard the religion and traditions of their ancestors. They became known as the *Hasidim* or "Holy Ones". Judas, the eldest son of Mattathias, took the surname of Maccabee (the Hammer), and led these fanatics into battle, to win two resounding victories against the Syrians and march on to liberate Jerusalem. The crowning triumph of the rebels was the purification of the Temple in 164. Spurred on by his success, Judas aimed at consolidating the results of the religious revolution by gaining political independence. When he died a hero's death in the year 160, his brothers Jonathan and Simon made use of Syria's own troubles to further their total emancipation. Simon assumed the hereditary title of Prince and High Priest, and became founder of the Hasmonean dynasty.

Unfortunately the burning religious idealism which had

inspired the Maccabean revolt was soon dimmed by the possession of such power, and only two religious sects survived. One was the remnant of the Maccabean Hasidim. They developed into a kind of brotherhood, exclusively religious, bent on safeguarding the purity of the traditional faith and customs. Their austere way of life earned them the name of *Pharisees* or "Separatists". They included especially the laymen particularly skilled in matters of Jewish Law, called Scribes. The other sect which survived was the priestly aristocracy. They were called *Sadducees* and held strongly to the old political ideas of the hellenizing party. In a change of allegiance as complete as it was unexpected, Simon's son John Hyrcanus (135-108) went over to the Sadducees, and began a bitter persecution of the Pharisees. His successors continued to carry out his policy right up to the coming of Pompey, who put an end to the affair when he took the Temple by storm in the year 63.

This was the beginning of what was perhaps the saddest period in Israel's history. The Jewish people finally lost that independence for which they had fought, and fought the more strongly because they had for so long been without hope of ever finding it again. At first the yoke sat lightly upon their shoulders. By sheer intrigue a former minister of the Hasmoneans, a man of Idumean stock (i.e. from Edom) ingratiated himself with Caesar, and won the right to rule the country in the name of Rome. After the battle of Actium in the year 31 his son, Herod the Great, was given permission by Octavius Augustus to call himself king. Herod was a brave man, but tyrannical and cruel, and profane records corroborate the description of him in the Gospels. He died in 4 B.C. (in fact two or three years after the birth of Christ; our era is based on a miscalculation), and most of his kingdom was divided among his sons. Judaea was the exception. It was so unruly that it was placed under the direct supervision of a Roman governor. Hence the Gospels show us a Palestine divided into four distinct territories, Judaea, Galilee, Ituraea and Abilene (Luke 3 : 1), although in fact they were all under Roman jurisdiction.

AT THIS critical stage in the history of Israel, we must call to mind the recurring pattern of this people's evolution. It is the only way to understand the twofold drama that put an end to her existence as a nation with a religious mission.

When Christ began his public ministry about the year A.D. 27 (cf. above; he was born in 6 or 7 B.C.), the Jews were in a state of religious and political turmoil, the regular climax in their evolution. Chafing under the yoke of Rome, the great mass of the people were haunted by memories of the Maccabees, and they cherished fond hopes of liberation. The ruling class was divided. The Pharisees, the official representatives of orthodoxy, had the ear of the people, but their religious enthusiasm had degenerated into a formalism which, from the time of Ezra, had become increasingly hidebound. The Sadducees, the priestly class, sneered at the popular nostalgia and despised the fanaticism of the Pharisees.

Yet it was this fanaticism that prevailed. The Pharisees were not inclined to take up arms, nor did they sympathize with the aspirations of the people. Had they not been so proud in their strict system of caste, and had they not closed their minds to the idea of spiritual rebirth, they might easily have accepted the transcendent teaching of Christ, which was so like their own. As it was, Christ was sacrificed to their pride, and in plotting his downfall they did not hesitate to play upon the disillusions of the people, who looked not for a gentle preacher but for a warrior Messiah. Even the Sadducees gave unlooked for assistance. Their one concern was to prevent the growing unrest in the nation from clashing with the government. Judged by merely human standards, the drama of Good Friday was simply the outcome of a temporary truce between these rival tendencies.

From a historical viewpoint, this almost unnoticed drama was yet another sign of the impending catastrophe. Christ was the victim of a religious fanaticism which grew wilder under the pressure of Roman countermeasures, until in the year 66 the storm broke. A band of demoniacs, whose intolerance served to justify every excess, were even more fanatical than the Pharisees. Titus, son of the future emperor Vespasian, was sent into Galilee to crush the insurgents. In the year 69 he laid siege to Jerusalem.

This siege is one of the darkest episodes in the history of man. The account left us by a contemporary Jewish historian,

Flavius Josephus, is terrifying. It was the end of the Jewish people. There was to be one last desperate attempt when Hadrian was emperor. An adventurer named Bar Kokba, regarded as the Messiah by some of the Rabbis, led a rising in A.D. 125, but it was quenched in blood. All that remained of this strange Jewish people, in whom wretchedness always walked hand in hand with grandeur, were the few communities that had been scattered throughout the ancient world since the time of the Exile. These people of the Diaspora (or Dispersion) remained unaffected by their contact with Greek culture, and kept alive that religious independence with characterizes the whole history of Israel.

V

FROM JUDAISM TO HELLENISM

Christ's death ostracizes the disciples from Judaism; the Jerusalem community, heirs of the chosen people; the churches of St. Paul, the new spiritual Israel; St. John and the pagan world.

THE date of Christ's crucifixion (probably April 7th, A.D. 30) marks the decisive break in the continuity of the life of God's people. Yet the break was more apparent than real. It had happened so often before—Egypt, Canaan, the Exile—these so-called "breaks" were but the beginnings of an unexpected and astonishingly fruitful rebirth. Israel had been transformed from a tiny clan into a people, and from a warrior people into an isolated religious community. Now it was to reach its climax in the last transformation. Its religion was to be raised to a universal and divine level.

The disciples of Christ had not visualized this when they followed their Master as the Messiah awaited by Israel. With everyone else, they had looked on him as the providential Saviour who would restore the nation's glory by freeing her from foreign oppression and bringing the whole world to her feet. The Cross, for them, was the supreme catastrophe. But nothing less than the Cross could have destroyed their illusions. After Easter, and even after Pentecost, the early Christian community had only a limited idea of the future extent of this revolution. Salvation was only postponed to the day of the "Parousia", when Jesus the Messiah would come in all his glory on the clouds of heaven. The interval was a breathing space to give the Jewish people time to reconsider their refusal of Jesus the Messiah. Far from claiming to found a new religion, the members of the Mother Church at Jerusalem thought of themselves as the true Israel, the kernel of the ideal Jewish community. This new Israel was no different from the old, except that she now knew the Messiah.

This fond illusion of theirs was shattered by facts. The Parousia was long in coming. Judaism was further from admitting its mistake now than in the year 30. It became more and more hostile. The young community had to sever all connection with it, and judged it to have taken over the rôle of the renegade persecutor. Almost by chance, at the precise moment when the natural heirs to the Kingdom were refusing their heritage, the pagans began to hear of its existence, and unlike the Jews were anxious to accept it. To crown all, the most zealous of the little community's persecutors was converted, and began preaching to the Gentiles.

So unexpected was this widening of scope that the leaders of the Church in Jerusalem hesitated. The Master had warned them of this development, but for the moment his words were forgotten. For the man born a Jew, the pagans were a race of untouchables (cf. Acts 10:28). It seemed too much to ask that the Jewish Christian should overcome his age-old repugnance and accept the pagan as his equal. Such an invasion of new recruits could only create grave difficulties. What guarantee was there that they would leave behind them the sinful habits and opinions that were so directly at war with traditional Judaism? Without this tradition there could be no faith in Christ. How could the Gentiles ever come to understand the words "Messiah", "redemption", "sin", "covenant", "promise", until they had first been initiated into the Jewish way of life, in short until they had first been made Jews?

SUCH were the demands of some of the Christians of Jewish origin. For them, salvation and belief in Jesus the Messiah, Son of God, was necessarily a Jewish concern, applicable only within the framework of Judaism. They were happy enough to include the pagans, but only by extending to them the privileges of the Chosen people, only by integrating them into Judaism.

St. Paul first had the clarity of foresight to appreciate the fallacy of such a viewpoint, apparently so reasonable and right. Almost at once he saw that, if the Judeo-Christians were allowed to make Christ no more than the keystone of the house of Israel, then the very foundation of Christianity was imperilled, and the whole import of Christ's death and resurrection was jeopardized. If Christ was dead, then it was useless looking to him for the restoration of Judaism. If he was risen from the dead, then he was not only the Jewish Messiah, he was the Son of God, and his life was eternal. His mission and the efficacy of his salvation were not of this world. They belonged to a world where there are no Jews or Gentiles, but only sinners needing forgiveness. Christ was not the keystone of Judaism. He was the corner stone of a new building of which the old was only a preparation and a type.

This, then, was the logic of the all-important fact of Christ's death and resurrection. It meant that Judaism was now superseded, and its revelation must be transposed on to a universal and celestial level. The Apostles understood this when they agreed at Jerusalem, about the year 49, that Paul should preach to the Gentiles without imposing the Law on them. They went even further, and allowed Christians of Jewish origin to mix freely with the pagan converts, provided that the converts made certain concessions (Acts 11, Gal. 2:9, Acts 15).

ONE grave difficulty had still to be solved. The message of Christ could not simply by-pass Judaism and pay it no heed. It was in fact the continuation of Judaism, and would be fully understood only in its light. If the whole course of Israel's history was a canvas for the coming of Christ, then Christ could only be fully revealed against that canvas. The Old Testament was no more than a type of the New, but without an understanding of the type the New Testament lacked meaning. St. Paul was faced with this problem of interpreting the one in the light of the other. His solution to the problem bears the sign of divine inspiration.

He tackled the work from both ends. To make Christianity understood to pagans, he took them to the Bible. But he also translated into Greek equivalents the Jewish concepts of its original message. In this way he not only made the Christian message intelligible to the Greco-Latin world, but he also presented it to them as the answer to their own longing for salvation and immortality.

If we are to understand the Christian message in all its fullness, it is not enough to be conversant with the Old Testament thought on which it is built. We must also understand the aspirations of those Greeks for whom the New Testament was written. In other words, we will need some idea of the pagan religions that reflect these aspirations. We must for example know something of the mystery cults, and be familiar with their vocabulary. The pagan was more at home with "salvation" than with "redemption". "Lord" meant more than "Messiah", "immortality" more than "resurrection", and "sin" more than "Law". St. Paul kept the entire Jewish vocabulary, as it was used from the beginning, to express the message of Christ. But he implemented the significance of these words by giving equivalents which the non-Jewish mind could more easily grasp. It was not only a question of single words; he sought out ways of conveying the most universal and fundamental cravings of the human soul, which could be satisfied only by this divine message.

He was helped in his work by circumstances. It would never have been possible without the political and cultural unity of the ancient world. This unity, which was first realized by Alexander and later consolidated in the Roman Empire, was something more than a mere geographical and administrative unity. In this enormous organization there was a single mode of thought and a single stream of aspirations, built on the Greek ideal of culture. It was this that welded these varying nationalities with their own customs into a unified whole. The hellenistic civilization was not entirely ignorant of Judaism nor unknown by it. The communities of the Diaspora were tainted with it, just as they in their turn made a considerable impression on some parts of the pagan world. Christianity looked first of all to these communities to preach its message. They formed the first group of Gentile churches by offering ground ready prepared for the hellenistic conception of the Christian message.

EVEN though most things seemed to favour this transition to the Gentile world, it was not without its risks. The anxieties of the Judeo-Christians were seen to have some justification. The first crisis had concerned the growth of Christianity, and had given rise to the Judeo-Christian issue. Now Christianity's coming of age brought another crisis in the shape of an early form of Gnosticism. The first had tried to put the new movement back into the Jewish environment from which it came. The second tried to merge it into the pagan environment it was trying to conquer. It was inevitable that some converts from paganism had only a superficial idea of the framework and the main themes of Judaism. At Corinth, for example, there was a tendency to take the easy way back to pagan morality, and even the mystery of Christ took on all the overtones of Greek mysticism and was shorn of its moral implications. The Corinthians had been too literal in their interpretation of the Pauline idea of liberation from the Law by faith. In a word, they had been too Greek in their approach. This was to come up again in Asia. The Epistles of St. Paul's captivity show quite clearly the existence of a syncretism in which Judaism, Paulinism and Greek philosophy are all mixed up together to produce a vague and intangible pseudo-mysticism.

It became necessary to try to make things more precise. The tenets of the Judeo-Christian reaction and the Greek excesses of a misconstrued Paulinism were put side by side, and by uniting their orthodox elements it became possible to arrive at a true and fixed synthesis. St. Paul himself had begun to do this. But it was left for the Johannine writings at the end of the first century A.D. to make the final statement of the revelation that had begun back in the time of Abraham. The Judeo-Christian ghost, which still haunted the early form of Gnosticism, was finally laid by the Fourth Gospel's insistence on the absolute newness of the New Covenant. The pagan syncretism of those same Gnostic tendencies was answered in the Apocalypse, with its stress on the vital links that bind Christianity to its Jewish origins. Both of these books, in spite of their dissimilarity, give the lie to any suggestion of a breach in the development of God's people, whose history we have been tracing. With St. Paul they insist that the two Testaments cannot be divorced, because they have been joined together by God.

And to us readers of the Bible in the twentieth century, St. John still affirms that if the Old Testament has no meaning without the New, then neither can the New Testament be understood without a full appreciation of the Old.

CHAPTER IV

THE BIRTH OF THE BIBLE

ARMED with our knowledge of the country and the history
of Israel, we can now approach the Book itself. There
were certain periods of this history which were particularly fruitful from a literary point of view, and they mark the
chief stages in the formation of the Bible. It was a gradual
formation, in which certain books were singled out as works
for which God was directly responsible. This discrimination
was practised first by the Jews and later by Christians. It
was finally sanctioned by the Church when she set up her
"Canon of Scripture" to establish which books were divinely
inspired.

I

THE FORMATION OF THE BOOK

*Its complex character; the three main literary periods of
Israelite history; their origins; the part played by each
in the formation of the Old Testament; oral style and
memory; their influence on the formation of the New Testament; St. Paul's Epistles dictated by circumstance; the
primitive catechesis and the Gospels; conclusion.*

IT WOULD be childish to imagine that the Bible was made
simply by collecting together the various books as they came
from the hands of individual writers. The Ancients, and the
Semites in particular, were not concerned as we are with copyright. To them, anything that was written, like the truth it
expressed, was public property. It could be freely added to or
modified to ensure that it best suited the particular needs of
time and place. In practice there is very little, in the Old
Testament at least, which can be attributed with certainty to
a specific author. For the most part the original texts have
suffered considerable modification in the course of time. Some

101

of them are a meticulous and scholarly amalgamation of earlier existing writings, others the gradual fusing together of the most varied kind of documents.

Several of the Old Testament writings can be dated with sufficient accuracy to enable us to determine the literary and doctrinal characteristics of the period from which they come. Almost all exegetes agree, for example that 2 Samuel 9-20 and the parts of the book of Kings that deal with Elijah and Elisha, are important fragments of chronicles almost contemporary with the events they describe. They agree similarly in attributing to the Prophets of the eighth and seventh centuries many of the prophecies that bear their names. The prophecy of Ezekiel and the second part of the book of Isaiah are valuable records for the history of the Exile. Lastly, the vast collection of Chronicles-Nehemiah-Ezra gives us an accurate picture of the post-exilic religious tendencies, and the literary trends which obtained in the Jewish community of the third century B.C. These works give us a yardstick for measuring three main periods in the literary history of Israel.

The first is the period of the ancient monarchy, about the time of David or the early Schism. The literary works of this epoch consist principally of history and anecdote. Here are gathered the religious traditions and the popular accounts of a golden past. As would be expected, the confidence and hope of a growing civilization are reflected in this literature. The chronicles of the House of David have the freshness of youth, and the earnestness and the zest for life that is reminiscent of Herodotus or Bede's *History of England*.

The popular traditions of Israel usually offer us two points of reference at this stage. They survived in parallel forms in each of the two kingdoms which resulted from the Schism of Jeroboam.

The prophetic writings belong to a later period, and show a marked contrast with the period that went before. The confidence of a young nation has given way to the preoccupied reflections of a people that has grown weary of the sophistications of civilization and is disquieted by social troubles. The prophetic literature is given to moralizing, and its religion is exclusive, lofty and transcendent. Moral uprightness and fidelity to the Covenant that Israel made with her God are its main themes. So characteristic is the admonitory tone of this period that its literature can easily be recognized.

With the book of Ezekiel we find ourselves in a third period. As this period progresses, its style and thought differ more and more from those that preceded. After the Exile, when the community was rising from new foundations, Jewish literature comes to its most prolific stage. Here we find the greatest output of biblical writings. There is hardly a single work from the previous periods which was not recast or at least retouched during this time of religious peace.

Even so, the writings of the third period seldom reach the same literary and religious heights as the older ones. The Jewish preoccupations of the time are well reflected in the book of Chronicles, a symposium of older documents selected with a definite purpose. The author clearly demonstrates his interest in matters of worship and law. For him and for his contemporaries, religious life is dominated by the fulfilment of the prescriptions of the Law. The spiritual outlook of the prophetic period has not entirely disappeared, and is still noticeable in the so-called sapiential writings which appeared at this time. But even they have caught the same emphasis, and are preoccupied with the moral problems of the individual and the personal aspect of justification. The social element of Israel's faith is reduced to a mere matter of worship.

These three main periods enable us to recognize the successive stages, or distinct schools, in the literary development of God's people. There is just as much difference in style between the stories of Elijah, the oracles of Jeremiah and the memoirs of Ezra, as there is between a medieval ballad and a speech from Shaw, or between one of Newman's sermons and a five-minute instruction. A person who had no more than a superficial familiarity with English literature would have no difficulty in recognizing the period from the style. The same is true of the Bible. One does not need a penetrating critical faculty to see the characteristic qualities of the different types of literature, ancient, prophetic and post-exilic. A constant reading is enough to show the obvious. The critics of the nineteenth century have been a little pedantic in the names they have given to the different schools. The ancient school of the kingdom of Judah is termed *Yahwistic* or *Jahvistic,* and abbreviated to J. The corresponding school of the northern kingdom of Ephraim is called *Elohistic* or E. The later literature of the prophetic period belongs to the *Deuteronomic* school (D), and the post-exilic writings to the *Priestly* school (P).

If the aim of these categories is to make watertight compartments in a development which was in fact complex and varied, then they must be called arbitrary. But if it is understood that they are only general classifications, intended to bring out the chief features and underline dominant characteristics, then they unquestionably give an accurate analysis of the main stages in the formation of the Bible.

THE reader may have noticed that nothing has so far been said of the period that preceded the monarchy, the period covered by the first seven books of the Bible. The reason is that here we leave the world of what is universally accepted and enter the realm of controversy.

Only a few years ago, the great majority of independent critics refused to admit even the possibility of an Israelite literature before the time of the kings. They decided that the Heptateuch (Genesis-Judges) was no more than a post-exilic compilation of four successive documents, the work of the literary schools J, E, D and P mentioned above. This famous *Documentary Theory* was a violent attack on the accepted view that the Pentateuch was Mosaic in origin. More recently, epigraphical studies have shown that an enormous amount of writing existed from the third millennium onward. In the Palestinian corridor in particular, various kinds of alphabetic writing were known from the fifteenth century B.C., and it is no longer possible to contest the possibility of writings prior to the tenth century. If a group of nomads from before the time of Moses were responsible for the Sinaitic inscriptions, then there is no difficulty at all in granting that the Hebrews, who came from civilized Egypt, knew how to write.

The Pentateuch contains many obvious indications of more recent work. But a deeper study of its stories and legislation has revealed that it also contains data belonging to a time well before Israel had abandoned her nomadic way of life. Much of the law has no meaning outside the desert. Some of the narratives, those in the first chapters of Genesis for instance, record religious traditions which are paralleled, in a degraded form, in Babylonian texts going back to the third millennium B.C. Chapter 14 of Genesis is an example of the remodelling of a document written very soon after the events it describes.

In view of all this, it is reasonable to allow that some of the material in the Bible comes from the time of Moses and before. It must also be granted that this material had been partially committed to writing even before it found its present form in the Pentateuch. The Mosaic origin of the Pentateuch is not a matter of faith. The ancient tradition does not give that degree of certainty which is required for a revealed truth, and the fact that Scripture itself attributes it to Moses may well be explained by the literary forms of the Ancient East regarding legislation. All the same, it is historically beyond question that the tradition of the Mosaic origin of the Pentateuch is based on very solid foundations. In the words of a non-Catholic scholar: " Moses can claim the rôle of initiator in every sphere of national life, whether it be political, legal, social, moral, religious, judiciary or military."

It is practically impossible to give any precision to this literary and juridicial activity of the founder of the people of Israel. His work has undergone the development common to all legislation. Every primitive code of law is added to and modified and transformed by a nation's need to adapt itself to changing circumstances. This anonymous adaptation is particularly true of biblical legislation. Every page of history and law in the Pentateuch gives evidence of material which dates from Moses and earlier, but it also gives clear indication of the slow work of adaptation by later ages. The parallel accounts that occur so frequently in the book of Genesis are probably an indication that the ancestral traditions underwent two separate editings, in the literary circles of Judah and Israel, during the time of the Kingdom. Deuteronomy is an oratorical paraphrase of these traditions, in the warm and vibrant style of the great Prophets of the eighth and seventh centuries. Leviticus too has handed down the core of desert traditions, but they have obviously been developed and framed in a later legislation, whose spirit is identical with the spirit that inspired the post-exilic reforms of Nehemiah and Ezra.

We might say that the Pentateuch enshrines the whole literary and religious history of Israel. The scholar quoted above says: "We can conclude that this is, in substance, the work of Moses. What we cannot do is to draw lines, and say this is definitely primitive, or that clearly much later." The most that we can do is to give certain sections, like the Book of the Covenant (Ex. 21-23) and the Decalogue, a place of honour; all the rest has been subsequently remodelled and enriched. But since the transformation has always been spontaneous and from within, the whole remains an organic unity. The Semitic mind found no difficulty in putting the name of Moses at the top of a work which received its whole impetus from his genius.

Popular tradition and memory also played a significant part in the formation of the Old Testament. The "oral style" is fundamental to Semitic literature. Before they ever came to be written down, many parts of the Bible had been recited and spoken after a set rhythmic pattern, in the form of poetry or sayings. When these were eventually committed to writing, great care was taken to preserve the flavour of the spoken word. Most of the old historical narratives, and the poetry of the Psalms, of the Song of Songs, and of the Prophets were handed down in this way.

It is this process that so utterly distinguishes biblical literature from our own. For the Hebrew, the written word was no more than a transcription; the content had been there long before it was expressed in writing, and it remained independent of its publication. The Semite did not know the typically modern cleavage between the spoken and the written word. His culture kept alive that spontaneity and sense of community which our own civilization has killed. It did not matter to him whether a thought was expressed by word of mouth or in black and white—it was still the same thought, and its significance and meaning came from within. Writing was not more important than memory; they were just different ways of handing down the living word.

WE FIND memory and oral tradition playing the same rôle in the formation of the New Testament. The early Christians were not at first concerned with putting Christ's teaching into writing. In fact they did not do so until the first witnesses were beginning to disappear. The early communities received all their teaching by word of mouth, in the form of simple sermons on the events of Christ's life and the principal themes of his doctrine. If this Gospel was soon set in a fairly stereotyped mould, it was not simply from a concern to preserve it intact. It was from sheer force of habit: its first preachers were Semites. Matthew had his "catechesis" or teaching, and so did Peter, and Paul, and the other Apostles.

It was the sudden and unforeseen acceptance of Christianity by the pagans that called forth the first Christian writings. It is significant that the earliest of them were written to answer specific needs of the moment. Overwhelmed by the widespread success of his preaching, and unable to give all his converts personal supervision, St. Paul was forced to resort to a copious correspondence, and consolidate what he had started or prepare for future missions by letter instead of by word of mouth. He had not the slightest intention of producing literature in the Greek sense of the word, even when he tried to accommodate his Greek audience by adopting their literary conventions. This is so true that very often he was content to dictate his words at speed, or even leave his secretary to develop a scheme on his own. Only a proportion of this off-the-cuff correspondence has come down to us. The early communities seem to have had the custom of exchanging these letters. We see it happening between Colossae and Laodicea (Col. 4 : 16), and there must have been other partial collections dealing from apostolic times. It was probably in the same way that some other letters were preserved, connected with the names of the Apostle Peter, and of the early disciples James and Jude.

The rapid growth of Christianity brought more problems. Those who had seen Christ in person were no longer equal to the task of evangelization. They were getting old, and the eagerly awaited "Parousia" seemed to be no nearer. By the year 50, it was becoming imperative that the oral catechesis of the Apostles should be committed to writing, so that its content would be preserved. St. Luke tells us (Lk. 1 : 1-2) that several attempts were made in this direction, and his statement has been verified from the recently discovered fragments of hitherto unknown Gospels, and from a close examination of our canonical Gospels.

According to a tradition that goes back to Papias, Bishop of Hierapolis in the Province of Asia at the beginning of the second century A.D., the first attempt of this sort was made by St. Matthew, who wrote in Aramaic for the benefit of the Jews in Palestine. This work was soon lost, at least in its original form. It is not unlikely that similar works in Aramaic appeared about the same time, in the form of collections of sayings or narratives. The need for them must have been felt even earlier in these communities which were far removed from Jerusalem, as at Antioch, the first large Christian centre in the pagan world. This may be the explanation of the independent and free use made by the Gospels of Matthew and Luke of a work of this kind. It has been called Q (from the first letter of the German word *Quelle* or source), and held by some critics to be in fact the original Gospel of St. Matthew. Others oppose such a view on the grounds that our Greek Matthew is vastly different from what can be reconstructed of Q. But it is possible that our Greek translation is no more than a free adaptation of the original. These are the sort of delicate problems that go to make up the " Synoptic Question ".

Be that as it may, the need for some written catechesis must have been keenly felt by the converts in the churches of the Greek world, who could not understand the Aramaic of the Apostles and were bewildered by the Semitic flavour of their Greek. The catechesis preached by the Apostle Peter in Rome was consequently written down by his interpreter Mark, about the year 60. The Greek converts found it rather barbaric and forbidding, and a little later an unknown writer tried to translate St. Matthew into a more cultured Greek. He seems to have made use of both Mark and the lost Q. These two sources were also used about the same time by Luke, a disciple of Paul, who undertook a similar task. His Greek origin gave him an advantage, and by literary standards his work was more successful. Our three synoptic Gospels—so called because they can be put into parallel columns and read at a single glance— are therefore simply the written expressions of slightly differing forms of the one apostolic catechesis, with Matthew and Luke making use of earlier writings stemming from the same oral catechesis. Mark reproduces the more or less impromptu preaching of St. Peter. Matthew is a more scholarly work, although its good Greek does not hide its Semitic mentality. St. Luke has his own approach. Pauline in doctrine and hellenistic in presentation, he reproduces his sources almost word for word, but still manages to present them in a way which pleases the Greek mind and underlines the religious themes that would appeal to it most.

Between the years 65 and 68, St. Luke produced a second volume, the Acts. It tells how Christianity grew as a result of the labours of his master, St. Paul. His procedure was the same as before, and he made use of existing writings and personal memoirs that had been written in the first person plural.

The Johannine writings belong to a very different category. For one thing, they come from the end of the first century, and are therefore considerably later than the others. The Fourth Gospel is not, strictly speaking, the written account of an oral catechesis, even though it does show signs of oral composition and of gradual development. It is a profoundly personal work and reflects the genius of its author. A very ancient tradition attributes the work of correction in style and language to a secretary. On the other hand, it may well be that John first brought out his work in Aramaic, possibly at Antioch before he finally settled at Ephesus. This would explain the marked difference in style and language between the Apocalypse and the Gospel, even though their thought and literary conception are so similar. John might well have written the rough-hewn Greek of the Apocalypse himself, when he was a very old man, about the year 96, whereas he would have left his Gospel, composed at leisure in his native tongue, to be polished and translated into Greek by someone else.

THIS rapid survey of the composition of the Bible is enough to show how complex and varied it was. Side by side with works which came from a single source and which clearly reflect the author's personality are others which are apparently the work of succeeding generations. Our own literature rarely raises the problem of the sources that have been used; in the Bible it faces us at almost every turn. The whole approach is typical of the Semitic mentality, where the written word is subordinate to the spoken word, and where truth is an objective reality rather than the property of an individual. When a thought has once been committed to writing, it takes on an aspect of finality. The Semite would not understand our care to change a phrase for the sake of style or to cover up a borrowed idea. He is quite happy to take the work of others and incorporate it into his own. Nor does this approach in any way prevent the emergence of distinct literary personalities. It is precisely the skill of the author which determines the way he uses his material.

This makes it extremely difficult and sometimes impossible to fix the precise origin of each book. It also means that much of our preoccupation with authors and dates is without real purpose. But it is the source of that complex unity and rich abundance which is the hall-mark of the Bible. The Bible grew in successive stages, but this does not mean that one completed work was simply tacked on to another. All the books have something in common, and this forms a bridge between one stage and the next. A number of converging lines run right through the collection, from one end to the other. All the writers, whether they are geniuses like Isaiah and St. Paul, or unknown compilers like the Chronicler, all are under the constant influence of the living community for which they are spokesmen. The Bible is the residue of a much vaster body of literature, which itself never pretended to be more than the reflection of Israel's religious personality. The purpose of an enquiry into the formation of the Bible should be to search for the history and development of this personality. Compared with this, dates, names and philological details are of little importance. From the human viewpoint alone, there is a profound unity running through all the various books of the Bible. As the Bible unfolds, the unity becomes more marked, and this alone is enough to give the Bible a character which lifts it high above the literature of all time.

II

THE FORMATION OF THE INSPIRED BOOK

Development of the idea of inspiration in the Old Testament; its social and religious character; the prophetical, legal and sapiential " streams"; secondary streams; in the New Testament, primary inspiration of Christ, handed down to the first Apostles; New Testament gradually placed on the same level as Old Testament.

GOD unfolds his plan through the pattern of human events. To some extent this explains how only part of Israel's literature was preserved while the rest perished. Much of it must have been lost, for instance, in the great upheaval of the sixth century B.C. and the Exile that followed. But it was a purely religious factor, subconscious for the most part and therefore less obvious, which played the decisive part in this work of discrimination. This was the firm belief in the divine authority, or inspiration, of the writings.

In itself, inspiration is due to the direct action of God. It is not, therefore, immediately perceivable. How then did the people of Israel come to know which books bore the stamp of divine authority? That is the problem we shall now try to solve. Not that we intend to prove the inspiration of the Bible thereby. The fact of inspiration we accept on faith. But given that fact, we still need to understand precisely how this divine activity was manifested. We still need to examine the historical events and providential circumstances through which this belief was introduced into the religious thought of Israel.

TO UNDERSTAND how the Jewish people could so easily accept this mingling of the divine word with the human, we must take into account two correlated facts. The first has already been hinted at in the section on the formation of the Bible. There we saw how literature in Israel, as throughout the Semitic East, was a kind of by-product of the living word and the human activity which went to produce it. In such a context, biblical inspiration could only be one form of the wider inspiration that affected the whole life of the people. If God was thought to intervene in the production of a book, it was because he was believed to intervene in the whole of Israel's national life. A book was said to be inspired because the author was acknowledged to be an inspired man. The author was seen to be inspired because he served the community in a social capacity that had been given him by God. This is the first fact.

The second fact is the willingness of Israel to accept this constant and almost tangible intervention of God in the affairs of man. This too they held in common with the whole of ancient civilization. Our modern outlook does not appreciate the religious intensity of the ancient world. If the modern man believes in God at all, he tends to think of him only as " Prime Mover ", and no longer sees his creative power in secondary causes. The ancients went almost to the other extreme. The Semites in particular were so profoundly religious that they often seem to have neglected created causes altogether in their anxiety to attribute everything to God. They had, in fact, a strong sense of reality, but they never for an instant lost sight of the sustaining power of God, in which reality ever " lives and moves and has its being ". To such minds as these, there was nothing strange in the idea of God participating actively in the affairs of his creatures. His hand was manifest to them on every side. Since Israel grew up in such a religious atmosphere as this it was natural that she should share the common outlook of the East and be keenly aware of the guiding intervention of divine Providence in human affairs.

There was one important characteristic which singled out Israel from her neighbours. Where the religion of Babylon was a sort of cosmic pantheism, and the religion of Canaan a deification of the forces of nature, Israel's religion by contrast was centred on a God who was transcendent and personal, and who alone was creator of all things. God's activity permeates the world, but it still remains distinct from the world and surpasses it. " Yahweh is a living God ", not just a nameless force. He had fixed his choice on his people, and he meant to guide them to a prepared destiny.

This guidance was made clear enough by his continued Providence and his miraculous intervention. It was made even clearer by the way he raised up, at every stage in Israel's history, leaders who would speak in his name and declare his will. All ancient peoples believed that divine authority was invested in their leaders. But in Israel this conviction was intensified by their belief in Yahweh as a personal and interested God. This no doubt increased the prestige of the person in authority, but it also subordinated him more thoroughly to God. Israel was a theocracy. Yahweh's people were ruled by Yahweh alone. His human agents were entirely dependent upon him. In his eyes they were only intermediaries between himself and his people, and they could be removed at his will. Yet in the eyes of Israel, they were bathed in the light of Yahweh's own glory.

AMONG the many on whom this divine light fell, one group was entirely peculiar to Israel, and they left an indelible mark on her history. These were the Prophets. Their strange demeanour, their aloofness, their unpredictable behaviour, their fearless daring, the impact of their ecstasies, the fierce exclusiveness of their religion, in short everything about them illustrated the direct intervention of Yahweh and his desire to replace men's activity with his own. The very fact that the phenomenon was peculiar to Israel gave tangible evidence of Yahweh's participation in the life of his people. It was prophetism, more than anything else, that taught Israel her divine mission, and convinced her that she was in some special way the messenger of God. "I have put my words in your mouth," said Yahweh to Jeremiah (1:9). When the Israelite heard the burning words of the Prophets, he experienced all the independence of God, his almighty power, the incomprehensibility of his ways, and the inevitability of his will. He understood that the Word of God was unique and unknowable, and yet that in some way it became incarnate in the Prophet. The Israelite's reaction to prophetism is best expressed in the close relationship he saw between the Prophet and the Spirit of Yahweh. If God spoke, he did so through the living and life-giving Breath of his mouth. If he communicated his Word to man, man could not help being shaken to the root of his being, to become the source of an activity that was superhuman.

IT WAS prophetism, then, more than anything else, which brought the idea of divine inspiration to the light of day. It was the prophetic oracles that first fostered a belief in the incarnation of the divine Word. But even before the time of the Prophets, Israel had learned to recognize this divine intervention in many other forms, though less clearly. Of these, the authority of the Law was without doubt the most important. Right up to the time of Christ, the distinction between "the Law" and "the Prophets" remained in Israel to recall the period when the books of the Bible had yet to be collected under the uniform title of "Scripture". The ancient Semites had a highly developed sense of law. Moreover, the code that governed their national life had a marked religious significance, because they made no distinction between their religion and their national existence. There was no aspect of man's behaviour that was not subject to God, and if their religion had necessarily a social and political value, then the most mundane of civil regulations were in their turn based on divine authority.

If therefore the legislator was to regulate the social and religious life of his people, he needed divine help. To ordinary people his work seemed so much beyond the powers of man that they often thought he owed it to a revelation from on high. The stele of Hammurabi in the Louvre depicts the king in an attitude of supplication, receiving the already written code from the hands of his god Shamash. In this context it is easier to appreciate the incomparable prestige enjoyed by Moses, and to understand why he left such an indelible mark on Israel.

It is this belief in the divine authority of all law and ritual that explains the progressive importance of the Law in the religious life of the Jews. The characteristic transcendence of God was stressed as much as it had been in prophetism. Yahweh was a God who did not ask for opinions: he simply gave his orders. The early Prophets already had a strong conviction that the Law was an express command of God (1 Sam. 28:18). By the time of the Exile it had so grown that it overshadowed everything else. Fundamentally, the idea was there from the beginning. It was Moses who based Israel on an essentially juridical foundation. At Sinai, Yahweh made a true pact with his people. It was a bilaterial contract, which bound Israel to her social, ritual and moral legislation, and by the same token bound Yahweh to give himself to Israel, his "inheritance". At the same time, the contract was made on God's own initiative, and it was his free gift. It was not just an alliance, it was a divine Covenant. Under both aspects, alliance and Covenant, the Law was seen as the expression of God's dealings with his people. It was only a step further to see it as the "Word of God".

IN THE concept of Wisdom we come to a third manifestation of the divine activity. It takes us back earlier still in the life of the chosen people. In the East, the authority of the sage existed long before the social development of kingdom or tribe. It goes back to the time when the structure of society was patriarchal and based on the clan. Even to-day it is fundamental to nomadic society. In these exclusive social groups which live close to nature and are hemmed in by the desert, personality is all important. When clan affairs are discussed at the tent door during the long night watches, every man is expected to voice his opinion. Where the sky is broad and the desert has no limits, there is a familiarity with eternity which prompts reflection. The conversation is punctuated by long silences, which encourage each man to argue out within himself the nuances of those ideas which are no more than stated in the dialogue. In such an atmosphere a man will show that sense of reality and life, clearsightedness, and fearless prudence that go to make the sage.

Wisdom has been called the embellishment of an active mind, but it is still subordinate to life and living. It is therefore often the fruit of experience, and the characteristic of the old who have learned to know the world and its ways. It can also be the mark of a bold leader, even a young one like David, or of an exceptional woman like Jael or Abigail. In such cases it is seen to be something singular, and evidently a special gift from Yahweh. David was said to be "as wise as a messenger of God" (2 Sam. 14:20). Such wisdom is clearly also given by the Spirit of God and communicated by his life-giving Breath. Israel found it easy to see here another source of the "Word" of God, expressed in human terms.

THE Law, Prophetism and Wisdom, these are the three fundamental streams. There were others which were subsidiary and often complementary. The priesthood, for example, had from earliest times the right to determine the will of Yahweh by casting lots. Its almost undisputed power after the Exile gave it an opportunity to leave its sacred mark on Israel's legislation. Military leaders and kings also shared the character, and therefore the privileges, of the lawmaker and the wise man. The Wisdom of God's Spirit was recognized in art and poetry (cf. Ex. 31:3). Finally there was the scribe, who enjoyed the prestige which had been accorded to his noble and wise profession ever since the Israelites first met him in Egypt. It was his delicate duty to preserve the records of the past and to hand on its traditions. His writings must keep fresh the memory of God's good gifts. After the Exile he became Israel's theologian and interpreter of Law. His words of wisdom also drew their authority from the Word of God on which he commented.

Priests, leaders, kings, artists and scribes, all had some share in God's own guidance of his people. They could all claim to be his spokesmen, although in a less obvious and a less personal way. More often than not, their sanctioning of a literary work as the Word of God came about as a secondary aspect of one of the three fundamental manifestations of God's Spirit. Nevertheless it was they who were responsible for the preservation in the Bible of such important works as the historical books, the Psalms and the Song of Songs. Of course, there were other factors at work here. The very content of the historical books and the liturgical use of the Psalms in the Temple helped to secure their inclusion.

IN THESE varied forms Israel gradually became conscious of God's intervention in her affairs. The different manifestations of God's activity were at first seen in isolation, and no conscious attempt was made to refer them to a common purpose. It was only later, when they were put into writing, that their correlation became more evident. When the various forms of divine teaching through Moses, the Prophets and the sages, had received this set written form, it was almost inevitable that they should be commonly called the divine " testament ".

It had been clear enough from the beginning that these various mediators were all God's messengers, but the emphasis was centred on the actual mode of mediation rather than on the message itself. The Law was God's Word, the Prophet was his oracle, the sage was the chronicler of his design for living. When these were committed to writing, the written word itself came to bear the divine stamp, and the expression enjoyed the respect due to the message. But, as the volume of writings grew, the characteristics of the individual contributions inevitably tended to become less marked, until in the end they faded altogether, to give birth to the single concept of the divine Scripture.

It was not until after the Exile that this final stage in the development of the idea of inspiration was reached. The levelling down of individual characteristics to the single concept of divine authority was due without doubt to the extension of what is called in the Schools the *principale analogatum*, or the most prominent feature. Of all forms of divine intervention in human affairs, the most striking was that of prophetic inspiration, and it was this, as an abstract point of reference, that was chosen to be the model of biblical inspiration. All other forms of Israel's religious literature were eventually considered to share in the prophetic Spirit. Such an idea led to a transformation of the concept of inspiration itself. Prophetism lost nothing of its own unique quality, but that quality was now applied to all the sacred writings, and the whole of Scripture was seen as a divine message to the people of Israel, delivered by an intermediary acting under the influence of the Spirit of God. In New Testament times, the evolution of this concept has already reached its term. The whole body of the religious writings that Israel accepted as the Word of God had become one indivisible whole. It had become " The Scripture ", and its very letters bore the stamp of divine authority.

The seal of God's authority was most obvious where a single person united in himself a number of these various aspects of divine intervention. Thus Moses was always considered to be the model mediator. Not only was he the supreme legislator, he was also the military leader, the first of the sages, the divine scribe, the priest, and above all the prophet. The same was true of David, as the ideal Anointed One of Yahweh, messianic king, sage, prophet and leader. As time went on, their prestige stood even higher in contrast to the unworthiness of their successors, and the hope for the future was centred on a new Moses or a new David, who would renew their work and bring it to completion. The Messiah, the supreme Envoy of Yahweh, was pictured as uniting in his person all the forms of religious mediation which had been shared among so many representatives in the course of history. He would be, in the most perfect sense, the Messiah, the Anointed One of the Spirit of God, endowed with the Spirit of wisdom and the Spirit of government, with the Spirit of justice and the Spirit of love, with the kingly Spirit and the prophetic Spirit. He would be the Son of David (Mk. 10:48) and the Supreme Prophet (Deut. 18:15-19), the Teacher, Spokesman and last Interpreter of the divine message of peace.

CHRIST was the term of this evolution, and belief in him must be seen in this context. The first disciples were not ready to express this belief in such an abstract word as "divine". Theirs was a more concrete outlook, and they summarized all its richness when they acknowledged Christ as the "Son of the living God" (Mt. 16:16). In doing this, they were not merely recognizing him as the Messiah. To them he was more than one who had received, in a more perfect way, the Spirit of God which Moses and David and the Prophets had shared. By their confession they acknowledged Christ's full and complete possession of the Spirit, and registered their assent to the words of the Father at his baptism: "This is my beloved Son, hear him" (Mk. 9:7). For them, he was the incarnate message of God, his living Word, the full Revelation of the Father, the Inspired One of God, the fulfilment of all that had been prefigured in the mediators of the Old Covenant.

After the coming of Christ, no Christian could conceive of anyone speaking in God's name except through Christ, the Son of God made man. In his person, the content of the divine message and the authority to speak it had reached its full expression. Acclaimed the Word of God and born the Son of God by the sanctification of the Spirit (Rom. 1:4), he summed up all the ancient revelation by his accomplishment of it. He was, above all, the *living* Word of God, not to be circumscribed by words. But if it had taken many hesitant centuries to spell out the letters of the divine Word and prepare the people of Israel for its incarnation, the Word had now to be transcribed anew and translated, so that its incarnation should extend to the entire world. The process had begun when the Spirit of Yahweh chose men out of Israel to prepare for the coming of the Son of God. To complete the process, the same Spirit, now the Spirit of Jesus, would pick his disciples out of the new Israel of God, and take possession of them. The old theophany of Sinai had guided the people of Israel to the Word. The day of Pentecost saw the Church established as the prolongation of that Word incarnate. This dawn of salvation was fittingly marked, as Joel had foretold, by a new outpouring of the prophetic Spirit. It was now for the witnesses of Christ to present him to the world both as the envoy and as the living message of God. Their authority came direct from Christ: "He who hears you hears me." When they were gone, personal historical contact with Christ was broken, and nothing more could be added to the content of his revelation. Henceforth it could only be a question of preserving the message. The Christian dogma that revelation ceased with the death of the last Apostle may at first sight appear strange, but it is founded on the deep conviction, which the Church has had from the beginning, that nothing can be known about God except what his Son has revealed.

The embodiment of Christ's authority in the persons of his chosen eye-witnesses seems to have been the guiding principle in the formation of the New Testament. The New Testament contains only those writings which stem directly or indirectly from these personal witnesses. In their first experience of Christianity and in the charismata, the early Christians had almost tangible proof that the Spirit of Christ lived on in his Church. There could be no doubt in their minds that the Apostles, who spread Christ's Gospel in word and in writing, were being directly influenced by the same Spirit. The Apostles possessed the fullness of charismatic power. Their gift of government, and above all their gifts of teaching, of revelation and of prophecy put them on the level of the greatest of the

Prophets of old. From the very beginning, the letters of St. Paul were received as coming from the hand of Christ himself. When later the oral teaching of some of the Apostles was committed to writing, it was accepted only because it bore their authority. Thus Mark was accepted because he was the interpreter of St. Peter, and Luke because he was the companion of St. Paul. The Gospel according to St. Matthew was received because it was a translation of Matthew's own work, and the Fourth Gospel because it came from the beloved disciple. The writings did not have to come directly from the pen of the Apostles. It was appreciated that the Spirit had been poured out on all Christians, especially on those who enjoyed the charismata. But if the work was to be accepted without question, there had to be incontestable evidence of direct contact with Christ through his first witnesses. It was by this criterion that the Acts of the Apostles and the Third Gospel were put under the authority of St. Paul, and that the Epistle to the Hebrews, the Second Epistle of Peter and the Epistles of James and Jude came to be received.

It must not be imagined that these new writings were immediately and consciously grouped together as "Scripture". Before they could be put on a par with the writings of the Old Testament, they had to go through much the same sort of process that the Old Testament had undergone. The first generation of Christians had as keen an appreciation of the divine authority of the Apostolic writings as they had for the Old Testament, perhaps keener. But while the memory of the circumstances in which the writings had seen the light of day was still fresh, they could not dream of putting them on the same footing as the sacred Book they venerated. Some lapse of time was needed for the circumstances to lose their transient aspect and for the divine to stand out more clearly. Only in that way could an analogy be made between the charismata of the Spirit of Christ in the new Covenant and the manifestations of the Spirit of Yahweh in the old. Already, in the first half of the second century, some Christian writers were quoting from the books of the New Testament, giving them parity with the books of the Old, and sometimes even designating them with the consecrated title of "Scripture". Towards the end of the century the practice had become general, and the New Testament gradually found a fixed place alongside the Old, to form the one Scripture inspired by God.

III

THE DEFINITION OF THE CANON

Gradual consciousness; the Old Testament Canon in Judaism; its two forms and their survival into the history of the Church; uncertain beginnings of the New Testament Canon; the rôle of heresies; hesitations and results.

IN THE foregoing pages we have seen something of the various influences which were at work in the unfolding of revelation, and which governed the gradual formation of a collection of religious books bearing the seal of God's own authority. In these books, certain stages of a wider and living movement have, as it were, crystallized. They are a particular form of the overall inspiration which made the people of Israel and later the Church of Christ the special objects of God's care. Sometimes, as with the Prophets, inspiration was so clearly and almost tangibly present that God's authority was seen to be inherent. More often it was the other way round, the divine authority standing as guarantee for the inspiration. It remains for us now to give a short explanation of how this vast and often subconscious work acquired the precision of a well-defined corpus of inspired books. The history of Israel and of the early Christian Church has left no trace of either a divine promulgation of such a definitive list or of any official pronouncement on the matter. God does not work in that way. He reveals himself through the ordinary pattern of human affairs. In this way the idea of inspiration was born: in this way the Canon of Scripture would receive its definition.

The word "canon" comes from a Greek word meaning rule or measure. From the beginning of the Church the Canon of Scripture meant the collection of books which were the rule of Christian faith. At first there was naturally some uncertainty as to what exactly should be included in the list. The ideas analysed above had not reached such a degree of precision as to preclude controversy. The clear-cut realization which the

Church now has on this, as on other aspects of divine revelation, was only slowly achieved. With the end of the apostolic age, there was no further addition to the content of revelation, but that does not mean that revelation was dead. The Spirit still preserves the living Christ in that Church which is his continuation. Although the constituent members of an organic body are present from birth, they still have to grow, to change, and to take shape. In a similar way the inspired books were all present in the Church from the beginning. But since they were cradled in a much vaster body of literature apparently sharing the same undefined inspiration, the line of demarcation was necessarily vague. Now it is a psychological fact that when two distinct things are in practice treated as one, only a conflict or a contradiction will help the mind to make the distinction. The Church came to her final definition of the Canon of Scripture only by the piecemeal process of eliminating or including the borderline cases.

As far as the Old Testament was concerned, this process of delineation was already well advanced by the time the Church was founded. The 38 books written in Hebrew, and only these, were received by the whole of Judaism as the divinely inspired rule of faith. From that time, inspiration and canonicity become terms with precise meanings, which the Church made her own simply by accepting them. Nevertheless opinion was still divided on whether or not the Canon was closed. The orthodox and rigorous Jews of Palestine maintained that the age of inspiration was past, and that the Canon had reached its definition. The Jews of the Diaspora, at Alexandria especially, were more pliant in their outlook, and with their idea of a religion that lived and continued to develop, they accepted the inspiration of later writings. There were consequently several works, written or preserved in Greek during the last few centuries B.C. at Alexandria, which the Jews of the Diaspora put on an equal footing with works accepted by all, even though they never quoted them as Scripture. The Greek Bible, compiled at Alexandria and known as the Septuagint (LXX), contains seven books over and above the 38. These are *Tobit, Judith, Wisdom, Ecclesiasticus, Baruch* and the two books of *Maccabees*. There are also some additions in the books of *Esther* and *Daniel*.

THE Church was born in Jerusalem, but it grew up in the Greek world in the wake of the Jewish Diaspora, and naturally enough it adopted the current Greek version of the Bible and the current hellenistic outlook on the Canon of Scripture. The New Testament writers quoted as freely from the books which the Hebrew Canon disowned as from those it acknowledged, although they too generally refrained from calling them Scripture.

Even this refinement was soon to vanish in the West, where the Old Testament was read in the Latin translations of the LXX. The East preserved the distinction, and even underlined it. In the middle of the fourth century the Council of Laodicea, following in the footsteps of Origen, Eusebius of Caesarea, St. Athanasius and others, recognized as canonical only the books of the Hebrew Bible. Not that the other writings were frowned upon: the Greek Fathers applauded their use in the churches, and their description as " ecclesiastical " writings has remained as the title of the most important among them (Ecclesiasticus). Latin scholars like Rufinus and St. Jerome, who had to some extent become hellenized, tried to preserve the same distinction in the West. But they had to contend with the immense prestige of St. Augustine, and when the Council of Carthage affirmed the canonicity of 45 books in 419, it followed Augustine rather than Jerome.

Slowly throughout the Middle Ages the two opposing views were resolved. While the East began to minimize the distinction between the two categories, the West under the growing influence of St. Jerome began to introduce something of the eastern nuance into her overall acceptance, a nuance which was preserved in the sixteenth century distinction between proto- and deutero-canonical books. The Council of Trent condemned Protestantism for recognizing only the Hebrew Canon, but did not apparently wish to make any definite pronouncement on this distinction, which was still being debated in the preliminary sessions of the Council. It did no more than affirm the inspiration of the 45 books which it named.

The Canon of the New Testament underwent a similar though more complex development. As long as the Apostles were still alive there was no great concern to group their writings into a single volume. Each church was the jealous guardian of the writings specifically addressed to it. At the same time, in those areas where the memory of an Apostolic visit served to forge a link between the various local communities, there was a constant exchange of these writings. It was this devotion to the memory of Christ's first witnesses that made the faithful eager to possess everything that came from them, and partial collections began to be made of whatever Apostolic writings were locally to hand. The Fourth Gospel, the letter of St. Clement and the letters of St. Ignatius all vouch for the fact that by the end of the first century St. Matthew's Gospel and the great Epistles of St. Paul were already widespread, no doubt by way of such exchanges.

A little later, the principal churches were forced to take more careful stock of their traditions in order to defend them against the new heresy of Gnosticism, which tried to bolster its own position by questioning the value of many writings accepted by the Great Church, or by promoting the growth of apocryphal writings. Marcion, about the year 140, accepted only the Gospel of Luke and some of St. Paul's Epistles. The Gospel of Peter, the Gospel of Thomas, the Apocalypse of Peter, and many other apocryphal works appeared about the same time.

In the face of heresy a strict uniformity was essential. From the first half of the second century definite lists of books began to appear, and the title of each was checked. About the year 125 Papias, Bishop of Hierapolis in Asia, collected the available references on the Gospels of Matthew and Mark, and perhaps also on the Johannine writings. The Roman church countered Marcion by issuing an actual edition of the works she recognized, and this included the four Gospels and all the Epistles of St. Paul. Towards the latter half of the century complete catalogues were drawn up. The Muratorian Canon and St. Irenaeus list almost all the books which are now accepted. At this stage the New Testament reached the degree of precision which the Jews had already accorded to the Old.

At this very moment, when the conscience of the Church was at last beginning to crystallize, a characteristic uncertainty appears. All the lists compiled at this time are either too long or too short. Either they contain writings whose canonicity was questioned and later rejected, or they fail to include something which was accepted by many and later canonized. In fact these fluctuations were confined to a few books only. Among those that were added to the lists were the *Epistle of St. Clement* of Rome (end of the first century), the *Didache* and the *Shepherd of Hermas* (about the year 140), the *Apocalypse of Peter* and the so-called *Epistle of Barnabas* (middle of the second century). The books which are now received but were then contested varied in East and West. Until the fourth century the Latin Church did not accept the *Epistle to the Hebrews* as the work of St. Paul, nor even (sometimes) as an inspired writing. The *Apocalypse* was vehemently attacked in Rome at the beginning of the third century, and although about the year 150 Justin had strongly asserted its Johannine origin, it was the subject of increasing argument in the East throughout the third and fourth centuries. The Epistles of *James, Jude, 2 Peter*, and *2* and *3 John* were frequently omitted from the lists.

Like the deutero-canonical books of the Old Testament referred to above, these disputed works came to be looked upon as possessing a kind of secondary inspiration. They were read in church, they were quoted even as Scripture, but each church kept to its own official traditions. By the end of the fourth century, however, the 27 books which we now have were almost universally accepted, and the Council of Trent did no more than confirm their undisputed use. In the event, the Protestants as a whole accepted them too. The old designation was nevertheless preserved and the *Epistle to the Hebrews*, the *Apocalypse, 2* and *3 John, Jude, James* and *2 Peter* are still called deutero-canonical. In practice, however, this has made less difference than in the case of the Old Testament.

IV

INSPIRATION AND CANONICITY

Distinction between the two notions; their interaction; difference in the evolution of the Old and the New Testament.

BEFORE we close this chapter we could profitably go back to the ideas of inspiration and canonicity, and seek for a more precise understanding of them by examining their final development. Not that we intend to read into the embryonic stage all the fullness of the riches acquired later, but an appreciation of those riches will help us to pick out the inherent potentialities. Whatever conclusions we come to now will be of great service to us when we come to deal explicitly with the problem of inspiration.

Biblical inspiration is in essence a religious phenomenon of the internal order. It is entirely different from any other sort of communication from God, private or mystical. Its existence was an established fact long before the coming of Christianity. The Jews of the time of Christ had a thorough understanding of it, as is evident from their absolute reverence for the sacred text itself, which was for them a communication direct from God. This clear-cut idea was inherited by the Church. Gradually she extended it to the writings of the New Testament, which then took its position of equality beside the Old.

From this abstract point of view canonicity is something quite distinct from inspiration. Here it is not a question of any divine and interior reality, but only of the external recognition that a given piece of writing is a measure of faith. A book is canonical when religious authority officially pronounces it to be inspired. Canonicity therefore comes after inspiration and is subordinate to it. A work could be inspired and yet not be declared canonical. In fact this has happened more than once in the course of the Bible's history. The lost Epistles of St. Paul are cases in point. On the other hand it would be impossible for a work to be declared canonical unless it were inspired.

From the historical point of view, however, the distinction is not so clear-cut. The actual reality of a thing is not the same as its appreciation by the human mind. In the event, the two notions of inspiration and canonicity were reciprocal, and each helped the other to develop, though in different ways. In the case of the Old Testament, the vivid awareness of prophetic inspiration seems to have played the decisive part in the actual formation of the book, whereas its canonicity was only accepted and extended to all its parts as an inevitable corollary. In the New Testament, the decisive factor was the authority of the apostolic writings. So clearly were these seen to govern faith that the early Christians considered them as something to which Scripture itself must be subordinated. This kind of super-canonicity only slowly revealed its identity with inspiration, in the technical sense of the word.

At the same time, the evolution of the New Testament did not really follow so different a course from that of the Old. The difference between them is almost entirely due to the fact that the New Testament was so very much later than the Old. In fact the technical concept of inspiration reached maturity in Judaism only as a result of canonicity. It was the semi-official and almost juridical recognition of the Sacred Book that made Judaism so conscious that it was unique. Inspiration itself was understood in the very act of living in that great and powerful stream which was the divinely inspired life of Israel as a whole. At first, Scripture was only the account, the log-book of God's dealings with his people. It was when it came to be established as a sacred code that its objective value began to appear. The New Testament evolved along exactly the same lines. In the early Church, the breath of the Spirit was too keenly felt for an immediate identification to be possible between the charismatic inspiration of the Apostolic writings and the more staid inspiration of the Old Testament, inherited from the Synagogue. It was only with time that these writings became the precious relics of a glorious past, and that their kinship with the books of the Old Testament became clear. Their analogous origin was spontaneously expressed by giving to both the sacred title of Scripture.

If we are going to grasp the precise import of Scripture, therefore, we will need to appreciate both the particular inspiration which gives it its sacred character, and the place it occupies in a much wider, living and flexible divine movement. The fact that it is written down makes it static and fixed, but it is fed by a living stream. Insofar as it is a book, it has the appearance of something distinct and independent, but its origins and its whole purpose give it a vital link with the more complex evolution of the whole of revelation. The Bible is the rich deposit left by a flood of living water.

CHAPTER V

THE HUMAN ELEMENT

SLOWLY we have come to the threshold of the real problem. The preceding pages have only served to lead up to the main question: What is the origin and real value of the Bible? The question has already been touched upon in our discussion of some of the human aspects of the Book, and in our examination of Jewish and Christian beliefs about its divine character. Both of these concepts must now be analysed more fully if we are to have a better appreciation of how God and man co-operated in the production of the Bible. Only when we understand how these two are fused together will we be able to read it in the Spirit in which it was conceived.

The Bible comes to us first and foremost as the record of the history and fortunes of a people. Essentially it belongs to a definite time and a definite place. Its content shows it to be an intensely human document. But we must go further than the mere content. We must study the whole framework which confines and supports it, its literary forms, its variations of style, the personalities of its heroes and the temperaments of its different writers. These alone can discover to us the origin and nature of the Book, for they are the pointers which reveal the milieu in which it was born.

I

THE HISTORICAL METHOD

Its importance; absolute truth and its relative expressions; each civilization has its own styles and literary forms.

IF A thing is to be understood properly, it must be seen in its right context. Readers may recall the panic that was caused in America a few years ago when a radio programme was suddenly interrupted with the announcement that the world had been invaded by men from Mars. The broadcasting station was immediately besieged with telephone calls. Listeners in their hundreds fled from their homes in terror, to make for air-raid shelters or the open country. The victims of this practical joke had done no more than take something out of its proper context. The "space-scare", then at its height, prevented them from being on their guard against the exaggerated style of radio, however accustomed they had previously been to it, and under its influence they mistook a radio play for a news bulletin. In other words, they had misjudged the *literary form.*

The example is an extreme one. Yet such misunderstanding is frequent enough, even if it has not the same repercussions. We are quick to smile at anyone who is naïve enough to mistake a novel for historical fact, but all of us are liable to make the same sort of blunder once we are outside the well defined limits of our own bailiwick. The man who is terrified by a medical prescription which reads: " *c. aq. bis. per d.*" is simply ignorant of the technical jargon. The man in the crowd who really expects the prospective candidate to fulfil all his election pledges is simply ignorant of the mechanics of election campaigning. The further we go from our own familiar surroundings, the less we understand the language of others. It is a commonplace to say that we live in a world of misunderstanding, where people call the same thing by different names, or different things by the same name. Our daily lives are made up of innumerable little conventions which we take for granted. Because we were born into them, we are inclined to think of them as necessary and permanent. Only the progress of time shows us how ephemeral they really are. Every civilization and age, every place and race, every society, in fact every individual, all have their own peculiar ways of thinking, behaving and living. Self-centred as we are, we all think that our way is the standard way. But an understanding of history and psychology, or even mere contact with other people, will force us to recognize the existence of other standards and to become aware of the constant evolution of all things.

This relativism in time must not be exaggerated. Under all this constant movement and change there is still an abiding permanence. In all human thought there is a fundamental element which transcends time and place. It is the same human nature which brings all men of all time to a knowledge of truth. Yet it would be wrong to think that the spiritual essence of man can be entirely divorced from his native world of experience and sensation, for it is precisely here that he is formed and moulded. This is where he learns how to express himself. It will always be impossible to devise an absolutely universal language, because the most abstract of expressions will always be tied to a concrete image, which by its very poverty will in turn weaken the idea. Had the Bible been written in Scholastic terms, it would be even more of a closed book than it is now.

In fact the Bible is subject, like everything else, to the laws of human psychology, and its origins will not be understood at all unless this fact is kept clearly in mind. It comes to us in a literary style that is two thousand years old. Without preparation, without preface, we are suddenly plunged into that lost world as soon as we open its covers. The whole context, the life and thoughts and interests of its people are strange to us. It offers no clue to the understanding of this context. The writers were no more concerned than writers are to-day to make it easily intelligible. On the face of it, the Bible is a closed book. It cannot be understood without the effort that is required to understand any book written in an age and language not our own.

A GOOD translation does not really overcome the difficulty. A translation can only put the words into another language, and mere words can easily mislead. If a person does not know, for instance, that for a Semite the " heart " is not the seat of his affections but the centre of his life and thought, he will do violence to many a text and miss its beauty. Even an understanding of the original language is no help unless there is also a sympathetic feeling for the mental make-up of the culture to which the author belonged. We cannot really understand him until we read between the lines and get inside the ambit of the life which he unwittingly portrays in his writing. The scientific method itself cannot arrive at the true reality unless it takes history and psychology into account. What is needed is a new approach based on this feeling for history and appraisal of man in his context. Until we have this concrete wisdom, we shall not even begin to approach the mystery of Scripture.

Obviously this is going to require a great deal of effort. The modern mind is more at home with the Q.E.D. of geometry than with the imponderable subtlety which the proper approach to Scripture demands. It feels a repugnance for this historical relativism in any context, and suspects that it is a veiled attack on the prerogatives of clear reasoning and abstract thought. To apply such relativism to the Bible involves further complications. The very fact that we believe it to be inspired provides us with an even better excuse for refusing to discuss it at this level. Surely the Bible, the Word of God, is not subject to the ordinary rules of human literature! If that is our attitude, then we are in effect refusing to tune in to the exact wave-length on which God has transmitted his divine revelation. We are searching for it on our own human wave-length, and distorting the signal itself, which is God's Message. The Bible is a pre-incarnation of the Word incarnate. We will never come to grips with its divine character unless we first accept the fact that it is human too.

This human element is something that affects the very words of the Bible. Generally speaking, all its books reflect the one literary mentality, even though this manifests itself in a variety of ways. It is essential to be familiar with the laws of this literary style, and to appreciate the variations they can undergo when they are applied to the different ways or "literary forms" in which the author may express himself. His purpose cannot even be grasped unless this particular literary form is ascertained and its peculiarities understood.

To clarify this point, we might well take an example from our own literature. Among other things, Chesterton wrote both detective stories and essays in religious controversy. Unless the reader is to be completely at sea, he will do well to realize that the Fr. Brown stories are the detective novels and not the controversies. Chesterton did not think to point this out in his Prefaces, nor was there any need. It is obvious enough that the books belong to two different types of literature, and that each follows the laws proper to its own literary form. And yet it is easy to see a common style. This is not only because they are from the pen of one author, but because they reflect a particular world which is unique and altogether different from the world of any other milieu and any other age. Nobody with the slightest knowledge of English literature would confuse Shakespeare's world with the world of Christopher Fry, even though they both use drama as a literary form.

Mental outlook and literary form are bound up together. But in themselves they are quite distinct. For an understanding of the Bible it is not enough to determine the literary form of each book. It is perhaps even more necessary to get inside the mentality which informs the biblical style and makes it different from any other literature.

II

THE SEMITIC MENTALITY

The meaning and the limits of this expression; Semitic and Greek mentality; Semitic and Greek dialectic; the Semitic style, symbols and parables.

WHEN we were dealing with the language of the Bible we pointed out the contrast between the Semitic and our western mentality. As we proceed we shall make constant appeal to this contrast. So that there shall be no confusion, we must define what we mean by " Semitic ". To the modern reader it may have an unfortunate connotation, and call to mind the Zionist controversy of our time. The term " Semitic East " may even conjure up a picture of the Arabian Nights, with its overtones of sensuality and cruelty. The Semitic world which concerns us has little or nothing to do with either of these. It refers simply to the civilizations which flourished in the Middle East from 4000 B.C. to the time of Christ. It includes all those peoples who made these civilizations: the people of Accad and their Babylonian successors, the Assyrians, the innumerable smaller races which lived on the borders of the Arabo-Syrian desert, and even the Hittites and Egyptians who, although they were ethnically quite distinct, enjoyed more than a casual contact with these civilizations.

When we speak of " Semitic style " and " Semitism ", we are

not thinking of the individual and transitory elements of these lost civilizations, but rather of the broad outlines common to all of them. We are thinking of the background and atmospere in which these civilizations were set. Again, when we contrast the Semitic mentality with the western mentality, we have no axe to grind. We do not condemn the West, nor infer that the Semite is the only representative of a type of human spirituality. The "sapiential" frame of mind reflected by the Bible is far from being the prerogative of the Semite. In some ways it is more characteristic of the Far East, the Chinese and Hindus for example, and of the Slav peoples. It is not unknown in the West, as the present vogue of existentialist philosophies bears witness. Nor is the Semitic world, for its part, completely unversed in the scientific way of thinking. It is common knowledge that the sciences of astronomy and mathematics were invented by the Semites, even though their approach was entirely different from our own. Our real concern in this question of the Semitic and the so-called western mentality is to analyse the fundamental tendencies which, by taking shape around different centres of interest, have made the two peoples quite distinct even though the tendencies stem from a humanity which is common to both. Every man carries the seed of this diversity within him. His aim should not be to concentrate on one trend to the exclusion of the other. He should try to discover their relationship with each other and effect a synthesis. Strictly speaking the two trends are not fundamentally opposed to each other. Their diversity is a superficial one, and concerns only their outward manifestations insofar as they can be described and compared. Nor is it our purpose here to examine, on a metaphysical level, how it comes about that men who have identical human minds are in fact so different. It is enough to point out that this is so.

History shows that all civilizations, however different they may be, have followed one or other of these two trends, according to the centre of reference they have taken—the technical side of human thought or the moral and sapiential side. This explains why the modern reader who opens the Bible for the first time will suffer the profound uneasiness of a man discovering a new world. Unless he can rid himself of the conviction that his own culture is the norm to which all others should conform, and unless he allows for the vast differences of environment and mentality hidden behind the deceptive simplicity of words, then he will get little benefit from his reading. He may even find it offensive.

The word " Semitic " is not, therefore, just a convenient label. It may indicate only one particular form of the sapiential civilizations, but it stands for a definite world, more extensive than the world of the Bible. We use the word with this express purpose, to show the reader that the biblical world was not sealed off from all contact with neighbouring peoples. The Bible is part of a great stream of culture, a culture which has in common certain basic characteristics and peculiarities of outlook which distinguish it from our own modern cultures.

THIS is best expressed in the difference between eastern and western *dialectic*, a difference which is at first sight irreconcilable. Here we have the breeding ground for a great deal of the modern misunderstanding of the Bible's true character. People who cannot think except in the logic of Aristotle or Descartes are disconcerted by what they call the " incoherence " and " obscurity " of the Bible. If they are critics or philologists, they tend to see every break in logic as a sign that the text has been tampered with, or a new source introduced. If they are philosophers or moralists, they harp on the Semitic inability to be abstract or speculative, and welcome the advent of the Greek mind which was able to put some precision into this childish babbling. If they are historians, they carefully catalogue all the " contradictory " themes, untangle the various systems used, and point out what has been " borrowed " from where. And finally if they are theologians, they set out to reduce the inspired author's poor ideas into some sort of order, and they card-index the rich themes which they happen to find scattered throughout the sacred pages. All of them agree in deploring the lack of precision and clarity. They do not see that they are trying to force a square peg into a round hole.

The uniform obscurity of biblical literature is not due to any desire on the part of the authors to be mysterious for the sake of mystery. Such a uniformity of expression argues to the use of a dialectic different from ours. The very rhythm of thought is different, because its object is different.

The Greek (and the rest of the western world after him) uses his mind and his words to *express* ideas, as succinctly as possible. He believes that such expression is possible because he uses as his starting point the world of external reality, which is itself distinct and measurable. The Semite, on the other hand, does not separate himself from the world in which he lives. He is not detached, he does not stand outside that world, he is part of it. His starting point is within himself, his own personal experience, which he cannot contain in words because words have no place there. He does not attempt to *express* what is in his mind, he simply tries to *evoke* it.

The Greek reconstructs and re-creates the outside world within the framework of his mind. The Semite takes what is already in his mind and tries to transmit it by suggestion. The Greek abstracts and arrives at a universal idea; the Semite fastens on to the particular and tries to absorb it. The Greek is concerned to conceive truth and demonstrate it; the Semite seeks to receive it and make other people want it. Conceiving and receiving, active and passive, these are the words which best sum up the two attitudes.

They describe too the type of *logic* which characterizes the different dialectics. The Greek dialectic is remembered for its perfection of the syllogism. Starting with abstract principles, it goes on to deduce hard and fast conclusions for concrete application. The subordinations which link the clauses of a sentence are meant precisely to reproduce the hierarchical order of these deductions. The Greek " period " is the masterly result of this logical process. A treatise is planned in exactly the same way, and the different paragraphs of a discussion or demonstration must follow each other in an orderly manner. Points must be dealt with in sequence, and a new idea must not be broached until the first has been fully disposed of. Everything proceeds with discrimination, precision and clarity, in an effort first to find adequate expression for the mind's concept, and then to set it down in irrefutable form. It is in fact the application of the science of mathematics to the field of the mind. Reason is an infallible thought-machine, supreme, incorruptible, objective and calm even when it contemplates itself. " What can be clearly conceived can be clearly expressed."

The Semitic dialectic is the exact reverse. At the outset it rejects demonstration, at least in the realm of thought. The important thing is not to compel the mind, but to give it a feeling for life and reality. The Greek mind is governed by a sense of the diversity of things, the Semitic by a sense of their oneness. The Semite will not translate, but tries rather to convey an idea, knowing well that words are clumsy vehicles, and that they are not the only signs and symbols by which the concrete thought of the speaker is evoked in the listener.

It is more or less of set purpose that this sort of dialectic rejects abstraction. To abstract is to weaken and amputate and eventually to kill. In its place the Semite builds up a concept by superimposing one suggestion on another. His thought does not proceed in a straight line but in concentric circles, where one affirmation is the repetition or antithesis of the one before. The Semite states what he has to say, and then says it again, and then several more times, adding each time another touch, another stroke, constantly enriching this or that aspect of a thought which was already present in its entirety in the first formulation. The process has much in common with the Hegelian method of thesis, antithesis and synthesis, and is rather reminiscent of the nineteenth century Impressionists. Like these painters the Semite first draws a quick sketch of the whole, and then proceeds to add a number of apparently isolated and even unrelated details, which need the mind's eye to co-ordinate them into a finished picture.

To describe the Semitic style as poetry and the western as prose would make too facile a distinction between the two. It is true that with us poetry is a kind of holiday from discursive reasoning and that the Semite is always something of a poet. But the spirit of pure poetry can fire the soul of Greek and Jew alike. Yet a comparison of Greek poetry with biblical poetry will immediately illustrate the gulf that divides the two. When the westerner turns from prose to poetry he changes from everyday clothes into formal dress. When the Semite turns from poetry to prose he only girds his loins a little tighter. Western poetry is prose in formal dress; Semitic prose is poetry in working attire. The greater the inspiration, the more stringently is the Greek tied to his technique, and the more freed is the Semite from all restraint.

THE *characteristics* of the Semitic style are few and simple, and flow naturally from the dialectic. They can be reduced to three: parallelism, juxtaposition and antithesis.

Parallelism is the natural mould for an idea which can only be evoked by repetition and suggestion. Its purpose is not only to enrich the primary statement by giving it precision, but also to create a gradual and insistent rhythm. The result can be compared to a succession of waves ebbing and flowing over a rock, or to a series of concentric circles rising in a spiral around an axis. There are examples of this on every page of the Bible. It is so characteristic of Semitic poetry that it is often imagined to be its hallmark. But a closer study will show that Semitic prose is governed by the same process, though in a freer manner. The Beatitudes provide a typical example (Mt. 5:3-10, Lk. 6:20-23). They are often imagined to be a eulogy of separate virtues, each with its appropriate reward. In fact Christ is only describing the different facets of one and the same outlook, which cannot exist without its component parts, and which is the basic qualification for entry into the "Promised Land", or "Kingdom of Heaven", or "Peace". The same thing is repeated over and over again (four times in Lk., eight in Mt.). But these repetitions have a rhythm and power which the finest Greek period could never attain.

The same passage will illustrate the second characteristic of the Semitic style, *juxtaposition*. Semitic syntax is based on co-ordinate rather than subordinate clauses. This is generally taken as an indication of the immaturity of Semitic languages. This is true enough, but it is even more an indication of Semitic psychology. The Semite refuses to analyse. Nearly all his phrases are simply linked together by a conjunction which we invariably take to mean "and", but which conveys for him an infinite variety of meanings whose richness is safeguarded by the very lack of logical precision. The whole art of juxtaposition consists in giving the sentences the order which will bring out the required shade of meaning. To us the phrases may seem to be thrown together haphazardly. In fact their sequence follows the intuitive progression in the author's mind. Sometimes, as with St. Mark, this will be spontaneous; sometimes, as in the Apocalypse, it is the fruit of careful thought. Always the aim is to create the living context in which each sentence will be seen at its true value.

The third characteristic of style, *antithesis*, is a variant of the last. The theme is stated and its opposite is placed next to it in contrast, the reader being left to form a synthesis. The Semite enjoys a paradox. Nothing pleases him better than to throw cold water on the conclusions of logic. He is by instinct suspicious of the syllogism with its shallowness and inherent ambiguity. He objects to the mental laziness that this way of thinking often encourages. The purpose of his thinking is to invade the citadel of the mind. So he employs shock tactics, and repeats and stresses and if necessary even marshals contrary ideas in order to force the mind to by-pass the discursive and penetrate to the intuitive. There is nothing artificial in this process; it is part of the very nature of thought, which can only see reality when it is thrown into relief by non-reality. All created knowledge is provoked by the psychological awareness of contrast. Man cannot see the shape of things at all unless they are placed against the background of infinity.

BESIDE these literary figures, which are capable of many variations, the Semite makes great use of symbolism. If he is to convey concrete reality, he must use language which is itself figured and concrete. But even in his use of the symbol he differs from the Greek. For the Greek, the symbol is a sign-post which points to an abstract idea, a mere convention which enables the writer to express his thought. For the Semite it is something more. One could almost say that for him the whole of reality, of thought and of life is a symbol. All creation is one hierarchical unity. All things have their proper place, but they are intimately linked with each other. Lower levels of reality are a first and symbolic expression of the higher levels. The one cannot be reached without passing through the other. A symbol is consequently no mere convention, but a valid sacrament of the thing it signifies. The sensible world is a reflection of the invisible world, and words themselves embody something of the reality of the things they signify. Their purpose is to convey a positive suggestion of concrete life and living thought, not a colourless and dead abstraction.

The highest development of the Semitic use of the symbol is

the *parable*, so often misinterpreted because so often misunderstood. We are apt to treat the parable as if it were an allegory in the Greek style, where each detail has its counterpart in reality. The Greek allegory is a pictorial representation of a thought already conceived in the mind. Its whole aim is to clarify the thought, and so it must itself be concise and clear. By contrast, the Semitic parable is never meant to be split up into its constituent elements. The individual elements do not, generally speaking, have an independent meaning. In the parable of the Ten Virgins, for instance (Mt. 25 : 1-13), neither the virgins themselves, nor their number, nor the oil, nor the lamps represent anything in the world of reality. They are no more than necessary properties for the telling of the story. It is only the story taken as a whole that has a meaning, an admonition to be vigilant. Some further elements have been grafted on to the central idea, and have their own particular significance (here for example, the bridegroom represents Christ, and the wedding eternal life). But on the whole it is true to say that a parable is never just a simple comparison or an allegory. It is a cross-section of life, presented as a silhouette of the life beyond the world of perception. It is a discreet invitation to find the deeper meaning of things. As soon as we try to draw logical and systematic conclusions from it, we distort it. Far from seeking to clarify, the parable tries to show that there is a mystery beneath the surface of things. Its aim is at once to catch the attention, and to force the hearer into one of the two inevitable categories, those who " have ears to hear ", and those who " hearing do not hear ".

There is, then, a certain technique to the Semitic style, although contrasted with the virtuosity demanded of our western writers and poets, who have to master a very complicated literary code, it is elementary and simple. With his constant use of imagery, the Semite simply rings the changes on the few basic literary constructions we have mentioned. The only limits to his freedom are set by his own intuitive inspiration. So long as he can convey the movement in his soul, expression matters little.

On closer examination, it will be seen that these elements of Semitic style (parallelism, antithesis and simplicity of construction) are exactly the characteristics of the spoken word, the natural expression of the rhythm in thought. Père Jousse, the psychologist, has explained this rhythm as the outward expression of the biological rhythm. But it goes deeper than that. The "explosions of energy", in which he finds the origin of the oral style, are themselves only a manifestation of a deeper spiritual rhythm. Syllogisms and measured verse are artificial things. At our deepest level it is not in these forms that we express ourselves. What is natural to us at our deepest level is a vivid awareness of contrast. It is here that thought is conceived, and it is consequently in passionate reiteration that thought is expressed. The style of western prose and poetry has no direct contact with the spontaneity of this spoken word. The Semitic style has; in fact its written word is not really distinct from its spoken word. The one is only a formal transcription of the other.

Clearly, then, Semitic literature is something that grows spontaneously out of the life of the people, and is never divorced from it. It does not create a literary or artistic intelligentsia. It is simply the highest expression of the soul of the people. Those scholars who try to elaborate a science of Hebrew poetry would save themselves much effort if they would recognize this fact. There is no point in looking for metre and stanza and rules for versifying, since these things do not strictly speaking exist. The only thing that exists is the pulsing rhythm of the poet's own overflowing soul, and the transmission of the vibrant waves that radiate from his intuitive genius. Parallelism or antithesis, concentric or linear thought, all are no more than the outward manifestations of the writer's inward experience.

To recapitulate, the Semite pays far more attention to his inspiration than he does to his style. His dialectic both shocks and charms. It lays open a world of thought which is impatient of syllogisms. For all its poor machinery, it has an appeal which the most passionless rationalist will find hard to resist. The Fourth Gospel, as the *chef-d'œuvre* of this style, will serve as an example. Even those who complain of its thin vocabulary and its rambling logic are unable to escape its serenity and compulsion. The secret of its attraction lies in the simple rhythm of its thought. An analysis of the discourse on the Bread of Life, for instance (Jn. 6), will reveal as many as six or seven parallel cycles, where thesis and antithesis are resolved into a synthesis which is itself the gateway to yet another cycle. From its starting point in the physical multiplication of the loaves, the discourse slowly rises to the sublime level of the Spirit and the mystery of the Bread of Heaven. As it progresses, so the cadence becomes more and more compelling. The richness of the concept contained in the first statement is gradually released, to reveal all its beauty and colour. Deeper and deeper it finds its way into the soul. At first surprised and disconcerted, the reader is irresistibly drawn, attracted, and finally committed to the truth which sets him free.

III

LITERARY FORMS

Variety found in the Bible; relation to western literary forms; lack of precision in Semitic forms.

T H E very fact that there is such a thing as a Semitic style (and every page of the Bible bears witness to it) is proof enough that this book is rooted in humanity. It belongs to a particular literary period, and if we are to understand it we must be prepared to examine the human background against which it was written. Nor is that all. Even though the Bible belongs to a particular tradition, it does not mean that all its literature will be homogeneous. In common with all human achievements in the field of literature, it will make use of a variety of literary forms. These we must know if we are to discover the author's aims.

A writer has a wide selection of literary forms at his disposal. His choice will depend on his temperament and on what he is trying to achieve. If he wants to write history he will not choose the poetic form; if he is to write a novel he will avoid the form of high drama. Every kind of writing has its idiom, which must be taken into account if it is not to be misconstrued. Inspiration does not do away with the normal rules of literature. If God speaks to men in the language of men, then he can inspire any of the means of expression capable of carrying his message, whether it be poetry or history, fact or fiction.

The Bible unquestionably makes use of a variety of literary

forms. We find histories like Samuel and I Maccabees side by side with collections of popular stories and with works of edification like Judith and Tobit. The prophetical books are quite distinct in form from the sapiential books, despite their common didactic purpose. The book of Psalms has a character of its own which distinguishes it from the Song of Songs or Lamentations, though all three are poetry. The Song has more in common with our own dramatic form. The Fourth Gospel, too, in achieving its thrilling climaxes owes something to drama, although clearly its main purpose is historical. We might say that the modern world knows of hardly any literary form which is not found somewhere in the Bible. Prose and poetry, history and romance, annals and legend, lyrics, epics, and straightforward teaching, all are to be found in the Scriptures.

HERE we must take heed. In this matter of literary forms we can be easily misled by the apparent similarity between modern and biblical usage. There are similarities, but these are offset by profound differences in method, purpose and spirit. Those scholars who have attacked the historicity of the Gospels erred precisely in failing to take this into account. They discredited St. Mark because he did not obey the rules for the scientific writing of history. Could anything be more of an anachronism? The Semite had his laws for writing history, but they were those of his own time, not those of the technical twentieth century. To apply one to the other can only lead to misunderstanding. In this respect the biblical science of the nineteenth century burned up a tremendous amount of energy to no purpose whatsoever. Of the whole mass of stuff that it produced scarcely half a dozen pages will endure; with a little common sense they could have been achieved with far less labour.

What is true of the historical books is equally true of the doctrinal and poetical works. It is just not possible to read St. Paul as one would read St. Thomas. To try to do so is to make nonsense of him. Nor can the verses in the Bible be indexed like the canons of the Code, except for amusement. There is no common ground on which Ecclesiastes can be compared with Montaigne, or Proverbs with Aristotle's Ethics.

Even in the field of fiction we must make allowance for

difference in usage. Ruth, Tobit, Esther, and in a different way Jonah, are all works intended for edification and they clearly contain elements of fiction, but that does not put them in the same class as modern novels. The fiction of the ancients was never purely imaginative. The Semite always kept one foot on the ground. His fiction was based on a core of reality even when it was coloured and embroidered by popular legend. The East has consequently never recognized our western distinction between the historical genus and the purely fictional one. The idiosyncrasies of each case can be understood only in the context of the Semitic mentality and of the literary forms to which it gave rise.

The problem of the reader becomes even more complex when he meets literary forms which have no modern counterpart. His first contact with the Prophets, for example, will dismay him. Even the Psalms do not enjoy among Catholics the esteem accorded to the comparatively uninspired litanies and devotions. As for such books as the Apocalypse. . . .! This short book, the very synthesis of all revelation, has troubled more minds than it has encouraged hearts. Yet it is the finest example of a literary form which was much in vogue towards the end of the Old Testament period, both in the Bible (the book of Daniel is an apocalypse) and in the apocryphal writings. But the conventional idioms and stereotyped turns of phrase which go to make up this literary form do not come easily to an analytical frame of mind.

In some cases the uninformed reader can easily mistake one literary form for another. Appearances are deceptive. We have already quoted the example of those books which at first sight seem to be historical. Even a more classic example is to be found in the first eleven chapters of the book of Genesis. Here we have a form which is quite unique and found nowhere else in the Bible. Elements of history, legend, parable and apocalypse are all combined, but it can be called neither strict history nor pure legend. Still less is it myth. The ancient Semitic conception of the creation of the world, built up on a nucleus of real happenings, has here been stylized, enriched and purified from the lees of polytheism. Into this framework have been woven the threads of the great religious themes—the creation, man, the fall, sin, and the promise of redemption. It would be wrong to interpret these chapters as symbols, without foundation in fact. It would be just as wrong to seek in them a scientific account of the pre-history of man. They are a graphic and concrete presentation of the beginnings of the human drama and of the plans of a merciful God. These wondrous pages are the gateway to the Bible, the first glimpse of the heavenly Temple which is to form the Book's climax in the Apocalypse.

WE HAVE said enough to give the reader some insight into the characteristics of the biblical literary forms and their relationship to our own. A more exhaustive analysis is made difficult by their multiplicity. Hardly one of them is used in isolation: always it is modified by its neighbour.

Especially is this so with the historical form. The biblical chronicler was not hampered by our concern for writing scientific history. Nevertheless the whole range of historical literature is represented: prosaic annals, official documents, detailed accounts (Samuel, 1 Maccabees), popular traditions (the stories of the Patriarchs), biography (David, the Synoptic Gospels), memoirs (Nehemiah), narrative in doctrinal form (Fourth Gospel), doctrine in narrative form (Genesis 1-11), and edifying legend (Tobit). These all come under the heading of history, and all make use of anonymity, compilation of sources, juxtaposition of doublets, glosses and simplification, with a facility denied to the modern scientific historian. This is true even of St. Luke's Gospel and Acts, in spite of his subjection to the influence of Greek historiography. In all these forms, everything is subordinated to the doctrinal and religious themes. In none of them is history written for its own sake.

This literary licence is not confined to history. It can be seen at work in other fields, though not so obviously. The prophetical form has an affinity with the apocalyptic (which was developed from it) and both are allied to the sapiential writings. Thus Ezekiel stands half-way between Isaiah and Daniel.

Naturally the forms used in the New Testament are rooted in the Old, though they have been influenced by their own background and their contact with hellenistic literary forms. The Synoptic Gospels are the written form of an oral catechesis in the Semitic manner. The Epistles of St. Paul are modelled on

K

the style of Greek letter writing, but in some of them the didactic spirit of Semitic literature has so far modified the hellenistic form that they are more like treatises than letters.

If we may catalogue what we have already said, we would first of all put the beginning of Genesis in a class of its own. In the historical genus we would distinguish detailed accounts, anonymous compilation, popular epic and theological history. The imaginative genus would include the quasi-historical narratives and the Song of Songs. The juridical genus is also represented, but under an historical form. The doctrinal genus covers the field of prophecy, apocalypse, homily, the sapiential writings and the Epistles. The Psalms finally stand on their own, as the only example of lyrical literature.

It is not within the scope of this book to analyse or even to summarize the characteristics of each of these literary forms. We will come across some of them in connection with specific problems. When we come to deal with the divine inspiration of the history of Israel, for instance, we will need to know something of the characteristics of those records which relate the history. All that we wish to do here is to point out their utterly human qualities and the need to study these qualities if we are to understand the divine message. We must, for example, see the affinity between the cosmogony of Genesis 1-2 and the traditional Babylonian accounts. The historical books must be read in the light of the vast number of literary sources which were used in their composition. The legislation in the Pentateuch must be seen as the residue of 800 years of law-making. The sapiential books combine the maxims of the ancients with the fruit acquired by meditating on those maxims. The Bible comprises a complex network of men, facts and texts, of borrowing and lending. The influences at work have not been hidden; even now they can be seen between the lines of the sacred text, to show the Bible for the intensely human ferment that it is.

IV

THE MORALITY OF THE BIBLE

*" Immorality" and anthropomorphisms in the Bible;
ancient realism and modern puritanism;* autres temps,
autres mœurs; *social nature of biblical morality; its historical evolution.*

THE Bible is a human book not only by reason of its composition and style, but even more because it records the lives of
men of flesh and blood.

The fact that it is so soaked in humanity is one of the Bible's
greatest paradoxes. It is usually a stumbling block to the new
reader; it has always been an embarrassment to those Christians
who have sought in the Bible only the wonders of God and the
ideal of humanity. A certain misguided type of spiritual reading has encouraged them to expect in the Bible near perfect
models of human behaviour. It was this outlook which was
responsible for the allegorical and accommodated interpretation
so common among the Fathers. It was not seemly that God
should lend the force of his inspiration to so much that was
barbarous and gross. Many a page ripped from its literal context seemed to some to be unworthy of God, and their prejudices urged them to take refuge in the safety of what they
imagined to be the spiritual sense. St. Augustine's well-known
apology for Jacob's lie is often quoted as an example of this,
but it is not a particularly good example. The subtlety of the
great Doctor of Hippo was never completely divorced from his
sense of reality, and under all his rigid reasoning on this text
there is a real intuition of the truth of the matter. Origen was
more anxious to jettison the literal sense. His mind was grate-
ful for any possible escape, and without provocation he would
sublimate the " carnal " infirmities of the text on to a moral and
spiritual plane. His homilies on the Old Testament are marvels
of fantasy and penetration, but they are not strictly speaking
exegesis of Scripture. Without doubt the fashionable return to
this sort of interpretation is due to a similar outlook. It was
Paul Claudel who deplored the utter poverty of the literal
sense.

The reader of the Bible will search in vain for the ideal of human behaviour. He will not even be altogether edified by the actions of God. The God of the Bible is not the metaphysical God of Aristotle. He is an intensely personal being, one who is alive, fearsome, active, at times almost inconsiderate. He is unpredictable. Sometimes he seems to share our human passions, sometimes to condemn them. He enters into the very thick of things and his miracles blossom forth in the most mundane circumstances. Ordinary and marvellous, stormy and calm, of the earth earthy and yet charged with a heavenly light, this is the atmosphere of the Bible and of its people.

THE uneasiness we feel in this regard will be dispelled only by a return to a deeper understanding of the workings of man's soul and to a more Christian concept of the reality that is God. True reality is what God has done, not what we think he ought to have done. One of the prime effects of an enlightened reading of Scripture is that it shakes our complacency by introducing us to humanity in the raw. The Bible calls a spade a spade, and it is better so. The moral judgment of Christians is still warped by an element of Jansenism. Through a kind of psychological inhibition, they have a complete list of realities which are not nice. These realities are not only kept out of sight, they are not even talked about. These misguided souls feel that it is morally better to insinuate and hint than to call things by their names. All that they do is to increase the already heavily charged atmosphere.

It is a moot point whether man's moral consciousness is any keener now than it was in the time of Moses or David. Any improvement that has been made is due to the ideals of Christianity, of which they were ignorant. The legend of Lot's daughters in Gen. 19:30-38—which implies a moral judgment since it puts a stigma on the hostile tribes of Ammon and Moab, sister tribes of Israel—can hardly merit the justifiable censure of people familiar with the moral depravities depicted in our novels and films. The destruction by "anathema" in the conquest of Canaan (Jos. 6:17, 8:24, 10:28, etc.) did not involve one fraction of the innocent victims of a single big air raid during the war. It is strange how people will condemn the one and condone the other. The Bible is merciless in exposing this Pharisaic attitude. It will not be satisfied with anything less than God as he is, and man as we know ourselves to be.

There is, however, a certain relevance in the proverb *autres temps, autres mœurs*. The field of morals is governed by the same principle of context as that of history and thought. When we evaluate the moral consciousness of people living in an age and locality not our own, we must make allowance for a certain moral relativism. It is true that there is an absolute standard of morality just as there is an absolute standard of truth, and these are not confined to time or place; but it is equally true that the imposition of these absolute standards was a slow and piecemeal affair, consequent on the realization of Christianity. Standards do not exist in the abstract. They are always actualized in concrete conditions, which vary according to particular stages of development. Alongside the universal standards will be found a number of conventions and prejudices which carry their own obligations. Consequently there will be numerous distinct moralities. Some precepts will have more compulsion than others according to the emphasis imparted by particular circumstances. Jephtah, for instance, with his obsession for the inviolability of a soldier's word, was carried beyond any objective norm in his respect for his vow (Jud. 11 : 30-40). In another context, the law of " blood " and the demand of revenge for murder has to be seen as a security measure imposed by the conditions of life in the desert.

O N E of the things that ties the Semitic morality closer to the basic things of life than our own is its insistence on the *social* aspect. It is a morality born of the desert, where the individual cannot live except in the shelter of a community. His personal behaviour is measured by its effect on the clan. The scale of moral values is therefore different. He is judged by the gravity of his action and not by his intention. He is very conscious of the disorders which follow in the wake of sin. A balance has been upset and it must be restored whether the sinner is culpable or not. Those things which strike at the good of the community as such (theft, homicide, adultery, inhospitality, violation of oaths, etc.), are all judged with a severity which to us seems excessive. Whatever promotes the good of the community is approved and encouraged (the overthrow of enemies, double-dealing with the enemy, sexual relationships which ensure the family line, etc.). The community is absolute, the individual is subordinate. His subservience to the needs of the community seemed to him quite normal, even where we would judge it heroic, or reprehensible.

Similarly, some of the personal virtues which we prize highly meant little or nothing to the Semite. Sex so preoccupies the minds of many to-day that they regard it as the touchstone of virtue and vice. Such an outlook is only to be expected of a culture which puts so much emphasis on the happiness of the individual. The Semite looked at the morality of sex in an entirely different way. His criterion was again the effect his behaviour had on the community. Sterility was a blemish. A large family was God's greatest gift to man. This regard for the social aspect was a constant safeguard against excess. The responsibility of a family was itself a tonic and an absorbing interest.

We are not claiming that this made the Semite a model of virtue. Human nature is human nature. The fact that his passions were normally restrained by the ties of his social life means that when he broke out he did so with violence. The desert which curbed his opportunity also heightened the appeal of the pleasures of sedentary life. Give him a motive (sometimes even religion provided one) and the pent up forces inside him would break out into an orgy of brutality. All was fair in war, since Israel's wars were Yahweh's wars.

We insist that this is not a question of a more primitive morality, but simply of a different scale of values. The West condemns the duplicity and the sensuality of the Semite without realizing that they are natural consequences of desert life. His concrete dialectic imposed on him a delicacy in moral matters, but he still had to reckon with the absolute forces within him which were liable to erupt without warning.

This does not mean that the men of the Bible were all cast in the same mould. Their morality is affected not only by place but also by time, and it is continually changing. This progress towards a more perfect realization of the ideal becomes evident as the Bible unfolds. The discriminating reader will again

apply the historical method in estimating the morality of the
Old Testament. He will see a long and painful evolution from
Abraham to Christ. Sometimes there are temporary checks,
but on the whole it is a progress towards perfection. Under
the influence of the Prophets and still more of the Exile,
the social aspect of Israel's morality is refined to reveal
slowly the true worth of the individual and of spiritual
values.

The morality of Abraham is remarkable for its forthright-
ness and integrity (St. Paul calls it his faith) but it was confined
to his clan and his immediate surroundings. The morality of
Moses and the Judges was marked by the severity imposed by
the national conquest. In David we see the freshness and
warm-heartedness of youth, and there is something of the true
Christian spirit in the happy way he unites complete abandonment to Yahweh with competent human endeavour. Even so
his reward remains on earth. After the apostasy of the last
kings and the collapse in Exile, there grew up a feeling of
resentment. The sentence of Yahweh had fallen impartially on
good and bad alike, on his servants and on sinners who had
abandoned him. A gradual murmuring arose against the traditional idea of an earthly paradise. Job and the Psalms raise
the problem of the suffering of the innocent. Ecclesiastes points
with bitterness to the vanity of earthly happiness. The influence of Greek thought began to be felt. All these conspired
together to raise men's minds to seek the only true answer
in personal immortality and happiness, within the spiritual
community of God's elect. Not until the eve of the incarnation was this finally realized in the book of Wisdom (ch.
1-5), which forms a fitting climax to the long process which
had been the piecemeal manifestation of Wisdom pre-
incarnate.

It would not be right to judge these gropings and uncertain
victories of the human mind with harshness, for it is of these
that our security was born. "Let anyone who thinks that he
stands, take heed lest he fall." We would do well to retrace
this journey through the Bible, the better to appreciate what is
ours. The strict and rigid code of Sinai was a good teacher,
as Paul knew well. When we feel its sin-laden yoke on our
own shoulders we may perhaps show more appreciation for the

freedom we have in the Spirit of adoption bequeathed to us by Christ (Gal. 3:24–4:7).

WHEN once we have learned to see this complex pattern of unity and diversity in the Bible, we shall not be shocked by its frankness in portraying humanity in all its weakness. In fact we will be glad to find a God who is interested in men of flesh and blood. We will begin to see him as a Father appealing to his wayward children. We will recognize ourselves in those people, our aspirations and falls from grace, the beauty of our calling, and our failure to be worthy of it. They, after all, had to grapple with the same mysterious forces which are lined up against us. They all come to life: Abraham, the wandering sheik and silent man of faith; Jacob, the keen and resourceful bedouin; Joseph, the victim of his brothers' hatred, who yet wins through by his charm and wisdom; Moses, the mighty tamer of his band of wild and lawless wanderers; the Judges, great and small, Ehud, the shadowy conspirator, Gideon, the crafty and sensual potentate, and Samson, the colossus with feet of clay. Then there are all the women of the Bible, from Eve to Mary, the weak ones and the strong ones, the calculating ones and the affectionate ones, the desires of men and the models of purity: Rahab, the prostitute; Deborah, the prophetess; Jael, guardian of her husband's tent; the barren Hannah, whose reproach was taken away; the sad and tragic wife of Hophni; Abigail, of the lovely face and quick wit; Bathsheba, of easy virtue; Tamar, the maiden in distress; Athalia and Jezebel, firebrands; and Judith, whose courage knew no bounds.

Standing head and shoulders above them all, uniting in his person both strength and charm, is David, the brightest jewel in humanity's crown, with something of the divine in his bearing. It is hard to know what to marvel at more in this most natural of men, his triumphs or his failures, the beauty of his love or the passion of his lust, the depths to which he fell or the heights to which his love of Yahweh led him. Men had gone before him who gave some hint of the Messiah, and others would follow him to complete the picture. Isaiah showed us the future nobility, Jeremiah the throbbing sensitiveness, Nehemiah the tranquillity and the Maccabees the peace-loving and

heroic generosity. But David was all these things. In him was
achieved the paradox of man made to God's image and likeness, yet clamouring for salvation from the depths of his soul.
There would be none like him again until one came who took
on the "likeness of sinful flesh".

V

THE WRITERS

*Pseudonymous and anonymous writers and compilers; their
relation to the community; the synoptic Gospels; literary
personalities of the Bible; their wide variety.*

A FURTHER indication of the human origin of the Bible can
be found in the mark which each writer has left on what he has
written. To see these men as no more than secretaries is to
have a poor idea of their share in the production of the divine
Book. Every writer is bound to leave a record of his own
mentality, his own personality, and his competence or otherwise in the very way he writes, and the biblical writers are no
exception.

Sometimes it is not quite so apparent as it might be, but this
is due partly to the circumstances in which some of the books
were written, and partly to the peculiarity of Semitic style. We
have already seen its tendency to subordinate the written word
to the spoken word, and this alone is bound to restrict the
writer's literary scope. We find plenty of pseudonymous and
nameless works. There was no such thing as copyright, and
everyone considered himself free to appropriate the work of
others, to amplify, correct and modernize it. If a book had to
have an autograph (and a civilization so wedded to the concrete eventually demanded it) then there was little scruple about
the name it was given. Tribute has already been given when
it is understood that one borrows only from the rich. In practice a number of expedients were adopted. A work would be
attributed to an outstanding personality traditionally remembered as having played a decisive rôle in its composition (the
Pentateuch, for instance). Alternatively a work might be presented under the pseudonym of a person who was looked upon

as the type of the writer's own literary tradition (thus Solomon became the "author" of the sapiential books). A book might well be called after its principal hero, like Joshua, Samuel or the Judges. Finally, as in the second part of the book of Isaiah, the principal author's name could be extended to the additions made to his work after his death. We do not have to believe that Moses wrote the Pentateuch word for word, or that Samuel, Joshua and the Maccabees were the authors of the books named after them. Solomon had nothing at all to do with Ecclesiastes or Wisdom. The title of a book is only meant to jog the reader's memory. It may even be a pure literary fiction.

This sort of usage is enough to distinguish Israel's literature from any other, but it need not stop us from going on to analyse the various stages of development in the books, or from looking for the distinguishing traits that characterize the contributions made by different authors. Unless he thinks that the workings of inspiration are quite mechanical, any reader can become conscious of the various nuances which betray this long process of editing. He can see, without the aid of much scholarship, that even the most anonymous of compilations is thereby given a unity which is of more value than the contribution of any one generation. A constant reading and familiarity with the text will give an almost spontaneous intuition about the presence of those nuances which express the different tendencies of each age. These are the mirrors which reflect the extent to which the progress of divine revelation is tied to human progress.

IN SOME cases the work of a particular writer is easily recognizable in spite of successive elaborations. Very often we know everything about him except his name. A piece of literature may well be anonymous and still be a true reflection of its generation. It may even be the condensation of several generations. This does not imply, as some German scholars have pretended, that it is a concerted effort of the community. A community as such does not create. It may furnish the material, the background, and perhaps the incentive for a work, but the work itself is conceived and composed by individuals. They could be called the spokesmen for the community, but in any event their work will bear their personal mark. There is no spontaneous generation in literature any more than there is in nature. Homer's poetry and the Song of Roland are quite clearly compilations drawn from a number of sources, but the actual compiling and co-ordinating must be the work of individuals of genius.

The same is true of the Synoptic Gospels. All three are transcriptions of the one oral catechesis about Christ, but it is the individuality of each Evangelist that makes the three accounts so profoundly different. The graphic and simple approach of St. Mark is far removed from the seriousness of St. Matthew's Gospel. The charm of the one and the majesty of the other are in high contrast to the urbanity and clarity of St. Luke, even though St. Luke did little more than re-write St. Mark in the light of sources known to St. Matthew.

Even the oral catechesis which lies behind these three different Gospels has its own distinctive flavour. It is not just a haphazard collection of pious stories fitted into a ready-made scheme of religious propaganda. One can feel the incisiveness which is the hallmark of someone who was actually there. The utter simplicity of Mark clearly points to the fact that St. Peter, his master, was part of this story. The style of St. Matthew preserves the rhythm of the first teaching of the Apostles. St. Luke interprets the message of Christ by adopting those themes which are distinctly Pauline. In all this there is honesty and directness. All that these intermediaries have done is to fix on particular aspects of the incomparable personality of Christ.

The Synoptics are only one example, chosen deliberately to instance the case where the author of a book is restricted in his scope and has to play a very minor rôle. Some people would have us believe that any form of literary borrowing is necessarily a borrowing of ideas. But even a man who borrows sources only to compile them cannot be dubbed a clumsy editor or a brain picker. The Semite who borrowed another's words did not thereby steal his ideas, since he did not identify thought and its expression as we do. A work which has used and woven together a number of sources is not simply a conglomeration. A writer worth his salt will obviously assimilate the substance of his sources, and if the Semite does not go out of his way to hide the fact that he has borrowed, it is because he is vividly conscious of the continuous growth and development of thought.

WE HAVE enough information about some of the sacred authors to be able to assess the effect that their personalities had on their work. In the Old Testament, Jeremiah speaks freely about himself, and Ezekiel lets us see what an important influence he wielded over the people of the Exile. These two were almost contemporaries, but there is a vast difference between the excitable pessimism of Jeremiah and the poised calm of Ezekiel. Again Qoheleth (Ecclesiastes) and Ben Sirach (Ecclesiasticus) both speak from a long life of experience, but where one is a bitterly disillusioned man, the other is full of happiness and contentment. The New Testament offers similar contrasts. Much has been written about the "volcanic" temperament of St. Paul. His style throbs with the movement of a restless zeal which his Greek background could not keep in check. His impatience was a fire which could not be contained by words. Utterly convinced in his own soul, he must necessarily drive himself towards his goal. St. Paul is a man of spirit, dynamic and moody. The breath of the Spirit only serves to amplify the tumultuous rhythm of his great soul. He is essentially a Jew anxious to make himself acceptable to the Greeks, and only partially succeeding. In contrast St. John is calm, peaceful and measured. There is no conflict in his soul or in his mind. The Greek world has given him only his vocabulary, it has not affected his Semitic outlook. He has already won the battle of words in which St. Paul is still engaged. His is the serene realm of the Spirit, and he is happy to radiate the victory and the peace of the risen Christ. In parallel, St. John is reminiscent of the second part of Isaiah. St. Paul is more like Moses, and St. Mark has the freshness of the second book of Samuel.

IT IS not difficult to discover many contrasts and many unlooked for harmonies in the Bible. It reflects the whole range of human temperament, all its wealth and all its poverty. Inspiration does not relieve Leviticus of boredom, nor does it give style to the clumsy and pedantic books of Chronicles.

It does not provide the author of the Apocalypse with a knowledge of Greek syntax, nor does it make St. Paul any the clearer, as the author of 2 Peter (3:15) had already discovered.

These hallmarks of the author's personality are further proof that the Bible is a book dictated by circumstance. There is not a single book which does not reflect the world of the author and the scope of his human environment. The second part of Isaiah needs to be read in the light of the ended Exile; St. Paul will puzzle those who do not know the story of his life as recorded in the Acts. The Gospels and many of St. Paul's Epistles can only be understood in the context of the topics that preoccupied the first generation of Christians; it was such problems as the binding force of the Law, the Judeo-Christian question and concern over the delayed Parousia that dictated the form in which the New Testament was written. Where St. Mark is content to give a straightforward account of the facts, St. Matthew and the Epistle of James express the prudent and cautious position of the conservatives, and St. Paul and St. Luke are frank and clear about their break with Judaism. When we come to St. John, this troublesome question has taken a new shape, and his writings reflect his concern over Gnostic mysticism and the promise of contact with a pagan world. The Old Testament is governed by the same law of circumstance. It was the prevailing political and social situation which dictated the preaching of the Prophets. The book of Ruth would seem to be a lesson in some points of law disputed during the Exile. The plight of the deportees in the Exile created the special needs which occasioned the book of Tobit. Whether the purpose of a book was didactic or polemic, historical or apologetic, juridical or liturgical, always it was circumstance which evoked the determination of the writer and compelled him to answer the needs of his people.

We may justly conclude that the Bible is utterly human. Not only does it reflect the best and the worst in man, it also tells of his hopes and his disappointments. Whilst it sings of his high calling it does not soft pedal his fall. All this it expresses in human terms of space and time in answer to prevailing needs. If one were to group together the works of Homer, St. Augustine, Shakespeare, Milton, Dickens and Newman, one would still not compass the drama of the human soul in the way the Bible does. One would have a collection of bits and pieces, but nothing of that unity which welds together the Bible's varied books and to whose power the man of faith cannot fail to succumb.

CHAPTER VI

THE WORD OF GOD

I

HUMAN AND DIVINE

The free gift of faith and reasons for believing; the Bible, human without and divine within; faith and reason in the study of the Bible; the Bible, object of faith and motive of credibility.

THE profoundly human character of the Bible is obvious enough to anyone who reads it. The divine character can be seen only through the eyes of faith. Now faith does not come from man but from heaven: it is God giving himself. We cannot grasp God of our own free will unless he first bestows himself. We do not, therefore, intend to prove that the Bible is divine. It is part of our faith to believe that it is so, because we believe in the Church of Christ which gives us the Bible from God. We do not look to the Bible to justify our belief in Christ and his Church; other. than in Christ God does not give himself to us, and without Christ the Bible is deprived of its divine element. It is only because Christ has left it for a witness of him that we put our trust in it.

All the same, we must not imagine that faith is a thing apart, unrelated to human experience. The truth known by faith and the truth known from reason or experience are both elements which go to the making of the one divine truth. Faith can never be a product of human reasoning or intuition, but if it is to be true faith is must be fully reasonable and capable of enriching the human soul. Without this interaction of one sphere on the other there is no faith. There may be illuminism or rationalism, but in either case we stay on the purely human level.

Nowhere is this more clearly shown than in the Bible. To

the unbeliever the Bible is no more than a collection of unrelated books of unequal merit. The humanity of the Bible blinds his eyes to anything else. To the believer, its profound logic convinces him more and more that this strange book bears the stamp of God's hand. Those people whose faith was shaken some fifty years ago by the difficulties of the Bible were not clear in their minds about this relationship between faith and reason. If they had read Pascal they would have had a deeper understanding of their mutual interaction. Mere scientific and technical weapons will never allow a man to penetrate to the divine citadel hidden behind its human outworks; in fact they will only lead him astray. Only a spirit of burning faith and submission will enable him to turn those scientific and technical weapons to good account, and let him realize that the blemishes and surface inequalities are indications of a latent strength. Only a Christian, armed equally with divine faith, intellectual honesty and a willingness to look at the Bible as a whole, will be able to see its profound unity and divine direction.

Yet faith must not be appealed to indiscriminately. It is the easiest thing in the world to represent an opinion or a prejudice as a dogma of faith. Many an obvious fact has been sacrificed to this sort of " faith ". Intellectual honesty and common sense go for nothing if a man is really determined to stick to the " truth " he is familiar with. How can faith do anything but slumber in such an atmosphere? It is bound to become weak and unable to face reality. Real faith is fearless. It is confident that there can be no quarrel between God's right hand and his left. It knows that contradictions are only apparent, and are occasioned by a human weakness which has either obscured the divine element or misunderstood the human.

Faih like this will reach the very heart of the Bible. It will not vacillate on the fringe of signs and wonders, but will make straight for the heart of the matter which is God's overall action. Rather than risk getting lost in a maze of detail, it will seek to find the broad trends which flow smooth and unbroken beneath the ripples of human fortune. If it does happen to meet an extraordinary manifestation of God's power, it will treat it as a climax in the rhythm, a sort of " shock " given in moments of crisis, emphasizing a movement which was already present in principle.

In this light the Christian will see that the Bible with its two Testaments, distinct but complementary, is the key to the divine plan. Out of the raw material of humanity the Spirit fashions the Word of God. The Bible cannot give faith, but the open mind cannot fail to see in it the hand of God. It is not the source of our faith in Christ, but it is the Church's surest guide to that faith. It does not create faith, but it does dispose the soul to receive faith, since without Christ the Bible is a puzzle. Furthermore, without the Bible in its context, which is the Church, we would have no knowledge of Christ under the human aspect in which the Son of God became incarnate.

II

THE BIBLE'S CONVERGENT THEMES

The cycle of the divine plan with its themes of election, covenant, people of God; the cycle of the fall with its themes of sin, punishment, repentance; the cycle of redemption with its themes of mercy, messianic salvation, the desert; the cycle of accomplishment with its themes of setback, hope, the kingdom; the containing theme of thanksgiving.

BEFORE all else in this search after the true meaning of the Bible, we must accept the texture of the cloth into which the Word of God has been woven. It is made up of a number of threads tightly laced together. These threads are the doctrinal themes which run the whole length of Israel's history. Supported one by the other in a hierarchy of mutual dependence, they gradually converge and become identified with a single central theme—the incarnate Word. Each theme is a pre-incarnation of this Word, outlining its individual aspects and effectively preparing for its final revelation.

It will not be possible to mark the development of all these themes, for they are numerous and deftly interwoven. Often they are entwined with minor themes which serve to underline a particular aspect. It is equally difficult to range them in precise order of importance, because even that varies according to time and circumstance in Israel's history. The nearer they

L

come to their common realization in Christ, the more difficult it is to separate them. All that we can do here is to pick out those that seem to form the warp on which the complex unity of revelation has been woven.

FIRST among these is the *theme of election*. It appears in a number of guises, but whether it is social or individual, whether it is a miraculous birth or an unlooked for victory, a reversal of human precedence, a free gift, or a minor theme like that of the "faithful remnant", it always emphasizes the primacy of the divine initiative and the absolute sovereignty of God over the affairs of men. From the call of Abraham to the magnificent statement of Christian predestination in the opening verses of the Epistle to the Ephesians, this is the burden of God's plan. It rings out in the episode of Esau and Jacob, in the story of Joseph, in the passage through the Red Sea, in the conquests of Joshua and the Judges, in the choice of David and the rejection of Saul, in the preservation of Judah from the fate of the ten tribes of Israel, in the wondrous return from the ruin of Exile, in the unexpected triumph of the Maccabees. It gives significance to the birth of John the Baptist, to the conversion of St. Paul, and to the phenomenal growth of a movement which had its humble beginnings among a handful of Galileans.

Throughout, God's strength is shown in weakness, in the exaltation of the lowly and the humbling of the mighty, in the triumph of life over death. Throughout, outlines are being sketched of one who was to take flesh from a Virgin and be born the Son of God, the archetype of all those who are predestined, whose humility and abandonment to the Father lifts them up to the right hand of God. Throughout is prefigured his Mystical Body, embracing all those on whom he has freely bestowed his Spirit and Life. The theme of divine election begins with the account of creation in Genesis, and achieves its fulfilment in the song of the blessed in the Apocalypse. Without doubt this gift of God is the most profound, the most revolutionary, and the most distinctly divine theme in the Bible. From it stem all the other themes.

Another fundamental theme is that of *Covenant*, flowing directly from the idea of divine gift or testament implicit in the theme of election. This is not a covenant in any ordinary sense. If it involves a sort of bilateral contract, it is only because the divine initiative demands a response. God's gift is entirely free. It puts him under no obligation to man. Yet those who receive it are necessarily bound by certain obligations, and this interchange forges between God and his people a bond so close that there is communion between them. The elect shares in the holiness of God: he is a man apart. For his part, God binds himself to ensure happiness, on condition that he is acknowledged as the highest good.

It is a legal covenant insofar as it implies conditions for both parties. But its truest terms are bonds of love. It is already present in its first beginnings in the patriarchal religion, where God is looked upon as the Father of the clan (a concept which forms part of the religion of the people from whom Abraham came). With Moses and Sinai it assumes a more formal aspect, though the intimacy of individual piety is not altogether forgotten. After the Exile, so much emphasis is placed on the remoteness of God that the element of love seems at first to be compromised. But both themes are needed if they are to be harmonized in the revelation of the Father in the Son, under the new law of the Spirit.

Together the two themes of election and covenant give rise to a third. The recipients of God's favours are set apart: they are *God's people*, stamped with his seal. The religious exclusiveness which made Yahweh the private possession of Israel and Israel the heritage of Yahweh may surprise and trouble us. Yet the very transcendence of Christianity, this religion of revelation and superhuman life, is the product of the tension in the apparent contradiction of the *exclusiveness* of a God who is *one*. *Yahweh* is the God of Israel, but he is the only God and all the world is his. He chooses Israel, but only that through her he may assert his claims over all mankind. The people of Israel are, like the Church of Christ, a theocracy. They were very keenly aware of their mission to the world. It is the explanation of their intransigence, and the cause of the invincible dynamism which they have handed on to the Church, the new Israel of God. From the tribes wandering out of Egypt for the conquest of the promised Land to the kingdom of David pushing out its national frontiers, from the post-exilic community awaiting a miraculous victory to the eschatological kingdom of Christ established through the preaching of the Church, always there is this theme of God's chosen people, the divine leaven which must transform the whole world.

THESE three themes, election, covenant and the people of God, form the basic trilogy which underlies the whole unfolding of revelation. But as a cycle it is not closed. In its themes of covenant and conquest there is room for development: covenant implies the co-operation of man, and in his conquests man is liable to suffer setbacks. Thus a new cycle opens out of the first, in the *theme of sin*. Sin in the Bible does not mean the scar left on the integrity of arrogant human nature, as it does in the pagan conception of morality. Sin is a defection of loyalty to the Covenant, a rejection of God's love and God's Gift. By sin, man breaks away from the charmed circle of God, and is thrown back on himself and his own nothingness. It may assume many forms: in Eden it is a blow struck for independence, in the desert it is the apostasy of the idolaters, with Saul it is a failure to observe the prescribed ritual, during the period of the Prophets it is moral corruption, after the Exile it is the pride of the ritualist or the self-sufficiency of the materialist, in the time of Christ it is the rejection of the Messiah, among the Pauline converts it is blasphemy against the Spirit. Whatever shape it takes, it is always a breaking of the Covenant of love and a rejection of God's courtship.

It involves the necessity for *punishment*. This too varies with the aspect of the sin. The almost arbitrary and unaccountable vengeance of God is expressed at the height of Israel's victory in terms of temporal misfortune and national catastropne. At this stage there seems to be no connection at all with what we conceive to be the primary effect of sin, namely the loss of God. After the Exile a deeper understanding of the interior life and the personal implications of the problem of evil brought new light to the question of temporal retribution. For Job, human suffering is not inevitably the result of sin. In the book of Wisdom the punishment begins to be regarded as something immanent—the eternal loss of God.

In Christ, the theme reaches its perfect expression. It is he who finally revealed the depth of the void left in man by such a loss. Those who were inspired to interpret his message did no more than clarify this revelation. For St. John, the gift of eternal life means accepting the Father in his Son; for St. Paul, sin is the utter emptiness of the man who has cut himself off from the Spirit of Christ. Thus the Bible grafts the problems of evil and pain and death on to the theme of punishment, whether it be personal punishment or social, moral or material, spiritual or eschatological. Always the problem is set against the background of God, always it emphasizes man's absolute need of God. No other book has so pointedly depicted in "existentialist" terms the confusion of man without God.

In the depths of his nothingness, there is one course left open to man, the acknowledgment of his guilt. The very nothingness to which he is reduced impresses upon him the knowledge that this is all he has. And so the *theme of repentance* is of cardinal importance in the development of the plan of redemption. It is the fallen soul's only way back to God. It may be motivated by contrition or merely by self-interest. Sometimes it is the poignant experience of the disasters which follow his breach of the Covenant; sometimes it is the misery of the man who knows he cannot escape God's wrath; sometimes it is the melting of a sinner's heart before the infinite love of the Father in his Son. The one theme embraces such apparent diversities as the moralizing book of Judges, the weary disillusionment of Ecclesiastes and the passionate appeal for love in the Song of Songs. From all of them comes the same cry of man's acknowledged nothingness, a cry which is echoed in the New Testament by Mary's *Magnificat* and the vibrant doxologies of Christian thanksgiving. This confession of need with its awareness that all men are "under the bondage of sin" (Gal. 3:22) completes the sin-cycle and introduces the cycle of redemption.

THE God of Scripture hears the cry of man's distress. If he is a jealous God and one who punishes harshly, it is because he is a loving Father. The *theme of mercy* is the pivot around which all other biblical themes revolve. It is an echo, a poised overtone of the election theme, a new and richer development of it. A gift is twice-blest if it has already once been refused. In Scripture God "repents", he relents, there is no limit to his love. He has pity, and is moved with compassion for his well-beloved. He swears he will not harm mankind again, he mourns for his trampled vineyard, and he weeps over the holy city which has rejected him. From the infinite treasury of his divine pity he reveals his breathtaking plan, determined from all eternity in "the hidden purpose of his will" (Eph. 1:9). From Paradise lost to the first Christmas night, he re-asserts his promise in ever more glowing terms. Noah, Abraham, Moses, David, the Prophets, John the Baptist, these are all its witnesses, the forerunners to the Angels' song "Glory to God in high heaven, and peace on earth to men that are God's friends." The whole Bible is the detailed publication of the "good news" which reaches its climax in the Gospel.

This mercy of God is not an empty word. It is infallible and efficacious. The Word of God does not return to him until it has accomplished its task (Isa. 55:11). God's pity is translated into action and his promise is made flesh. To bring his people out from the bondage of Egypt he raises up Moses, a leader for his people, strengthened with the power of his Spirit and commissioned to make with his people a covenant of blood. Joshua conquers the "Land" in his name. Each of the Judges is an incarnation of God's desire to rescue Israel from the plight to which her sins have reduced her. The long line of divine mediators, the instruments of Yahweh in the founding and restoration of his Kingdom, culminates in David, a second Moses. Henceforth God's captain is a King Messiah, the Anointed of Yahweh's own Spirit. It is David who gives direction to the *theme of messianic salvation*. Before him Israel had always looked for a second Moses. Now Judah would look for a second David to be both King and Prophet. The darker the gathering clouds in the political sky before the Exile, the more eagerly did the Prophets turn their eyes to the day of wrath when the Messiah would eventually appear as the hoped-for Saviour. When that hope became dimmed in the pallid Restoration after the Exile, Daniel looked to heaven to see the Son of Man coming on the clouds in a victory which was to be the consummation of all things.

As these glorious messianic traits are more precisely developed, so are they unexpectedly modified. Persecuted like David, like Jeremiah hated by God's enemies, like the Psalmist the victim of wicked men, like Job the innocent in the power of Satan, so the Servant of Yahweh will suffer for his people, their guilt imputed to him. He will be the new Paschal lamb, led to the slaughter. The salvation of his people will not be won by force but by the shedding of his blood. He will give them God's life at the price of his death. He will carry them along in his triumphal glory, but only when he himself has drained the cup of the divine anger. The poignant songs of the Servant of Yahweh are a symposium prefiguring those of St. Paul and St. John on the mystery of Christ. Jesus, son of David and son of God, unites and synthesizes in his own person all the characteristics of the long awaited Mediator. He is the expression of God's love, the firstborn of his beloved children, the scapegoat for God's anger over his sinful people, the supreme lawgiver of the new Covenant in his blood. He is the harbinger of new life by his victory over death, through sanctification in the Spirit of God.

The cycle of redemption is not completely achieved by the work of Christ. He is the mediator, joined with his Father, but joined too with those whom he has redeemed in his blood. Therefore he is the firstborn of the new race of God's people and his victory is not communicated to his own except by their sharing in his death. This brings us to the "in-between" theme or the *theme of the desert*. It completes the third cycle and opens on to the fourth. Noah's ark must wander for forty days on the bitter waters; forty years of pilgrimage separate the Red Sea from the entry into the promised Land; before he is king in Jerusalem David must go to earth in the hill country of Judah; before he receives his commission to anoint the kings Elijah must fast for forty days in the desert of the Negeb; the Exile is a painful confinement for the eventual rebirth of God's people. Christ himself finally inaugurated his own mission with forty days of lenten fast and so hallowed the custom he gave to his Church. In the symbolism of the Apocalypse (12:6) he consigns the woman in childbirth to the desert for three and a half years (half of the perfect seven) so that she can escape the persecution of the Dragon and bring forth her Son to triumph.

The desert theme gives point to the *theme of life through death*. This paradox is truly the fundamental principle which gives biblical morality its supernatural quality and distinguishes it from the so-called "natural" morality of paganism. Judged by wordly wisdom, the morality of the Cross is folly. There is no promise of happiness but only of future suffering, death and perhaps martyrdom. It is a divine promise that biblical morality offers the Christian, God's wisdom that it prepares him for, and the Spirit of sonship that it breathes. For entrance fee into this world of God's fullness a man has nothing to offer save his own nothingness and the confession of his misery. Christian morality is a morality of death to the old so that the new man may be born. It is only to babes that the Father reveals the splendour of his Son, only to those who are parched that he gives the water of life. With set purpose Christ turns upside down the world's accepted design for happiness (Mt. 5:3-12) and smashes the proud code of human perfection. The justification preached by a humanism of good works is not pleasing to God. Man was created to be satisfied not with himself but with God.

The humble whom Christ calls "blessed" are those whom the Psalms have called the "poor" and whom St. Paul will call believers, the true sons of Abraham. The faith which brings salvation is the passionate surrender of that nothingness which is all a soul has to give when it is faced with God's own gift of his Son. To believe in the Son of God is to die to one's own self-sufficiency, to make over the whole heart to the call of the Spirit's love. Thus the life of a Christian here on earth is a constant battle, where the forces of the world are straining to check his escape into the joy of the Spirit. The Christian suffers Christ's own agony, completing in his body what is lacking in the Passion of Christ. In the Church he is in the world, but not of the world. It is here that he goes to earth to be transformed from death to the life which was won on the first Easter morning. The Church is in the Desert, waiting for the harvest to ripen, waiting for the Body of Christ to achieve that absorption of Death by Life which was begun by Christ, and which will not be complete until all men belong to him as he belongs to God.

THIS brings us to the last cycle in the fullness of revelation, the *cycle of accomplishment*. To every advance in the realization of the messianic hope there corresponds a qualifying disillusionment and *partial set-back*. Abraham was not to know

his numerous posterity, Moses was not to see the promised
Land. Joshua's conquest was not the fondly imagined military
rout, David saw portents of ruin in the civil war of his own
lifetime. Judah was confident of resisting Assyria, but like
Israel she was led into exile. The Restoration saw little of the
grandeurs promised by Isaiah. Even before it finally collapsed
under Pompey, the triumph of the Maccabees was compromis-
ized by the successors of the early heroes. Finally Christ himself was put to death. . . . Where was the end to this insistent
rhythm of failure and success, of defeat and victory? With
Easter morning the disciples thought that it had reached its
climax, but instead of the glorious Parousia they were given
the Consoling Spirit. There was to be no victory in fire and
thunder, but only a slow and painful conquest in teaching and
blood. Their Kingdom turned out to be a Church. *Disillusion*
is the very first theme in this cycle of accomplishment.

But disillusion is only an aspect of death to the world. Out
of that death God's people are to be reborn to God's life. Each
failure is a prelude to the rebirth of a stronger and more vibrant
hope. The Bible is constantly looking beyond what is, to the
wider scope of what will be. With Christ that scope becomes
present, it is begun. Yet it too lacks completion; Christ's victory has not yet realized its accomplishment. The *theme of
hope* is the Bible's expression of the believer's last resort, the
living synthesis of his faith and love, of his death and life, of his
need for salvation and his thirst for the Kingdom of God.

The Kingdom of God is begun, the seed has been sown and
it grows. But there are tares among the wheat. The combat
between Good and Evil, between Christ and the Devil, between
Light and Darkness, this is not the supreme battle. That has
still to be fought when all these preliminaries are done. The
Serpent in the Garden, Pharaoh and Assyria, false brethren of
Moab and Edom, Philistines uncircumcised, Balak and Mesha,
Gog and Magog, Antiochus Epiphanes and Herod the Great,
these are just names, incarnations of Antichrist, personifica-
tions of the "man of sin", agents of the *Mystery of Iniquity*
(2 Thess. 2:7). Before the end comes, Satan will all but prevail
and apostasy will be widespread, until the Son of Man appears
in all majesty to destroy the Enemy with the Breath of his
mouth. Resurrection and judgment will follow to set the final

seal on the Kingdom and restore all things in the harmony of divine fullness.

So the doctrinal themes of the Bible come back full circle to their starting point. From the eternity in which mankind's election is first planned, they carry us through to the vision of *eternal life*. In the very first pages of Genesis, the Bible portrays the memory of this vision: God in the garden of Eden talking with man in the cool of the evening. It is with the same thought that the Book closes in the Apocalypse: a picture of the heavenly Jerusalem. If the earthly Paradise was only a nostalgic memory of a home that was lost, and the promised Land only a narrow strip in the Middle East, they yet expressed a yearning for the place where God has pitched his tent. It was Christ himself who showed the significance of these images when he gave to his own Kingdom the titles of "Land" and "Paradise" (Mt. 5:5, Lk. 23:43). If the Kingdom is prefigured in a way which is human and inadequate—the clan of Israel, the twelve tribes, the kingdom of David, the religious community of the Restoration after exile, even the Church which rules the earth—the reader of the Bible knows that they are but pale reflections of that everlasting glory which the Father has destined for his elect, through the life-giving Spirit of his Son.

WE CONCLUDE this section with a theme which is outside the scope of those we have dealt with. It will serve as a frame to contain them: the *theme of thanksgiving*. This is the form in which the Bible most happily expresses the overall view of salvation. Here the organic unity of all the themes is underlined. Whether it is expressed in a simple formula of praise like "Blessed be God", or more fully as in some of the Psalms, always there is an attempt to draw a picture of God's great "mercies" in the three or four successive movements which correspond to the cycles we have described. First there is the statement of praise. This is followed by a description of some favour, pictured as one aspect of salvation. Thirdly this favour is connected with a promise made in the past, and so becomes part of God's hidden and eternal design. Finally the purpose and effects of the favour point to the last times, of which these present times are a presage.

There are classical examples of such doxologies to be found in both Testaments. Some comprise a single short stanza, like Christ's song of thanksgiving in Mt. 11:25-27 and the *Nunc Dimittis*. Others, like the *Magnificat*, the *Benedictus*, and especially the opening of the Epistle to the Ephesians, repeat the theme time and again with continual variation on the original four movements. These are perhaps the most perfect examples of the circular movement which characterizes the poetry of the Bible. When the first Christian liturgies came to express their own thanksgiving in the "eucharistic act" (the climax until Christ comes again of God's eternal mercy incarnate in his Son) they found here a ready-made and natural framework.

III

THE GRADUAL TRANSPOSITION OF THE BIBLICAL THEMES

The organic development of revelation;
1. The Cycle of the Promises: the Patriarchs and God the Father.

2. The Cycle of Mosaic Law: the God who is; his Covenant with a nomad band; purification in the desert; Yahweh the warrior God and the agricultural Baals of Canaan.

3. The Cycle of Royal Law: David the founder of the Kingdom of Yahweh; moral decadence after the Schism.

4. The Cycle of Prophetic Law: the Prophets, traditionalists and pioneers; religion of the Spirit; collapse of a national religion.

5. The Cycle of Priestly Law: cult of the Law and the law of cult; a community consecrated to the God of Heaven; personal and interior religion of the Wisdom literature.

6. Final Bearings: the three currents at the advent of Christianity: messianic, legalistic and sapiential.

The organic development of revelation

THE doctrinal themes of the Bible can all be reduced to a few closely knit cycles, each leading to the next, each incomplete without the next. An outline of these themes in their mutual relationships should resemble a series of concentric circles, and illustrate both their organic unity and their living complexity. To see revelation thus in its entirety is to see a perfect blueprint of the eternal plan of God. Yet it has its dangers. Such a view is so rich that we are liable in our fascination to be unaware of its dynamic progression.

In fact such an outline must of its nature be abstract, and its value can only be relative. The fact that we have caught it poised in the order of logic must not blind us to its movement in the order of time. Revelation is necessarily bound up with its development at any given moment in history, and the concentric circles of the different biblical themes open out historically into a spiral. The explanation of the themes given above was a bird's eye view. It showed the inner structure, the fixed woof across which the shuttle travels. What we must do now is to give this view a third dimension, to see it in its side elevation. In this way we will see its gradual unfolding. The four cycles and the dozen or so themes which we have singled out are present in embryo from the beginning of revelation, just as all the organs of a man are present in a foetus. If we pluck revelation from the perspective of history in which God wished it to grow and develop, if we level out all the different themes and forget their dimension in time, we will pervert the full sense of revelation. Our contact with the eternal is made at some point in time, and we cannot think of it except in that context. There is indeed a similarity of proportion between the different human expressions of the divine thought (they are related to each other by analogy), but they retain their essential differences. There is a world of difference, for example, between Yahweh's Covenant with a roving band of bedouins bent on the conquest of the land they covet, and the transcendental design in which the Spirit of Christ sanctifies the union between the Father and his elect, and bestows on them the eternal life of the Son.

All the same, the similarity between the different expressions is not merely superficial. The realities they represent are cognate, and one is the flowering of the seed contained in the other. Though it is something less than identity, there is more than mere analogy between the Covenant of Sinai and the Covenant

ratified in the Spirit by the risen Christ, between the crossing
of the Red Sea and Christian baptism, between Abraham's race
and the royal race of the elect. Between these realities there
is a living unity, which progresses but is constant, which is able
to effect change without itself changing, which can operate on
different levels without losing its irresistible and unifying dynamism. The external similarities are simply the spontaneous
manifestations of this dynamism. They are the confining shell,
the kerbs which define the road. To rip up the kerb-stones and
set them side by side to show their similarities is to lose both
the confines of the road and its direction. The Bible is like a
reel of film which shows the different forms assumed by a living
tradition through the ages. To cut this film in order to re-
arrange the sequence of its frames is to take all meaning out of
it and destroy the possibility of it ever being screened. *The
Bible will have meaning only if its sequence is preserved and
its upward movement understood*. This cannot be done without the living Spirit which continues to breathe this tradition in
the Church.

It is difficult to know which to admire most, the constancy
of the themes or the rich variety of the ways in which God has
taught them. It is of the utmost importance to mark this divine
technique as one stage succeeds another. With infinite tact
God moulds his approach to suit prevailing needs. He will
fasten on disillusionment to raise men's hopes to a higher level;
he will turn a material failure into a spiritual victory; he will
try every expedient that a Father's love for his child can fashion.
The rationalist's microscope will discover here nothing that is
not human; the eyes of faith alone will see beneath the surface
the guiding hand of God, weaving this mass of humanity into
the unity of his plan. It is not a heavy hand—more often than
not it is imperceptible and almost furtive. But it is always
there, interlacing the divine thread into every section of the
human pattern, showing itself occasionally to impart a twist to
the direction or stimulate a new beginning. Generally the
movement is scarcely noticeable except as a gradual upward
trend. Now and again, when a hidden snag has fouled the
work, a sudden acceleration of pace is a sure sign that the divine
hand is there. When the work of revelation is eventually
viewed as a whole, it is seen to fall into a number of clear-cut

stages. In each the same basic pattern may be recognized, sublimated and transposed as one stage leads to another. In each transposition it is possible to see the human element at work, but under the direction of God's firm hand. It is this hand alone which can explain the unwavering continuity of the movement, and the overwhelming transcendence of its final achievement.

St. Paul divided the two thousand years of revelation's development into three main periods. We could do worse than follow his example and mark the progress towards Christianity in three stages, the *cycle of the Promises*, the *cycle of the Law, and the cycle of the Spirit*. Alternatively, we could lay emphasis on the historical, geographical and spiritual aspect of these stages by calling them *patriarchal*, *national* and *universal*. Or again if we wish to mark the development in the concept of the God who is the pivot of this evolution, we could see them as the cycles of the *God of the clan, absolute monotheism*, and the *revelation of the Father*. Finally, by underlining the unique influence of God's Word on the human founders of these three stages, we could call our three cycles *Abraham, Moses* and *Christ*. The name is not important. What is important is that we realize the length of the road between the stages and the unswerving unity of its direction. In the last two stages especially, we should take notice of a number of secondary themes which define more closely this direction.

The Cycle of the Promises

ABRAHAM is well named the Father of those who believe. If there was a rudimentary revelation made before his time, the patriarchal traditions are the only evidence we have of it. Some historians are inclined to believe that the prehistoric religion of the Semitic peoples had a monotheistic bias. This may well be: they were all of nomadic race, and the constant use by the whole group of the name *El* to designate the divinity may be an indication of a common monotheism. The crowded pantheon of Babylon was a later development, and in any case more symbolic and imaginative than real. Even so, the possible existence of an ancestral monotheism which may have survived to Abraham's time does not in any way detract from him. His

Babylonian background was one of polytheism, and his own clan most likely paid cult to the moon gods of Haran. His sudden determination to break with his clan and its gods may have been made under pressure of historical circumstances. Even so they were subordinate to a religious experience which was the real cause of the break, for which the world will ever stand in his debt. This was the first of those divine "shocks". Abraham retired to the desert under the spell of the mysterious call, a call which was to take hold of him and dominate the rest of his life. In this call he became aware of his vocation. He was to be the chief of an autonomous clan; the fact that it was called into being by a new and unknown God would ever be the mark of its uniqueness. That is all there is. But in that little is contained the germ of the fullness of revelation.

The Patriarchs were not theologians or metaphysicians. They were simply sheiks of the steppe land, occupied with their flocks and fully intent (as was all mankind in the dawn of history) on ensuring the power and growth of their clan. We see their numbers growing but making no great mark on the naturalistic polytheism of the Corridor. Now and again the Experience is repeated, sometimes brutally, sometimes graciously, but always insistently. Those who suffer the Experience are possessed, for it is a shock which has no parallel in the petty religions of their neighbours. But the first feeling of terror is followed by a more reasoned calm. The shock has rocked the foundations of their religious ideas, but they still keep to the old religious forms, and they try a little clumsily to make these old forms contain their new emotion. Thus Jacob erects a *menhir*, and Abraham is prepared to sacrifice his only son. But these are surface things. Beneath is the forceful grip of a new and mysterious God who has captured their imaginations and established a new claim in their hearts. They express their feelings in the only way they know, and see themselves as the children of a *divine Father*. When the shock of the first impact has passed, their childlike candour reasserts itself in the sly and self-interested familiarity engendered of this new relationship. Whatever profit there is in being adopted by this rather disturbing God, it must be turned to the account of the clan. It is a down-to-earth sort of religion, with little or no appreciation of the transcendence of God. Yet this same infant candour which babbles to the God-Father about the good of the clan is more than the germ which will later develop into the formidable Covenant of Sinai. Already it has the flavour of that filial piety which will mark the feelings of the true sons of Abraham for God, their Father.

The Cycle of Mosaic Law

THE promises of the nameless God were fulfilled in Egypt. The Israelite clan had become a great people there. The God of their Fathers had not fared so well: a demoralizing slavery had almost destroyed their national identity and religious personality. The Experience had ceased to grip their souls. The smooth waters of the Nile had washed away the clinging sand of the desert, and the heavy hand of Pharaoh had speeded the work of time. Then, suddenly, the shock came again. Moses had fled into the desert and there, before the burning bush, he found once more the faith of his Fathers.

This second manifestation of God's design is not just a return to the past; it bears the hallmark of a new departure. The God of their Fathers at last speaks out his name. The name of Yahweh, "He who is" or "He who causes to be", is not a metaphysical abstraction. It is a name which distinguishes him from the impotent gods of other nations. This is the God *who is* as opposed to those others *who are not*. This is the living God who causes all things to be. And this God has chosen the race of Israel for his own people. Until now, they had been only separated groups without a bond of unity; but now Yahweh would snatch them out of Egypt and lead them into the desert, and there, in the crucible where their ancestors were fashioned, he would weld them together by giving them a leader, a law, a religion, a God, and a destiny. The Covenant of Sinai was a strange and unprecedented contract. The God of their Fathers bound himself to be to this tribe of nomads what Kamosh was to Moab and Marduk to Babylon. For the Israelite, Yahweh was an exclusive possession, and yet also (though less articulately) a God who had sovereign rights over all the earth, the living God who is and who created all things. Israel's stupendous destiny stems from this belief. In the matrix of this tiny people, hemmed in both geographically and mentally, there lay hidden an intuition with infinite possibilities. The history of this people is the gradual opening of the matrix under the pressure of divine force.

At first the achievements were modest enough. All that these wild bedouins expected from their formidable and strange God, whose claims they hardly understood, was immediate military success. His power was like the elements: he was Yahweh of Armies, the warrior God with lightning in his hand. The burning faith which energized their dynamic power was tribute enough to his transcendence. All other gods were dead. This was the living God who must conquer his land, and Israel was certain of victory. Canaan must fall into their hungry hands like a cluster of ripe grapes. Yahweh would bring his people back to Canaan, where he had first revealed himself in the promise made to the Patriarchs that they would one day share this land which was his home. The cycle of Egypt had closed with the crossing of the Red Sea; the cycle of the desert closes on the banks of the Jordan, with the coveted Paradise in sight.

But just as the rescue from Egypt was followed by the despair of the desert wanderings, so too the victories of Joshua were succeeded by the long and disappointing period of the Judges. Quite clearly Yahweh was not like other gods. His jealousy had already kept them wandering in the dry southern steppes. Now he again deserts his people: alone they must grapple with the difficulties of a slow campaign of infiltration. He had undeniably proved himself to be a God of war, and occasionally would raise up a captain to "wage the wars of Yahweh". But why did he not now rise up, and with one fell blow smash these peoples on whom he had pronounced his anathema? Why must he be so fastidious, why the moral demands? The Baals of Canaan were easier to please and had a better understanding of flocks and herds than the rough warrior God Yahweh. What harm could there be in consulting them in this new and settled life which they must learn to live? Hardly had the little band of invaders become united before they were in danger of crumbling before the sensual gods they had vanquished. At the end of this period they are back to where they were under the Egyptian oppression. The Philistines have them by the throat,

M

for all the allegiance their Fathers swore to Yahweh. Even the
Ark, the symbol of their Covenant and Conquest, the memorial
of their second resurrection, even that had fallen into the hands
of the uncircumcised.

The Cycle of Royal Law

THIS was the depth of despair for which Yahweh had waited.
Now he would return a third time to show his people the
dazzling prospect of an even more wonderful salvation. Backed
by the new prophetic movement, David not only crushes the
power of the Philistines but leads Israel under her king and
her God to a state of political, social and geographical significance beyond her wildest dreaming. In his Anointed One,
Yahweh inaugurates the Kingdom of God already inherent in
the terms of the commitment made at Sinai and in the promise
given to the Fathers. The national aggrandisement was based
on what was in essence a religious conquest. Israel's faith in
Yahweh has been tried and has become deeper, purer and
wider. Henceforth Israel is sure that Yahweh alone is the
living and omnipotent God. Henceforth she is open in admitting that boundless ambition which has been her secret hope
since Sinai. Yahweh would no longer be content to defend his
own against enemy peoples and strange gods: he would now
carry the fight to them, destroy those false gods and subdue
their followers. Through Israel the whole world must be
dominated and serve the Kingship which is Yahweh's by
right.

David's reign marks a climax in Israel's religious development. Two salient interventions of God have so far given it
direction: the call of Abraham and the revelation of the name
Yahweh. Yet in spite of the progress that has been made,
David's faith is still the faith of Abraham. Both are bounded
by the confines of this world; for both salvation is thought of
in terms of man's temporal happiness; both are primarily social
and national in outlook.

If Israel's faith during this period is something less than
monotheism, it is something more than monolatry. Yahweh is
more than one among many gods, to satisfy the material and
political hopes of his people. He is totally unlike the blind

tyrannical gods of other nations. He is a living God, who searches the reins and hearts of those he wants to possess. From Sinai onwards, Israel's religious outlook has a moral, personal and interior bias. There is only one God; his name is Yahweh and his will is binding.

The conclusions reached in these first stages mark a revolution in religion. They contain a seed that has the power to grow into the most supernatural of revelations. The one and only moral God will not be satisfied with outward observance. His object is the very soul of man: he will go to the very fibre of man's being and be his beginning and last end. He breaks the barriers which divide the human from the divine, and tears down the iron curtain of a "natural" religion, to establish between God and man the mystery of Fatherhood which Abraham had glimpsed, which the Covenant of Moses had consecrated, and which was the mainspring of David's unclouded love for his God. All this is inherent in the faith of Israel on the eve of the great prophetic movement.

Inherent, but not obvious. The ordinary man was still thinking in terms of a national and earthly kingdom. The cult of Yahweh is merely the highest expression of the political life of the nation. He is expected to vouchsafe human bounty to the nation as such. Whatever he may demand by way of moral injunctions and ritualistic prescriptions are simply his conditions for granting salvation. There is no intrinsic connection between the two. Yahweh is the desire of all hearts because he brings earthly bliss. It will need some catastrophe to swing the balance between the two axioms of their traditional faith. Only in this way will the more fundamental axiom win the day and the other sink back into its proper context. Prophetism marks the third intervention of God: its precise purpose was to achieve this swing of the balance.

The Cycle of Prophetic Law

THE Prophets up to the time of the Exile seem at first to revert to a merely national messianism, to be reformers conserving the work of the past. In fact, even the triumph of Yahweh in the time of David could not escape the downward trend to decadence, and Solomon's glory was thin enough covering for the impending ruin. If the nation had risen to great heights, it had further to fall. After the Schism the apostasy in both kingdoms was almost absolute, and the first impression given by the Prophets is that they were men who had arrived too late to prevent the apostasy and could only refer the realization of the disappointed dream to a remoter future. In point of fact, however, the Prophets belonged to the future as much as to the past. Not that they were innovators—salvation was still thought of on a national and earthly level, to be achieved by religious reform. But insofar as they championed this reform, they were forced to delve deeper than ever before into the real significance of the Covenant which had dictated earlier conceptions of salvation. In this way the glory that was Yahweh emerged from the twilight of polytheism. His moral requirements outgrew the ritual which had clothed them, and his political horizon reached to the ends of the earth. Salvation assumed a personal aspect, in answer to the tormented cry wrung from the heart of a people oppressed by sinners. In his love, Yahweh would make Israel his bride, with the nations for her dowry.

Thus these apparent survivors of a past generation became pioneers of the future. Incapable of understanding the new language they spoke, Israel and Judah went the accustomed way of infidelity. Then came the momentous disaster. Moses had staved it off once by his timely intervention. David, too, had managed to postpone it. But the slavery of Egypt and the oppression in the time of the Judges were as nothing compared with this. Yahweh's people were simply wiped off the political map, once for all. Never again, not even under the Maccabees, would the Jewish people have even a semblance of freedom and independence. They should have disappeared altogether, like the ten tribes of the northern kingdom. Yahweh himself had been conquered in the defeat of his people, and by rights his name should have been obliterated in the destruction of a nation whose only purpose was to perpetuate his name.

And yet the seed which the Prophets had sown bore fruit in the land of exile. For the fourth time, the dawn of salvation was to break, this time for the " Remnant " which germinated there in penance and the spirit of hope. Freed from the confines of its national and ritual framework, its faith was slowly re-fashioned and purified. Shorn of its national and earthly ties, religion went deeper and its perspectives became wider. Salvation was no longer national but personal; the things of the world made way for the things of the spirit; a narrow exclusivism gave way to a world-wide proselytism. Above all, there was a deepening of the concept of God. The name of Yahweh with its nationalistic connotation gave place to the almost too transcendent " God of heaven ". The Exile marked a profound stage in the history of God's people. They were no longer a nation but a religious community: here a national cult was transformed into a spiritual force.

The Cycle of Priestly Law

IMPORTANT though this metamorphosis was, we must not exaggerate it. The old nationalistic hopes were to endure for a long time yet. Even up to the fall of Jerusalem in A.D. 70 they would be for the ordinary people the most natural expression of that infinite happiness which is the inspiration of all religion. It was the fortune of history which gave these aspirations a new shape. The meagre results of the Restoration from exile sowed disillusionment in their hearts. Even the successes of the Maccabees were soon a bitter memory of what might have been but for the enslaving hand of Rome. Hers was a rod that no human Messiah could break. So it is to the clouds of heaven that they look for their messianic deliverance, and they live for the day when the cataclysm promised by their apocalyptic literature will create a new Israel and establish her dominion over the world.

This messianic hope, transformed though it was into an eschatological one, was no longer the only source of the Jewish community's religious energy. For the very first time the people are governed by priests. Under them, religion becomes a cult, and all the main themes of the past begin to shift on to a moral and juridical plane. The teaching of the Prophets in particular is taken up and made more precise. The idea of God's transcendence is pushed to its furthest limits, and the moral aspect of the Covenant is the only one that receives recognition. In fact the theme of the Covenant becomes the pivot on which all

Jewish thought turns, and the narrow confines of the community give it a new look: it becomes more rigid and polished, more legalistic and juridical. Whereas prophecy was a dynamic movement which looked forward, the cult of the Law looked back to the past. Where the interior religion of the Prophets made them hope for an actual historical Messiah to fulfil their ideal, the spirituality of the votaries of the Law was achieved and consummated by the letter of the law and its fulfilment. The Covenant becomes more of a contract than a testament. So compelling is the concept of God's transcendence that eventually all relationship with him is inconceivable, apart from the purely external one flowing from this contract. No longer does God give himself to men, he simply exacts their obedience and worship.

This conception is not without its splendour. The chosen people are the priests of God, whose office is to proclaim his transcendence and order his praise in all righteousness. The theme of accomplishment and eternal life is enriched by this new revelation. However, the conception contrasts too violently with the wretchedness of human misery for it to be sufficient. What is worse, it tends to upset the delicate balance of the whole of revelation on the very eve of the Christian era. In seeking to base the Covenant on moral perfection rather than on the free choice of God, and by setting God at an incommunicable distance from his people, this outlook threatened to split asunder the two basic aspects of salvation which revelation had constantly tried to bring together. In such an outlook, man with his free will has no absolute need of divine grace, and with his inner perfection he can look God in the face. In place of a religion where wretchedness called forth mercy, where nothingness gave birth to free election, where the cry from a child's heart stirred the love of a Father, there is substituted a natural and water-tight religion, where man has nothing to offer God but his own self-sufficiency, and nothing to hope for but what he has earned.

The cult of the Law was bound to be at loggerheads with reality. It was inconsistent with man's weakness in giving him no support save a code of rules. It was incompatible with God's goodness in making the existence of evil incomprehensible. In fact the " just " man did not inevitably receive his reward: not infrequently it was the sinner who prospered. Such a cult of the Law could never suppress that yearning for consummation and new life which was at the root of all messianic expectation. The yearning remained, and it was deeper than ever; the mere fact that ai. hope of political power was now gone and that the Law itself assumed a moral aspect only shifted its emphasis from an earthly and social level to a personal and spiritual one. The book of Job first showed the utter bankruptcy of the kind of Law and Covenant which automatically rewards man's perfection with God's happiness. Ecclesiastes went further, showing from experience that the very opposite is true; a soul filled with every human bliss could still be empty and famished. These "sages" of the post-exilic period remained true to the real current of prophetic revelation. While they enlarged its moral import and applied it to the problem of personal salvation, they still managed to preserve the prophetic conviction of man's inadequacy, and to insist on the need for a justice which came entirely from a merciful God. By admitting their own inability ever to achieve it, they underlined the traditional hope all the more.

Final Bearings

THUS the old religion of Israel had reached the threshold of Christianity in three distinct forms, the down-to-earth messianism of the ordinary people, the religion of the Law, and the ideal of the sapiential books. So clear-cut had these three become that they sometimes seemed to delineate three separate sects. The mass of the people were fired with hopes of national sovereignty. The ruling classes took refuge behind a religion which they claimed to be definitively closed, the Sadducees smiling at the popular illusions, and the Pharisees expecting nothing of the Messiah except his endorsement of the Law. Even the immortality promised by the last inspired books was seen only as a confirmation of their belief that revelation was to reach its perfection in the eternal cult of the Law. Certainty of an afterlife had done no more than take away their hope of receiving anything on this earth.

It was the third, the sapiential school of thought, that inspired the final surge of revelation, the greatest and most revolutionary yet. The triumph of the Maccabees had increased the anxiety and dissatisfaction of men like Job and Ecclesiastes. They were bewildered by the pointless sacrifice of men who had not lived to enjoy the fruit of their work. It was the Greek hope of a life after death that gave the eventual answer to these soul-searchings. Ben Sirach had already pointed to the solid foundations for such a belief; the book of Wisdom asserted it with God's own authority, and with a boldness and precision which left no room for doubt. In this new hope of immortal life was contained a conception that was to upset all previous ideas. The author of Wisdom appealed to it, drawing revolutionary conclusions as if they were self-evident. In making eternal life the end-term of personal salvation, of the last judgment and of man's happiness, he brought together the two parallel streams in which the old yearnings of Israel had by-passed legalistic orthodoxy and survived. Eschatological and interior, national and personal, earthbound and moral, historical and sapiential, these aspects were for the first time fused together. Unfortunately, this reconciliation in eternity left the present life empty, and this happiness with God still required a name.

To sum up then, on the eve of the birth of Christ, revelation had reached such a stage of maturity that it seemed to the more responsible elements among the Jews to have reached its term. And yet some vital thing was wanting. This happiness, whether it was given or promised or only hoped for, still had to be given a name. Official Judaism looked for it in the satisfaction of legal fulfilment; the ordinary people awaited it in the Conqueror who was to vanquish the Romans; the Sages turned to the un-known beyond. If this prodigious growth of Abraham's faith was to be given some unity, if this threefold harvest was to be gathered together, nothing less was demanded than the revelation of this happiness in person. God must name himself.

IV

THE CHRISTIAN TRANSPOSITION OF THE BIBLICAL THEMES

The problem of Christ, traditionalist and innovator; the new fact of a Messiah-Son of God; the indispensable set-back; renewal in the Spirit; the final illusion—Kingdom or Church; growing pains: St. Paul and Judeo-Christianity, St. Paul and Hellenism, St. Paul and Christian anxiety; the hostility of "the world" and the Johannine synthesis.

The Problem of Christ

SO FAR, we have tried to disentangle the themes which constitute biblical revelation. We have traced them in broad outline from the beginning to the period immediately preceding the Christian era. Enough has been said to allow the reader to assess the revolution occasioned by the appearance of Christ.

In a study like this, it is as important to underline the continuity of the two Testaments as it is to mark the differences brought about by the new leaven which is Christ. Anyone who has grasped the logical and upward trend of revelation will be able to appreciate the place occupied in the scheme by the fact of Christianity. Jesus of Nazareth is not only the term of the evolution; he so transcends it that its whole perspective is changed. He is not only the building's key stone; he is, in his own words, the "corner stone".

A merely human appraisal of the beginnings of Christianity will always boggle at this duality. Judeo-Christians of all time have looked upon Christ as no more than the fruit of Judaism at is best. By contrast the Marcionites have always made of him a revolutionary pure and simple, whose aim was to give the death-blow to a Judaism already on the point of death. Either he is put into an eschatological and social framework, and his scope restricted to the achieving of Israel's old hope for a definitive Kingdom, though on a higher level; or else only the moral content of his teaching is recognized, and he takes his place in the line of the ancient Prophets, an artist with a talent for communicating an intimate experience of God.

In point of fact, Christ did present himself both as the national Davidic Messiah of the Jews and as the supreme Prophet of renewal in the Spirit. His teaching embraces both streams of Israel's divided hope. At one and the same time he claims to be God's wonder-working messenger to his people Israel, and also the ideal of personal intimacy with the Father, the model for all men of good will. He is the answer to those who yearned for a Messiah, and to those whose hearts were heavy with dissatisfaction. He finds only one insurmountable barrier, the self-sufficiency of Pharisaism, which will not admit any need for hope and finds no room for one who claims to be the answer to all hopes. All the same, he is careful not to add fuel to the feverish expectations of the mob, and he paints his picture of the eschatological kingdom in colours striking enough to deceive even the "liberal Protestants" of his day. He puts himself at the very centre of the two streams, messianic and sapiential, so that he can the more happily embrace both and transform them in his own person.

The New Fact

IN ITS immense simplicity, the message of Christ simply put a name to the expectation of Israel. It is his own name—the Son of God—and he died rather than renounce it. This unprecedented claim sums up all that was new in his teaching, and in its light everything else is changed. Happiness, or "salvation" as the Jews called it, does not consist in the triumph of Israel, nor in human perfection, not even in immortal life. It is identified with *God himself*. The Covenant is no longer concerned with a promised land or a mere earthly paradise; it is a divine betrothal, a gift greater than the numerous posterity of Abraham, a favour more wondrous than the rescue from Egypt, an election more radical even than that of David or Solomon. It is God himself that Christ brings to a humanity waiting in the emptiness to which sin has consigned it, a God who, like a loving Father, bends down and begs men to open their empty hearts so that he may fill them with his fullness.

Christ alone can reveal this Fatherhood, for he alone is the true Son of God. But this sonship is to be shared by those who accept in Christ the witness of the Son of God, and so discover the Fatherhood of God for themselves. For Christ is both the Messenger and the Message of God, and the bond that ties his disciples to him ties them also to the Father. He is strictly the Gift of God to men: when God gives men his Son, he gives them himself as a Father, and thereby accepts them as his children, asking only that they open body and soul, mind and heart, to receive the fullness of his gift.

In short, Christ unites in himself all the themes of past revelation, *and thereby transposes them*. He answers the anxious cry of the masses for a Messiah who will found an earthly kingdom by bringing a heavenly kingdom into their midst. He meets the self-sufficiency of the Pharisees by showing them the deep void which can only be filled by the Father's love. The personal dissatisfaction of the sage he answers with his revelation of God's vast plan for a renewed Israel. He is indeed the promised Messiah, though his kingdom is from within—in the world but not of the world. To those who receive him he brings a gift from God, and that gift is himself, for he is the Messiah-Son of God, whose mission is to show forth his divine sonship as testimony to God's fatherhood. He has come to give to the world the life of the Father, which he shares by right, as the pledge of a new Covenant, to which man is asked to contribute only his nothingness, and commit it into the hands of God.

The Indispensable Set-back

THERE is nothing in the above outline of Christ's doctrine which cannot be gathered from an objective study of the oldest Gospel traditions, even if no account were taken of the miracles. But those who first heard Christ did not grasp the full significance of this doctrine. They coloured it with their own prejudices and pre-conceived ideas. Nor was Christ under any illusion about that. As he approached the end of his ministry, he foretold in ever clearer terms that there would be a fatal set-back. He had set himself to co-ordinate in his person all the traditional themes, and to raise them to a supra-terrestrial level. It would have been remarkable if such a programme had not led to misunderstanding and provoked conflict with commonly accepted views.

Those who saw this most clearly were the Jewish theologians. Their own instinct of self-preservation made them realize the revolutionary character of this seemingly traditional doctrine. If such a Messiah-Son of God should ever find his way into the already completed edifice of Jewry's official religion, even if it was only through a side door, then the whole structure was in danger of being blown sky-high. How could the barred and bolted framework of Judaism contain a Messiah whom the earth itself could not contain? What would become of established traditions under the influence of such an unknown quantity? Born conservatives that they were, the Jewish theologians were not going to take chances. He must be put to death. It took longer for the ordinary people to reject him. Charmed by his miracles and his forthright approach, they found his preaching ambiguous and harmless enough. It was only when they decided that this gentle Messiah was an idealist incapable of striking a hammer blow for freedom that they, too, lost interest and dropped him. Even those who were attracted more by his personality than by his sublime wisdom were amazed that he did not clear away all misunderstanding by a dazzling manifestation of his apocalyptic glory. The disciples themselves understood little of their Master, except that he had looked into their hearts, and left a mark which would remain always.

So the inevitable catastrophe came. It had to come to shatter the illusions which had dogged this people from the beginning, from the racial ideal to the escape from Egypt, from the promised Land to the messianic Kingdom, from the Restoration after exile to the justification of the Law. The oppression of Pharaoh did not shatter it, nor did the arid desert nor the Philistine invasion. Deportation, exile, suffering, oppression, the promise of immortality even, none of these had destroyed it. What was needed was something that would pluck the illusion out by the roots. Man must learn once for all that his happiness does not lie *in himself*, that heaven is not to be found on earth, that God cannot be called upon to vouchsafe a perfection that is exclusively human. Christ must die, in order to reverse the scale of values established by the mummified laws of a paralysed Judaism. An unbridgeable chasm must be driven between man and the mirage of a happiness of which he himself was the centre. Man must himself be split in two, take a blind leap to the sublime level of the divine Fatherhood, without ever ceasing to plumb the sickening depths of his own nothingness. Man must learn to see death and suffering, evil and sin, as the springboard for this twofold leap. Christ must die, and show up the emptiness of the earthbound hope for a closed moral perfection or for material goods, and the futility of an ideal which would make man a god, or make God the unknowable mystery. Christ must die, if the Jewish masses were to die to their earthly messianism, if official Judaism was to be shaken out of its false security, if his own disciples were to be rescued from their intoxication. Judaism must die to whatever was perishable in the Promises and inadequate in the Law. Christ's death must kill the yearning born of the Promises and the hope based on the Law, in order that the letter should die and the spirit live. The ambiguity which made the Promise its own fulfilment and the Law an end in itself must be shattered. Shadow must give way to reality, and the fair copy replace the rough draft. The earthly set-back must become the pledge of a heavenly success. The human matrix must be cracked to reveal its divine content. Christ must tear himself away from the earth and so open the way to the Father. "Christ must suffer and die and so enter into his glory." (Luke 24:26)

Renewal in the Spirit

THE death of Christ is incomplete without his resurrection. Good Friday is the annihilation of all that was only human: it is Easter Sunday that begins the work of re-creation. For the disciples, the death of their Master would always be regarded as a catastrophe beyond imagining and the death blow to their illusions. It is not until Easter morning that a new faith is born, and that they discover a new world. If Christ is truly risen, then the enterprise is not doomed. It needs only to be taken up again, though on a higher and wider level than before. Hardly have they had a chance to glimpse this new world before it comes on them like a mighty wind, in the wake of a Christ ascending to heaven. The Spirit descends on the little band. There is no room now for hesitation. The very vitality of Christ, which had so captivated them before his death, is now surging through their veins. The glorious life which he now lived was being poured out on them. His mission from the Father had been precisely to share this new life with them, as a new gift of himself and a new mode of his presence among them. The Spirit filled them now, as the principle of an other-worldly covenant and the giver of heavenly life. Through the Spirit, Christ bestowed on man the privileges of his own divine son-ship. The Spirit was the very life of Jesus, the Son of God sitting at the right hand of the Father.

It is impossible to over-emphasize the effect that this experience of the heavenly Vitality of the risen Christ exercised on the infant growth of Christianity. Admittedly it was not an altogether unknown experience. Throughout its long history, Israel had known the Breath of God as the irresistible power behind his Word. When the Word commanded creation, already the Spirit of God stirred over the waters (Gen. 1:1). It was the breath of God which dried up the waters of the Flood (Gen. 8:1) and divided the Red Sea to provide a passage for the chosen people (Exod. 14:21). It was his fire that surrounded Sinai when God proclaimed his law (Exod. 19:15f), his strength that filled all those through whom the divine Promises were effected. In the Prophets, especially, it was he who gave a supernatural light and life, his Breath that energized the Word of God they proclaimed. But in the person of Christ the disciples had touched this vital power of God at its very source. No one else could have said with such truth " The Spirit of the Lord is upon me ". The new Moses had published the terms of the new Covenant. The son of David had been anointed God's Messiah from the womb of his mother, proclaimed Son of God at his baptism, and crowned as such from the moment of his resurrection by the sanctification of the Spirit. The Prophets had only been given the Spirit to speak of this Prophet. He knew the Father before ever Abraham was. This greater than Solomon had received the fullness of the Spirit. He had been singled out by the voice of the Father and the descending dove, as the one in whom the Father was well pleased, and on whom the Spirit rested.

Now, it seemed, the rôles were to be reversed. Up to this the Spirit had been the symbol of God's incommunicability and the mainspring of his holiness. If the disciples had seen Christ as the Son of God it was because they saw the fullness of God's Spirit in him. But now it was no longer the Spirit who pointed to Christ, but Christ who communicated the Spirit. It was no longer Christ who pointed back to the Spirit, but the Spirit who pointed forward to the hidden glory that was Christ's. It was no longer the Spirit who consecrated Christ as Son of God, but the Son of God who at his Father's right hand freely bestowed the Spirit. Pentecost had indeed turned the world upside down. The disciples found themselves suddenly transported from earth to heaven, lifted up by the Spirit into the incommunicable world of God, taken up in the risen Christ to the very centre of this new world.

To the Spirit, then, must be attributed the vast misunderstanding between Judaism and Christ. The Spirit alone, through Christ, was responsible for the friction from which the Church emerged. It was the Spirit who compelled his Anointed One to be untrue to the fossilized letter of the Law. It is the same Spirit who will now gradually make the disciples realize that by his death and resurrection Christ was faithful to the deepest meaning of Israel's revelation. If Christians to-day do not understand their faith, it is not because they have forgotten Christ, but because they have forgotten the meaning of Christ, which is the Spirit.

The Final Illusion: Kingdom or Church

AT PENTECOST the disciples learned only the bare essentials of this meaning of Christ. Although they were in contact with the divine through the person of Christ, their minds were still burdened by the cramping framework of a moribund Judaism. Far from making a clean break from this framework, they clung to it and tried to remodel it along new lines. The old illusions had died with Christ, but this new Spirit of Christ seemed to lend them a new lease of life. And indeed the unfolding of revelation was not completed at Christ's death, or even at Pentecost; it would not be completed until the last of the Apostles died. Until then the Spirit of Christ must work through Judaism like a leaven, must put new life into those old limbs and bring them to their full stature.

The New Testament writings bear witness to the fact that the first disciples took time to realize the change that the new Spirit was going to introduce into their traditional ideas. Only very slowly did the Spirit bring about that evolution of ideas which enabled the disciples to adjust their minds to the new outlook, and draw the line at the end of the verbal incarnation of the Word incarnate. They had accepted Christ as Israel's true Messiah. His death taught them that he had not come to deliver Judaism from the yoke of Rome, and his resurrection that his messianic rule had indeed begun but that it was an entirely spiritual one, the final flowering of Israel's prerogatives. The coming of the Spirit had convinced them that all things were now accomplished. In the little group of Christ's followers the Kingdom was established on earth in all its heavenly reality. The end could not be far off. Christ would soon return, to consecrate by his presence the triumph of his re-born people.

So the illusion came back for the last time. The first generation of Christians thought that the Spirit was the key to the Kingdom, the whisper before the storm of the Parousia. They were not entirely wrong. But the Spirit was no more concerned with earthly achievement than was Christ. Neither of them came to set up a heaven on earth, but to lift up earth to heaven. It was not enough that Christ himself should die: the sons of the Kingdom would have to die too. The life of the Spirit could be made manifest only in the death of all flesh, the Kingdom achieved only in the Church. The final combat was joined between Life and Death: the Kingdom itself must die if it was to yield its hundredfold.

Growing Pains: St. Paul and Judeo-Christianity

THE first delusion that had to die was that of nationalism. In its attempts to get the Jews to accept the promises, the little community met with failure and bitter opposition. All the hatred that had been vented on Christ was now turned in its direction, and there seemed to be little or no future for this tiny off-shoot of Judaism. It fed on a hope that grew weaker as the looked for miracle failed to materialize. By all human reckoning it could not survive for long. There was little point in being heir to the promised Kingdom if the Kingdom had no subjects. This was the moment for which the Spirit had been waiting. Out of this death he forged a new life, totally unexpected and tremendous in scope. It was almost by chance that the pagan masses came rushing headlong to inherit the Kingdom which the rightful heirs had abdicated.

The movement first started in Jerusalem. Peter had baptized Cornelius the Roman centurion, and Philip the Ethiopian eunuch. The Spirit had come down on the Samaritans and declared clean the Gentile food that no Jew would touch. But all this was insignificant compared with the revolution brought by St. Paul. For him, the surrender to the goad of Christ on the Damascus road meant the renunciation of his whole past. Cured of the blindness of Pharisaism, the scales fell from his eyes and he saw the dazzling vision of the mystery of Christ. He had not known, as the other disciples had, the slow development from the baptism of Christ to the day of Pentecost, from illusion to reality, a development which still held them in the clutches of Jewish preferment. For St. Paul the issues were clearer: his conversion was a complete break. Either Christ was a Jewish impostor, in which case all his claims must be denounced, or else he was the Son of God, who could not be the exclusive property of a restricted group. Paul envisaged the conquest of the world, and Jerusalem, dumb with astonishment, agreed that the Spirit was on his side.

This numerical emancipation was not enough. Before things could be finally settled there would have to be a spiritual emancipation too. Liberation from Judaism meant nothing unless there was a liberation from the Law as well. Considerable anxiety was felt among some sections of the Jerusalem community over this open invitation to the "lame and halt" to come and fill the places left empty by those who had refused the feast. As they had seen at Antioch, Gentile conversions inevitably threw convert Jews and pagans together. Jewish law forbade such contacts. The Jew, indoctrinated from early childhood, felt almost a physical revulsion against such proximity. Was he expected now to deny all that he had been taught? The Judaizers at Jerusalem maintained that it was for the pagans to submit to the law and adopt circumcision. Clearly principles were here at stake: the whole meaning of the Christian revolution was being questioned.

N

Judeo-Christianity was Pharisaism's last effort to absorb the Church of Christ back into Judaism by cutting her off from the Spirit that was her inspiration. If a baptized pagan must first be circumcised before he could consort with a baptized Jew, then baptism in the name of Jesus was not the passport to the Kingdom. It meant that sanctification by the Spirit was of no avail without the Law, and Christ was no more than the Law's complement. Salvation was achieved by the Law and its observance, and man was back where he started. Instead of the free outpouring of divine life into the empty soul of man, there is only the old juxtaposition of the two parallel perfections which never meet—that of the just man and that of God. The whole metamorphosis involved by Christ's death and resurrection, and the incorporation of man into that risen life through the Spirit, that was the point in question.

In his piercing wisdom, St. Paul saw the danger. His was the task of weaning the infant Church from the dried-up breasts of Judaism and imparting to her a consciousness of her own dynamism. In no uncertain manner he cut away the parasite growths of outworn ideas, and revealed the deep intuition which the first disciples had drawn from their faith in Christ. Christ was not the servant of the Law but its Master; not its fruit but its meaning. He was not only the keystone of the old Covenant, but also the corner-stone of the new; not only the Jewish Messiah but also the universal Lord. His Kingdom was not the privilege of one people, but the mystical body, in which Jew and Gentile have their place and receive the Spirit of sonship freely bestowed by the Father. All mankind, Jew and Gentile alike, stand in need of this justification—the Gentile caught in the abyss of his moral indigence and the Jew chained in the prison of his legal arrogance. It was not only from Judaism that Christ freed man by his death, it was from the whole law of sin which Judaism symbolized even while it denounced it. Christ's death undermined both Jewish righteousnes and Gentile corruption, to lay hold of the very root of man's insufficiency, wring from him the admission of his nothingness, and open to him through the resurrection the way to heaven and that free justification in the Spirit of the Son who makes him cry out, " Abba, Father ".

Henceforth salvation is not achieved by the works of the

Law, but by faith in Christ (the Epistle to the Romans is full
of the theme).   This means, first of all, that Christianity and
not Judaism is the way of salvation.   It means further that salvation is a personal and interior attitude of abandonment to
God in Christ, and not the automatic privilege of those who
observe the Law.   In the last analysis, it means that the very
adhesion of the believer to the salvation achieved by the Son of
God is the free gift of new life, whereby he becomes, through
the sanctification of the Spirit, a child of God.

Growing Pains: St. Paul and Hellenism

WHILE St. Paul was still occupied with the Judeo-Christian
problem, his attention was being drawn in another direction.
Before he had even begun to marshal the doctrinal justification
for his work among the Gentiles, he had organized the people
into independent "assemblies" or churches to take the place of
the synagogues which were now closed to them.   Here he had
spent much effort in trying to translate the Jewish message of
Christ into concepts which would be understood by the Greek
mind.   But at the very moment when he had finally settled the
emancipation of the churches from Judaism, he found that he
must apply his own brake to the movement.   One of the
churches had gone too far, and the great teacher of Christian
freedom had to insist that the pure spirit of Israel must be preserved in the Church.

To bring about the complete emancipation of the Christian
movement St. Paul had selected words, images, ideas and
themes which were more sympathetic to the Greek mind.   In
this way he tried to overcome the obvious difficulty which the
Greeks felt when they were faced with the Jewish vocabulary
of words and ideas in which the Gospel was written.   As we
have already seen, the primitive Christian faith had grown
naturally out of the national hopes and the religious themes
inherited from the Jews.   These would not mean very much
to the Greeks.   Their inheritance was one of a hope for immortality, for a new life to be found by rites of initiation.   The
inspired genius of St. Paul saw what could be achieved if the
finest elements of both these religious currents were combined
and boldly sublimated to a new level.   The Greeks would under-

stand the mystery of Christ if it was presented to them as a "wisdom" of divine life. The Christian fact would be accepted by them if he could show them that it alone held the true "mystery" of death and life. Moreover, the simple religious rites which the first Christians had brought with them from Judaism to express their new faith would translate immediately, without adaptation, to become the rites of initiation into the salvation of the risen Christ. With magnificent skill and tact St. Paul was able to change a thoroughly Jewish movement into a universal and hellenistic religion, without losing anything of the essence of primitive Christianity.

Such a transformation was not without its dangers. Would the convert pagans press the adoption of forms so far as to alter the content of the Christian message? Since they were dispensed from initiation into Judaism, would they think that they were also free to throw over the fundamental religious values of Israel which remained as the foundation stone of Christianity? In other words, would this process of the hellenization of Christianity threaten to cut Christianity away from its origins, and make it an easy prey for the prevalent syncretism? These were the dangers which had troubled the minds of the Judeo-Christians, and prompted their conservatism. It would be sheer folly, in their view, to bring straight into the Christian fold pagans who could not overnight shake off their legacy of idolatry and immorality. The decisions of the Council of Jerusalem in the year 49 (Acts 15) had given some support to these fears: the Corinthian crisis was to show how well founded they were.

St. Paul accused the Corinthians first of all of moral indifference: the case of incest and the question of idol-offerings were evidence of it. Such indifference was not only the legacy of their former paganism, it sought to justify itself in the very teaching of Paul, and in his proclamation of the Christian's emancipation from the Law and the man-made conventions of religion. So far removed was this interpretation from the true tenor of St. Paul's thought, and so obviously indebted to Greek philosophy, that the Apostle came down on it with all his vigour and denounced the "wisdom" that had inspired it. What had these pagans done but idolize "wisdom" as the Jews had idolized the Law?

Worse still, such moral indifference was based on a misconception of Christ's mission that was reminiscent of the Greek "mysteries". The whole religious yearning of the Corinthians seemed to be satisfied with the "experience" of salvation which they received from the rites of Christian initiation. It was to soothe the worries of the first Christians over the delay of the Parousia that St. Paul had gone out of his way to emphasize the "spiritual" reality of the Kingdom. What the Corinthians had done was to exaggerate this to the extent of losing sight of the essentially dynamic and moral aspect of Christianity.

To those Jews who wished to prolong the economy of the Law, St. Paul had preached the scandal of the Cross, which dealt the death-blow to hopes of Jewish nationalism. To the Greeks who now, with typical optimism, made Christ a salvation-myth he preached the foolishness of the Cross, and its lesson of the Christian ideal of suffering and self-immolation. It is this context of sin, suffering and hope that puts the "mystery" of Christ solidly in the tradition of Jewish thought. The Kingdom is not yet realized, except in faith (it is a variation on the theme of *Romans* and *Galatians*). It will be manifested in glory, but not until it has followed Christ dead and risen. It will reach its full stature, but not until "death is absorbed by life" and the day of the Parousia dawns.

Growing Pains: St. Paul and Christian Anxiety

THE Judeo-Christian crisis and its Corinthian correlative were not the only factors which gave St. Paul this wide view of Christianity that embraced both the New Testament and the Old. There were other factors to influence him, and of these the most important was the inner development of Christianity itself. The Judeo-Christianity which he was fighting outside had taken an even subtler form inside the Christian communities themselves. The spectre was still there, finding an unlooked for ally among the Greek converts, with their yearning for that tangible earthly happiness which he had condemned in the Corinthians.

For the élite Judaism had meant the cult of the Law, but for the ordinary folk it had always meant the expectation of a Messiah. Christ had supplanted the Law, but surely his title of Messiah still remained. Surely Messianism was the very soul of Christianity. For the Apostles and for St. Paul himself, the burning desire to see the Kingdom established for all time was the mainspring of their dynamism in the Spirit. And yet it had not happened, and any hope of it happening grew fainter as the ideal frontiers of the Kingdom were extended further and further in the Gentile mission. Christian faith was troubled. If Christ was the definitive Messiah, why was salvation delayed? Had there not been disillusionment enough—the long desert journey, the failure to subdue Canaan, the divided Monarchy, the Restoration that misfired? Were these now to be crowned by a disappointment more cruel still, that of a Kingdom which was given only to be taken away again? Was not the bitter blow of Good Friday disillusionment enough? How could it be said that faith in Christ had saved his followers if it brought them nothing but hatred from Jew and Gentile alike? Faithful but perplexed, the Thessalonians became impatient. The Corinthians gave up hope altogether and fell back on their Greek "wisdom": the delay and Paul's explanation of Christian freedom meant that the Kingdom was a Greek mystery, amoral, outside time, a mere serviceable pledge of immortality. The two attitudes were radically distinct. The first, typically Jewish, aggravated the all too earthly yearning for external salvation; the second, typically Greek, did away with the need and hope of salvation by making it no more than a spiritual pledge already given. Both had this much in common (and they always will have until the Parousia), that they made salvation something entirely human—an earthly crown which can be fondled and enjoyed. In St. Paul's words, both are "unspiritual". Both imprison man in the very way that the Law had done.

St. Paul himself had known the pangs of this evolution. In the Captivity Epistles he made the synthesis of ideas which were still unresolved in *Romans, Galatians* and *1* and *2 Corinthians*. His final solution lies no longer in Christ, but in the Spirit of Christ, and it is from the intimate experience of that Spirit that his synthesis springs. Those who wait impatiently for the Parousia Paul counters with a Parousia of Christ already established in the Spirit. Those who have given up all hope of Christ's second coming he counters with the unspeakable groanings of the Spirit labouring in a new creation in Christ. To both he shows the essential mystery of the Church, the new half-way stage of the "desert", where the people of God, the new Israel, are slowly transformed from the "flesh of sin" into the glory of the risen Christ. He emphasizes the utter necessity of this struggle between death and life, as a perpetuation of Christ's own death and resurrection, where evil and suffering serve as the catalysts essential for the Christian's spiritualization in Christ. He paints a bold picture of the unfathomable designs of the Father, begun in eternal pre-destination, slowly unfolded and transposed through the ages, and reaching their achievement in Christ and their full flowering in the Spirit. The whole human race and its fortunes are held in a complex rhythm of evolution. Already the last phase has uttered its birth cry, but it has not yet reached its full stature.

Having announced the death of Jewish exclusivism, the death of the Law's humanism, and the death of the Greek idea of happiness, St. Paul now proclaims the death of the Kingdom in the Church, until such time as the Church shall be absorbed in the victory of the Kingdom.

The Hostility of the "World" and the Johannine Synthesis

AT THIS point, revelation had reached such a degree of fullness in form and thought that its completion was imminent. In fact the Johannine writings, the last of the inspired Book, make no new advance but only a final review of precision, force and harmony.

The fall of Jerusalem was the signal for the last convulsive kick of Judeo-Christianity. The Church had spread so widely, throughout Asia especially, that Christians found themselves far more involved in the civil life of pagans than they had originally intended. What was worse, the fall of the holy city had not brought the return of Christ that his words had led them to expect, and they were left to face the gathering storm of paganism alone. St. John met their growing anxiety with the solution which St. Paul had offered, although his presentation is distinctly his own. He gives the Christian mystery the atmosphere of peace and certainty that Paul's genius lacked, and fixes his vision far above the shifting horizons of this earth.

Not without reason has he been called an eagle: he hovers without apparent effort, his eye fixed on the divine Sun. Not that he has no feeling for men: he is no metaphysician or dreamer. He can scale these heights only because he has measured the depths of his own heart, and has reached far beyond the void of his own nothingness to discover the Word of God which sets him free.

His first thought is to look back at what has gone before. To those who stand hesitating at the cross-roads he gives a warning —they must not go back. It is the whole purpose of the *Fourth Gospel* to render impossible, once for all, any such return to Judaism. By the end of the first century Christianity had reached a much fuller appreciation of its own meaning. In the light of this, and with his own astonishing power, John applies his mind to the life of Christ and recognizes it for the revolution it was. He picks out precisely the elements in this history which give promise of the way Christianity would go after the resurrection. He delves deeply into the essence of Christ's thought underlying the ambiguity of expression forced upon him by the mentality of his hearers. He singles out its message of eternal life in this world, gained by dying through faith in the Son of God. He offers that life to the Christians in Asia, in answer to their fears of the mounting persecution and their frustrated hopes of the Parousia.

In this sense, the aim of the Fourth Gospel is to allow the meaning of Christ's life to shine in its true light. The first catechesis, found in *Mark, Luke* and *Matthew,* had given a detailed account of the outward facts of Christ's life. Time was needed for the true import of that life to appear. At first sight St. John's Gospel seems far removed from the picture given by the Synoptics, but a closer study reveals that he has remained as true to the picture as he has penetrated deep beneath it. Not only is it an authentic interpretation of the basic facts of Christianity, it is also the key to the Synoptics. In his Christ, the Son of God, St. John shows the hidden meaning of the Scriptures as they are recapitulated in the person of the Word incarnate. The old Covenant had one purpose—to support the new; the new Covenant has one meaning—to transform the old in the Spirit. The final balance is struck between the Jewish revelation and the Christian revolution. Between them he establishes a unique rhythm of types and fulfilment. Grace answers grace, and the believer learns to die to justification by Law, and to be born again in the glory of the Father.

John stands between the past and the future, synthesizing the one and looking towards the other. Having cut off all possibility of a return to Judaism, he now faces the persecution of paganism, in the *Apocalypse*. The Church has been newly born from the womb of its Virgin Mother, but it still has to learn from her how to walk the hard way of the Desert before it can reach the fullness of maturity in Christ. It is a pity that the Apocalypse has so often been regarded as a secret code containing details of the whole of Church history. In fact the only prophecy that it makes is that there will always be persecution until the final triumph. It is much more than a cipher—it is a prolongation throughout time of that rhythm of God's plan which was conceived in eternity and gradually woven into the very material of this world through the double incarnation, verbal and personal, of the Son of God. The entire history of all ages in the framework of the Father's plan—that is the theme of the Apocalypse. The Father's merciful design has not been cut short, nor is his love in any way exclusive. Christ is infinitely more than the climax of God's plans—he is the beginning of a new cycle of redemption which penetrates heaven itself. Revelation is born: it must now grow. Redemption is achieved: it must now be applied. Christ is dead and risen from the dead: his death and resurrection have still to be fulfilled in his Church. The Parousia of the Lamb, slain but triumphant, is not, in the Apocalypse, something still to be achieved in the far future: it is *here and now, within us.* It begins and comes unceasingly, as new life is born out of death, and as the world's persecution blossoms into the liberation of the Spirit. How is it that we have been able to lose the meaning of this book, which is the only one that was ever written directly for us? Standing as it does between the two comings of Christ, its message is one of consolation and hope to a Church that will reach its glory through suffering. This book should be for us a most powerful encouragement to await with patience the fulfilment of God's eternal designs.

Thus the Apocalypse sets its seal on the Bible's message. It is the last "revelation". The long unfolding of man's yearning and God's answer comes to an end in the mystery of life in the Spirit. In one sense the Apocalypse is the least eschato-logical of all the books of the Bible, since it spells the end of the tormenting delusion which God was able to use to such effect throughout Israel's long history. Henceforth the Christian knows that he can expect nothing but suffering and death from without. He knows that within him this death will be exactly balanced by the life of the Spirit flowing to him from the throne of the triumphant Lamb. The ultimate victory over the forces of Evil will come, to establish the harmonious com-pletion on earth of the work begun at the creation. But already the victory of the Christ-life is announced in the death of the Christian. Already it raises him from earth to heaven.

V

CHRIST THE FOCAL POINT OF THE SCRIPTURES

Inner continuity and unity of the revelation from Abraham to Christ; Christ the historical culmination, logical term and sum content of the Bible.

IN THE light of what has been said, the reader will at least know what to look for when he reads the Bible. If he concen-trates too much on detail, he will rarely feel the touch of God's hand; he will even risk losing himself altogether in a welter of secondary causes behind which God is hidden. Revelation and the supernatural are rarely obvious in the Bible. It is frequently possible to explain things by natural agencies and causes. What the reader must look for is rather the constant, sure and irresis-tible movement of the whole towards one end, irrespective of human conditions. It is here that the hand of God is most surely in command. Every nation has a history of success and failure, but no nation has a history like this one, where success and failure alike conspire to produce a living and complex up-ward movement towards a single end. The call of Abraham can be explained by natural causes. So can the Exodus from Egypt, the Conquest, the success of David, Israel's survival after exile, even the "miracle" by which neither Persia nor Greece nor Rome were able to absorb this nation. What cannot be so explained is how all these events gradually and surely led this tiny, materialist and dull-minded people to the conclusion that the God of Abraham was the supreme creator of all things. What passes understanding is that a people as hard-hearted as this could pin their hope on an unbelievable manifestation of love, and see that hope realized in such splendour that their hearts could not contain it.

All the lines of this history converge. All the Bible's themes, whether we consider them horizontally or vertically, logically or historically, at rest or in motion, all meet at a single point. We might well compare the Bible to one of those elegant turrets which decorate the great towers of our Cathedrals. They are really spiral staircases, where each step fans out from a slender central column which is itself made up of the angle end of the successive steps. The whole turret is built on the base of this central column, and the roof is the fan-vaulting which springs from its top, and keys the outer walls. Every full circle of the spiral is a repetition of the last. The same number of equidistant steps lead from one floor to the next, and so to the top. The cycles of doctrinal themes in the Bible are rather like these winding steps. One leads into the next with a similarity of construction which argues to the constancy of the part they have to play. On different levels, each depends for its support and function on the basic central column which gives cohesion and vital direction to the whole. This central column is *Christ*.

Christ is the focal point of the Scriptures on an *historical* level first of all. He is the fan-vaulting which concludes the spiral. If we are to understand the Bible, we must before all else be absolutely clear about the line of direction of every single event and idea it contains. They have no meaning except insofar as they effectively prepare the way for the supreme event in this history—the incarnation of the Word and the revelation of his message. From this point of view, the call of Abraham and the revolt of the Maccabees are of equal value. The only difference is that one is at the beginning and the other near the end of a succession of events which produced a background on earth against which the Son of God could be revealed. Man could never have assimilated that revelation if it had appeared out of the blue, divorced from this movement through time.

It needed a favourable historical context (a people, a religious tradition, and a place in the economy of that tradition) and a favourable psychological climate (a faith inexorably directed towards a future revelation, a religious fervour, and above all a yearning). These were the components which God so slowly collected together when he determined to set apart the people of Israel in this particular corner of the Mediterranean to prepare a humble cradle for his Son.

Christ is not only the term of an historical sequence. He is there in germ at each of its stages, in the first as in the last. As the evolution advances, so his features become more and more precise. He is therefore the *logical* focal point of the Scriptures. At whatever stage they are considered, the various doctrinal themes are all centred on the idea of a divine and freely bestowed salvation, realized by an envoy sent from God. Basically each theme is only one aspect of this single theme, whose potentialities are not fully brought to act except in Christ. His foreshadowing in the Bible is not therefore merely a subjective one; he is prefigured on the objective plane of reality (whether potential or actual). Only rarely were its writers, the Prophets included, even implicitly aware of the person of Christ. It was not important that they should be. His presence in the Bible transcends the consciousness of men. God had himself infused it into the profound logic of events and ideas, and into the living flesh of his People.

Christ is consequently the focal point of the Scriptures on the even deeper and altogether supernatural level of *revelation*. The Bible contains both revealed truths and truths attainable by the unaided use of reason. But there is only one Truth, living and revealed, and that is the incarnate Word. Reflection on the concept of supernatural revelation will show that God can reveal nothing which is not his Son. God, alone and in himself, is beyond the attainments of created reason. Outside God there are many truths which man has not attained, but none that he could not attain. In this sense truth is natural to man, it is within his scope. God alone lies outside that scope, and everything else insofar as it is rooted in God. He alone bestows himself freely. The natural knowledge that we have of God brings God into our minds, but it does not place us in God as he is, in all his ineffable reality. If we are to know

God in that way (and our whole being cries out for it, since he made us for himself) then God must give us the knowledge he has of himself. This Knowledge of God, subsistent and personal, the eternal Word, is his Son. The eternal design of God from Paradise lost to the Parousia, the entire plan of salvation to which he invites us, consists precisely in this revelation of himself in his Son. Thus when God reveals " something " in the Bible, that something can only be his Son, reduced to human and halting symbols. That something can only be a logical and historical preparation for the revelation of his Son in person, in the flesh.

So we come to the final level: Christ is the focal point of the Scriptures as the *incarnation of the Word*. If God is to give himself to man, he must come to man's level, the level of fallen nature. When man wrenched himself from God's grasp, he had nothing but himself to fall back on. From that time onward he knew only himself, and whatever else he knew beneath him only led him back to himself. If God would now take a hold on him again, he must stoop down to man's fallen level, and there offer his hand. The divine Word must be spoken in sounds that the human ear can hear; the divine Light must shine in a way that the human eye can see. The Bible is the Word of God become audible, Christ is the Word of God become visible. Whether its function is to be heard or to enlighten, God has only one Word, and he speaks it only to give it. The pre-incarnation of his Word in the Bible is the prelude to the incarnation of the Word in the womb of the Virgin Mary. " This is eternal Life, that they may know Thee, the Father, and Him whom thou hast sent, Jesus Christ " (John 17:3).

CHAPTER VII

THE WORK OF THE SPIRIT

I

REVELATION AND INSPIRATION

Their relationship to each other and to the Trinity; their close connection in the work of salvation; distinct and yet parallel in their reference both to the human faculties and to the divine persons.

WE SAID at the end of the last chapter that God has only one Word. It is a statement that sums up the efficacy of the divine Word. With man, thought is not necessarily translated into act—we know it well enough from our own experience. With God it is otherwise. His Word never returns to him until it has accomplished its purpose (Isa. 55:11) because, in reality, it is the omnipotent Power of God. God's Thought is charged with action and translated into love. The Word which expresses him is actuated by the flood of his vital Energy. Necessarily the Son of God is the well-spring of the Spirit, who proceeds from the generation of the Son by the Father.

The Bible is the Word of God. This means that it is the living Word, energized by the Spirit of God. When God speaks, it is the Breath of his mouth that renders his Word audible. At the very centre of the mystery of the incarnation lies the eternal mystery of the procession of the Spirit in the generation of the Son. It is the Spirit who inspires those who preach the old Covenant, which is a pre-incarnation of the Word. It is again he who overshadows the Virgin Mary when the Word becomes incarnate. It is still he who transforms the Eucharist and the Church into the body of Christ by the sanctification of the same Spirit. Just as in eternity the Father's revelation of himself (which is the Son) gives to the Son, in his

Father, that vital inspiration which is the Spirit; so in time the revelation of the Word is achieved in Scripture, and in the womb of the Virgin, in the Eucharist and in the Mystical Body, by the efficacious inspiration of the same Spirit. As the incarnation of the Word in the Bible is prolonged in Christ, so Christ is prolonged in the Church and in the humblest of her children, and the same fertile love of the Spirit prevails throughout. In the rhythm of this Love we are brought to the splendour of the Son and carried to the bosom of the Father.

The Father is eternally at the centre of the Godhead. The Son is its immanent mediator and subsistent revelation. The Spirit lies, as it were, on the circumference of the Godhead, as the overflowing vitality which communicates the Father in his Son. Man's return to God must re-trace inversely the logical and historical order in which God gave his gift to man. Here the Spirit comes first. At his prompting man's heart is opened to the light of the Son who carries him back to the Father. It is the vibration of the Spirit that makes the Word of the Father audible to the ears of man. In other words it is the Bible's inspiration that guarantees its revelation.

It is important, then, to understand not only the profound connection between the notions of revelation and inspiration, but also the distinction between them. Revelation pertains to the intellect: it is the communication of an unknown truth. Inspiration pertains to the will: it is the vital activity which translates thought into action. Commonly, when we say that a writer is inspired we mean that he is compelled by an inner force to express his soul's vision. The vision itself will be called inspired if it is born out of the impact of a vital shock in his deepest level of consciousness. The same is true of the Bible, but on a religious plane. Biblical revelation is the communication of a truth which is proper to God. The revelation of the Bible means its content of revealed Truth, its manifestation of the Thought of God, the intellectual communication of his Son. Biblical inspiration is the divine operation whereby this Truth is spoken and made audible to the ears of man. It pertains to the divine Activity and is the vital communication of his Spirit.

To relate revelation in this way to the Son and inspiration to the Spirit will emphasize the distinction between them. It will also serve to mark their intimate connection. The Spirit is the very life of the Son in his Father. In the same way biblical inspiration is the divine vitality by which the revelation of God becomes actualized. One might object that the greater part of the ideas expressed in the Bible are attainable by unaided reason, and are not properly speaking revealed even though they may be inspired. It remains true, however, that these so-called human ideas are brought into service only to express the revealed truth, and thereby share the strictly divine light of the Bible. Exactly the same is true of inspiration. Very rarely is it a divine impulse which takes the place of man's normal literary activity, and yet it pervades the whole of that activity in the Bible. Thus revelation and inspiration are complementary and parallel aspects of the divine nature of the Bible. Both act on human activity at its very root, determining it infallibly, not by supplanting it but by informing it and raising it to a supernatural perfection.

II

THE NATURE OF INSPIRATION

Ideas that go beyond or fall short of Christian belief; living inspiration of the community; supernatural character of inspiration; its contact with the human will and its source in the Spirit; inspiration and grace; inspiration and the personality of the inspired writer.

THE dogma of the inspiration of Scripture was never seriously questioned until the birth of scientific criticism in the nineteenth century. Before that, the tendency had always been to emphasize the Bible's divine character and minimize the human. When this was taken to extremes, it led to such errors as the theory of verbal inspiration, according to which every material word was dictated by God, and the sacred writer was no more than an automatic recording machine. It was inevitable that the discovery of the human element in the Bible should at first seem to destroy belief in inspiration altogether. In fact it only destroyed the rigid framework in which the belief had been held prisoner. And here errors were made in the opposite direction, the rôle of inspiration being reduced to that of divine approbation, or of a mere general providence, or even of a simple guarantee against error.

In condemning these views the Vatican Council was content to re-affirm the traditional belief in a positive inspiration by the Holy Spirit. The infallible magisterium of the Church gives no technical definition. The Church's thought is nevertheless quite clearly enshrined in her ancient documents, and more especially in the encyclicals of Leo XIII, Benedict XV and Pius XII, all of which teach the following as certain: both the divine and the human character of the Bible is to be preserved intact; God is its principal author; by determining its content through the positive action of his Spirit he has made himself responsible for it; the sacred writer is equally author in the true sense of the word; he has contributed to its production through the normal human activity which God has employed as his instrument.

For the Christian, inspiration is a dogma of faith given him by Christ through the Church. The sacred author speaks the words of God because he has been moved by God to do so. That is the simple statement of his belief. The Christian who wishes to broaden his faith will not stop there; he will want to go into it more deeply. In an earlier chapter we described how belief in inspiration grew. We will now resume the conclusions we came to, and in the light of the Church's teaching we will try to define more precisely what is meant by inspiration.

WE SAW first of all that the inspiration of the Bible was a particularized form of Israel's general religious inspiration. We saw that it was not confined to writers properly so called, but extended to all those who contributed in some way to the slow and complex formation of the Book. The Bible is the expression of a living tradition, moulded into the life of the people by God's delegates, but developing in the community as such. These delegates, whether they were prophets, sages, priests, kings or scribes, were not only God's representatives to the community but also the community's representatives to God. Every single member of the community therefore participated in some way in receiving, transmitting, and enriching the growing content of revelation. By the same token, every single

o

member of the community walked, as he had done in the desert, under the luminous cloud of the Spirit. Anyone who enjoyed a special form of the Spirit's inspiration could be said to epitomize the privilege which God had given to all his people. God had chosen him from out of the midst of his people. As the life of the early Church was dominated by the Spirit of Christ, so was the life of the people of Israel dominated by the Spirit of Yahweh. The Spirit's continuous control over the historical development of revelation goes hand in hand with the divine Word's own growing manifestation.

Biblical inspiration thus falls under the general category of divine Providence. In both, God works through secondary causes, and does not replace them with his own activity, as he does in miracles. There is no miracle about biblical inspiration, because God does not upset the normal process of the writer's activity. There is no obvious intervention by God. Biblical writers wrote as other men do, and left the imprint of their personality on their work. For the most part they were not even conscious that they were inspired. Inspiration must not therefore be thought of as a *substitution* of God's action for the normal activity of the writer. There is no question of an artificial insemination of ready-made concepts into the author's mind, nor of any arbitrary interference with his imagination or feelings. Normally God acts here with a delicacy of touch that shows his respect for his own creation and his intimate knowledge of its mechanism.

What we have just said should not lead us to conclude that biblical inspiration is nothing more than a facet of the ordinary Providence of God, or the mere selection of an élite to form the focal point of Israel's religious life. Although to ordinary eyes the Bible is clearly and fully a human book, to the eyes of faith it is just as clearly a *direct* revelation of God. In the workings of divine Providence, creation always stands between God and man; in inspiration there is an immediate and personal contact between God and man. This element of contact is essential to the notion of supernatural revelation, in which God gives himself *as he is*, naturally incommunicable. If such a strictly divine truth is to enter the intellectual stream of a community, it must do so through the channel of a physical individual; for a human community is not an entity of itself, independent of the individuals whose physical and spiritual ties form its web and woof. God must actuate a privileged individual from within, to enable him to express to the community the ineffable content of the truth he has received in words they can understand. There must first be *inspired men*, in immediate and personal contact with the divine truth, before the Word of God can become incarnate in the community. Any other form of communication would not make known the divine Truth itself, but only its created reflection, and leave man cut off from the truly supernatural.

WHERE precisely is this contact made between the divine Spirit and the inspired man? Since inspiration is neither an indirect movement nor a miracle, we must conclude that contact is achieved at the only point where man is open to the direct action of God, namely at the root of his being, in that spiritual cradle which was created for the express purpose of receiving it. Man admittedly is incapable of touching God, but he is not incapable of being touched by God. If God had not so created this hidden aptitude for receiving the supernatural revelation of himself, then we would never be able to take any interest in it or receive it when he chose to give it. Supernatural revelation is not something added on to man to embellish his otherwise integral nature; it is the unique transcendent perfection of his nature, and the be-all and end-all of his life. An aptitude for the supernatural lies at the very root of his most spiritual faculties. His intellect passes beyond all that is finite and hovers in a void, face to face with the infinite God. His will is not sated by created good but always hungers for the Other. It is this insatiability of man that God created to find a way to man's heart; this is man's yearning which seeks God's free gift even though he must wait for ever. God has made of man's mind a cradle to receive his Son the everlasting Truth, and of his will a seed to be germinated by the vital energy of his Spirit.

Thus it would seem that biblical inspiration affects man on the level where grace affects him. Like grace its contact is direct, but like grace obscure and beyond consciousness, for it is consequent on the Fall by which man lost that delicate balance whereby he was directly conscious of the supernatural.

Like grace again, it is not a forced invasion of man's natural faculties, but the infusing of those faculties with a higher life.

In fact inspiration and grace do not merely resemble each other, they are closely inter-related. Grace is the restoration to man of the supernatural revelation of God, in the person of his Son and under the impulse of his Spirit. This is something that transcends consciousness: man's intellect since the Fall is too clouded to perceive it clearly, and his will too hardened to respond to it as it does to a sensible good. In other words it belongs to the realm of charity and faith. Now charity is based on faith, and faith on the teaching of the Church. This in its turn is based, by way of the Church's tradition, on the testimony of the inspired writer. In the last analysis therefore, faith puts man in contact with the truth which was directly communicated by God's inspiration. The act of faith infuses into the Christian the invisible Light which is the Son of God, even though it reaches him by means of the visible human form in which it first entered the world under the impulse of inspiration, and in which it has been preserved by the living tradition of the Church.

This analysis of the relation between grace and inspiration will also show where they are distinct. Grace belongs to the realm of faith; inspiration is more in the nature of a vision. Not a strictly intuitive vision, for the intellect is often not conscious of it, but still a real and direct psychological contact with God, producing a positive reaction in the consciousness of the sacred writer. Where grace is a permanent state, inspiration is of itself something temporary. Its whole tendency is to express itself outwardly, and it achieves permanence only by being embodied in a living tradition, for which the inspired person has acted as a sort of divine *medium*. Inspiration does not, like grace, bring about justification. All it does is to lift a corner of the veil which since the Fall has hung between God and man. It gives back to man the vision he lost, in terms he can appreciate, so that he may make that vision his own. But it will be only at the price of death to sin, only by being crucified in faith, only by accepting this incarnation, that he will reach the fullness of the vision which brings him justification.

IF WE may go even deeper into this mystery, we will see that inspiration produces a direct and radical contact between the will and God's Spirit. This contact with the vitalizing Energy of God rectifies the intellect and allows it to open itself to the Light of the Son. The first contact necessarily leads to the other—the Spirit is necessarily the herald of the Truth of the Father, which is the Son. Inspiration then is the direct action of the Holy Spirit on man's will, an action which necessarily involves a supernatural illumination of the mind by the Word.

This action, which takes place at man's most spiritual level, transcends consciousness. In his present state of fallen nature, man can think consciously only by means of images drawn from sensible objects, and can react only to a sensible good. And yet, precisely because his spiritual mind and will are tied to his lower faculties and through them to his body, whatever touches his spirit is bound to percolate through to his body in the form of conscious human ideas and feelings. In other words, the divine impulse of inspiration, registering on man's spiritual level, must pursue its course on to the plane of sensibility and is born in the form of human concepts. Revelation, ineffable in itself, takes shape in the images already formed in the human make-up of the inspired person. He reacts to it as would the community he represents. Revelation becomes concrete in the form of the answer to the community's yearning, a yearning which through the medium of historical circumstances has, as it were, provoked God to act through the prophet. By the same token, the divine impulse which is set up in the inspired writer's will and in the very muscles of his fingers is exactly adapted to his temperament and to the circumstances in which he lives.

From all this it follows that by inspiration God does not simply substitute concepts and images and desires for those of the writer, but infallibly informs the writer's faculties at their source. Thus the divine action respects every constituent element of the writer's intellectual, moral and social make-up, and at the same time governs them so decisively that they never cease to be under the influence of the Spirit. At every level of his being and at every stage of his activity, even down to putting pen to paper, the inspired person is dominated by the power of the Spirit. Throughout there is only one influence at work. It acts directly on the mainspring of normal human activity, and from there permeates through the ordinary channels. It is a radical and sustained impulse, informing every detail of the writer's activity, making up for his deficiencies, elevating his natural abilities and consecrating his function in the community. It is the transcendent principle which governs all his work without supplanting it. Of his own free will the inspired man conforms infallibly to God's Design.

III

INERRANCY

Inspiration commits God's authority and veracity; divine Truth and human truths; the Bible as divine truth become human; conditions and limits imposed on the divine guarantee by this incarnation.

THE fact that the activity of the sacred writer is grafted on to the activity of the Spirit gives rise to a most important corollary: by inspiration God assumes responsibility for the work of the writer and becomes its true author. Its first beginnings, content and ultimate purpose are all due to him. Not that the responsibility of the writer is thereby destroyed: he acts throughout like any normal writer, and on his own level makes his personal contribution at every stage of the work. He remains author in the full sense of the word. But his activity has been elevated to a divine plane and imbued with a new significance. Although the work is not altered it is transfigured.

This first corollary gives rise to another, of considerable practical importance. If God is its author, the Bible can contain no error. In overshadowing the sacred writer with his Spirit, God becomes one with him and endows him with divine authority and truth. The Bible becomes the Word of God. Now the Word of God is one; and since it bears the infallible efficacy of the Spirit, it is the criterion of all truth, the creative norm of all reality. To say that God is truthful does not mean that God conforms to reality, but that he created reality to conform to his own subsistent truth. The inerrancy of the Bible covers therefore in principle every field of reality—religion, philosophy, science, history, psychology—since all these individual aspects of truth must coalesce in the one truth of him who created them. While revelation and reason must never be confused, they cannot be altogether divorced. The formal objects of each are different, but they are united and joined together by virtue of their absorption into something higher.

Stated in their stark simplicity these principles are absolute. It is when we begin to apply them to the Bible, the Word of God become incarnate, that we see how problematic they become.

In the sacred Books eternal truth is expressed in human terms, and is necessarily limited by the adequacy or inadequacy of human language. It follows that the truth of the Bible must be judged by the same standards which are used to judge human truth. Its truthfulness is the truth of men not of angels. Nor is it a metaphysical truth but a concrete one, necessarily adapted to the limits of man's knowledge and his vehicles of expression.

Since it is incarnate in this way, the truth of the Bible is subject to the same contingencies as any human truth, provided of course that the absolute divine truth is not compromised.

Insofar as it is rooted in divine truth, all human truth has an absolute value. Again, its rational structure, with its permanent framework of the abstract thought common to all men, gives it an absolute value. But when it becomes articulate it loses its absolute quality, and becomes relative in extension, in content, in subject and in expression: in extension because, even as a concept, it cannot embrace the entire range of one thing's relationships with others, but must make a choice; in content because it does not necessarily consider the whole but only certain aspects of a given reality; in subject because the intelligence and powers of penetration and perception will not necessarily measure up to the fullness of the object of thought: and finally in expression because words which are inevitably drawn from sensible images are of themselves unable to express a spiritual truth. Words are conventions, which vary in meaning and value according to the milieu, the literary form and the mentality of the people using them. It is here that the relativity of human truth may be most compromising.

In the case of revealed truth, its slow evolution gives rise to another form of relativity. Revelation was progressive, and we must not expect the same degree of precision in the early stages of its formation that we find later on. For example, belief in the immortality of the soul does not come to light fully until Maccabean times. Assertions about life after death made before this time must be judged in their context, in the light of the evolution that this item of God's revelation was designed to undergo.

WHEN we say, therefore, that the Bible contains no error, we use the word in its human sense, and not with any metaphysical or divine connotation. Absolutely, error is the affirmation of something which does not conform to reality as it exists, independent of perception. If this is our definition of error, then the Bible bristles with errors. It states that the sun rises, and means this literally, as everyone else did before Galileo. It imagines the sky to be a solid fixed vault; it allows only 5,000 years to elapse between the creation and the incarnation; it divides the work of creation into seven days; it extends the Flood to cover the whole earth. There is not a page and hardly a verse which could not be pulled to pieces by philologists, philosophers, theologians, and scholars of every kind. But then to take each text merely at its face value is not scholarly: it must be interpreted.

The proper criterion of human truth was well defined by St. Augustine: "It is not the material meaning of the letters and syllables that is important, but the reality they signify and convey." In other words, error is present only when an author makes a deliberate *judgment* which is at variance with the reality that he means to express and that his contemporaries may reasonably understand him to mean. Two things are required for error: first a judgment, something formally affirmed and taught, and secondly an explicit intention to express that precise aspect of truth which is in fact not expressed. Where nothing is taught but only an opinion given, or where a universally accepted idea is received without judgment being passed, then there is no error. Where a given affirmation is erroneous only from a point of view entirely foreign to the formal intention of the writer and the demands of the readers he is addressing, there is no real error. In fine, error is part of the philosophical definition of evil. Evil is the absence of a good which is *due*; error is the absence of the truth which *may be demanded.* Nobody can be accused of error, of failing to express himself perfectly, if it was not his intention or his duty to his contemporaries to do so.

Later we shall see some practical applications of these principles. All that we aim to do here is to draw a general conclusion on the exact import of biblical inerrancy. Error is measured by the formal intention of a given writer in a given milieu. In the Bible this intention is strictly limited. Firstly God, the principal Author, has one aim only—to teach man *religion.* Admittedly this is conveyed by means of human teaching, and it would be a mistake to confine inerrancy to the dogmatic or moral parts of the Bible. But it remains true that this primary religious purpose subordinates all others, restricts the emphasis of all ancillary teaching and excludes any pretentions to science as such. Secondly, the divine teaching is given mediately, through an inspired author, and is thus made *incarnate.* It is, therefore, subject to those limitations of the writer's literary make-up which we mentioned earlier: his Semitic mentality, his literary forms, his aim, his peculiarities of style, the relative position he occupies in the evolving scheme of revelation, and so on.

To sum up, the divine truth, absolute in itself, is in the Bible adapted to the limitations of human truth. We attain the absolute truth of God through the medium of relative truth. The errors we find in the Bible are of our own construction. We have either misunderstood what it says or forced it to say what it does not intend to say. Either we are blinded by our own purely human curiosity and fail to see the divine content, or we look only for the Word of God and forget that it has become incarnate in human form.

IV

THE "THEANDRIC" NATURE OF INSPIRATION

Interdependence of the divine and the human in the Bible; theory of instrumentality; inspiration the act of the Spirit; the inspiration of Christ.

THE question of inerrancy brings us back to the very heart of the problem of the Bible. At one and the same time the Bible is simple and complex, human and divine, human although divine, divine through its humanity. Its two elements are to be neither confused nor separated; they are correlatives and as it were con-substantial. We can no more separate the divine content and the human shape of the Bible or absorb one into the other than we can isolate the Word of God from the man Jesus, or confuse his divine nature and his human nature into one. In the Bible it is not possible to confuse or separate the two authors, any more than it is possible to confuse or separate the levels at which they operate. We cannot say this is divine and that is human. Both activities work together in an order of harmony and balance to form a single work with a single meaning. The divine value of the Bible cannot be reached in isolation from its human meaning, nor can the human meaning be stripped of its divinity.

The ultimate reason why the Bible is con-substantial with eternal truth lies in the very nature of inspiration. Inspiration is essentially " theandric ". The divine and human activities are not set in juxtaposition, nor does one substitute for the other. The natural mechanism of the sacred writer's literary activity remains undisturbed, even though its motive force is the impulse given to his spiritual faculties. This basic impulse dominates him, and permeates down through all his work into the very last written word. In the ordinary writer this impulse (whether it is a psychological emotion or not) has a human explanation. Analysis shows that it is always a manifestation of man's natural desire for the infinite. In the sacred writer the impulse reaches him at the same level, but it is of an entirely different nature. It is no longer the desire for a God who is perceived through created things, but the direct answer of the Father in his Son through the Spirit. It sets in motion the writer's natural mechanism without affecting his make-up, his limitations or his freedom. It fills him completely with a superhuman activity and subordinates him utterly to a divine purpose.

Christian tradition from earliest times has chosen a happy expression to convey such a complex interaction. It compares it to an instrument in a man's hand. The Fathers used the particularly striking image of David and his harp. A musical instrument is a dead thing until brought to life by someone outside it, nor can the musician express himself without the aid of the instrument. The beauty and the manner of his expression will vary with the quality of his instrument, although a genius will be able to produce wonderful sounds even on a poor violin. It goes without saying that the musician's is the fundamental activity: the music is in his soul even before he has the means to express it. Similarly the inspired writer is only the divine Musician's instrument, but he is essential if we are to hear the music which the finger of God would play.

Exempla claudicant, and we must not push this one too far. The inspired instrument in the Bible is unique—a man, individual, conscious and free. Nothing less than the finger of God is strong enough or delicate enough to make this instrument sound truly. For the "finger of God" is no mere material contact but the living Breath of his Spirit which, at the passing of God's Word, stirs the living chords of his instrument to make their very fibres resound.

This was the Spirit which was God's voice when he spoke to Adam in the "evening breeze". It is still he who opens the heart of the Christian to speak the Son's call to the Father. Throughout the course of this history, which begins in the inspired Adam and culminates in the inspired Christian, he has chosen many instruments to attune men's ears to the song of the Son in his Father. This Breath from the mouth of God put the eternal Word on to the lips of his servants so that they could slowly spell out the Redeemer's name. He is the soul of all inspiration and revelation, and the long history of inspiration came to a climax in his solemn apparition on the banks of the Jordan, in order to make public the fullness of the Spirit by which Mary's son was consecrated from his conception as the Word of God incarnate.

At the end of the last chapter we enumerated the four titles on which Christ is the focal point of the Scriptures. We must now add a fifth, that of inspiration. In Christ all inspiration is summed up, because he is the subsistent Revelation of the Father. In him dwells all the fullness of the Spirit of God because he is the only Son of the Father, at once the divine source of the Spirit which is his life in the Father, and the human dispenser of that life to his followers. This inspiration of Christ was the inspiration that filled Adam, the Law and the Prophets. It is the same inspiration of Christ which now fills all Christians by grace, and in glory all the elect. For the Spirit is the eternal Life of the Son in the Father; and our own eternal life consists in knowing the Father in his Son only because that life is breathed into us by the Breath of love, wherein God gives his Son and the Son eternally loves the Father.

CHAPTER VIII

THE BIBLE AND THE CHRISTIAN

THE Bible is the Word of God, and obviously God meant people to read it. He does not act without purpose. Believing in the Bible as we do, it must surely cause us some sadness to see the indifference with which men greet this gift of God. There are Christians who are genuinely grieved when they encounter the general lack of interest in the mystery of love which is the incarnation, who are truly distressed when they come across the lukewarmness which will make any excuse to avoid Communion, and who yet feel no qualms at all when they themselves forsake the living waters of sacred Scripture. Yet, if Jesus, our Christ and Lord, is truly the Son of God made man, if he is really the incarnate Word (and this is the very essence of our faith) then he is present in the Bible as well as in the Eucharist. Communion with his crucified and glorious body in the Mass cannot be divorced from communion with his living Word in the scriptural readings of the fore-Mass. Christian vitality has a double source upon which to draw, the Bible and the Eucharist. These are the two forms assumed by the spiritual flesh of the incarnate Word so that he may feed our minds and our hearts. " Unless you eat the flesh of the Son of man and drink his blood, you shall not have Life in you " (John 6 : 53). These words of our Lord refer to the reading of the Bible just as surely as they refer to the eating of his risen body.

We must read the Bible, because it is the Word of God, and it is by keeping his Word that we possess eternal life. This conclusion, however, needs to be clarified. The Bible, we say, is the Word of life. The question arises, what life? Such a life, we say, is based on revealed faith. How exactly does the Bible give such faith? This faith, we say, is enshrined in history. What is the connection between faith and history? These are questions which must be answered if we are to know what to expect from our reading of the Bible.

I

THE BIBLE AND SCIENCE

Science not to be found in the Bible; concordism impossible in spite of points of contact with natural sciences; outlook and method different from that of philosophy and theology, in spite of common object; true interpretation untechnical, in spite of its doctrinal value for exegesis.

FIRST of all, let us clear the ground and say what not to expect. It is quite useless for us to look for any form of science, because the Bible clearly has no intention of teaching science. Its sole aim is to teach religion.

We must be clear about what we mean by science. The word comprises all intellectual disciplines that are concerned with the mastering of creation by reason, for its own sake. As a method, it requires specialization, impartiality and abstraction. Even though the scientific method has been extended and applied to philosophical and theological research, the proper field of science is the world of sense and matter, and its tool is reason. It is concerned with things that have nothing directly in common with the inner world of the spirit, and still less with religion. It is an achievement of Greek thought and more particularly of post-Renaissance civilization. Obviously there is no question of any science in this sense in the Bible.

THE Bible has nothing to say about the natural sciences, if only because there is no sphere of study so remote from the set religious aim of the Bible. It is our modern approach, so accustomed to reducing every manifestation of truth to a science, that finds it constantly necessary either to reconcile the Bible and science or to oppose them. The nineteenth century thought to destroy biblical revelation in the name of astronomy and geology. Towards the end of the century books like Fraser's *Golden Bough* won notoriety by maintaining that religion was the outcome of totemism and magic. To-day, hypothetical reconstructions of the prehistoric evolution of religion are still thought to compromise biblical revelation. As a counter measure, various forms of apologetic concordism have tried to reduce the Bible to a science. In the 1870's the Bible was "reconciled" variously with astronomy, geology and zoology, and the six days of creation became six periods in the Darwinian theory of evolution. Then came the turn of ethnology, and the beliefs of modern aborigines were examined for confirmation of a primitive revelation of man's beginnings, the fall and the dispersion. Finally, with the science of prehistory, an attempt was made to parallel the oldest biblical popular traditions with the vague hypotheses gleaned from recent discoveries about the life of man previous to documentary evidence.

Such attempts were doomed to failure because they did not face facts. Advances in the fields of geology and palaeontology have made it clear that so complex a thing as evolution could not be confined to the artificial framework of six days. Ethnology, too, bristles with difficulties. The tribal myths of the Zulus, for example, are now seen to have nothing in common with the profound and delicate psychology which permeates the biblical accounts of man's creation. Even prehistory has no immediate relevance. How can it, when the Bible's first smiths were descendants of Cain, even though Palestine's iron age did not begin until the time of Moses! The attacks on the Bible have proved equally pointless. The march of science has only widened the extent and demonstrated the complexity of scientific data, and the wisest of the scientists have learned to bow in humility before the manifold riches of creation.

These difficulties once caused many people to lose their faith. The crisis could have been avoided if sufficient attention had been given to the true character of the Bible, and to its literary forms in particular. The first chapters of Genesis do not pretend to be a scientific disquisition. They are simply a religious presentation in popular form of a belief in the creation of man, in God's plan for man, in the beginning and last end of man, in his fall and decadence. There is no possible ground for conflict or for concord between these concrete pictures of a faith and the abstract findings of a science. The two are worlds apart.

This does not mean that there is no contact at all between faith and science. It is true they have to do with different spheres of reality, but both spheres meet in the overall unity of God's design. Man receives God's revelation in the world

which science unfolds to him, and revealed truth must necessarily tally with the findings of science. It is true that the Bible
does not treat these findings with the precision of science, but
only with the approximate terms that an ordinary non-scientific
man will use. All the same, its contact with scientific data is
objective, and there is a real contradiction between the Bible
and any hypothesis which would rule out a creation *ex nihilo*,
or the original unity of the human race, or the reality of the
world of sense. There are many thorny problems here. At the
moment, for example, some students of prehistory are putting
forward the theory of polygenism, according to which man
descended from several distinct and independent original
couples. This theory cannot be altogether rejected, except insofar as it denies the specific unity of mankind. But even if it
conceded that point, it would still involve a complete overhaul
of the problems of original sin and its transmission.[1]

In fact, the natural sciences can be a real help towards the
interpretation of the Bible by shedding new light on certain
aspects of its framework. A better understanding of geography
and ethnology, for example, is bound to improve our knowledge
of the formation of Israel. Psychology, too, can with advantage
revolutionize our appreciation of religious phenomena and their
historical evolution, as long as it is careful to keep within proper
bounds and not deny the supernatural. Sociology has light to
shed on the actual conditions of life peculiar to the Patriarchs
and the people of Israel.

WE HAVE said that the Bible teaches no science. Now we
must add that it teaches no philosophy and no theology, using
these words in their technical sense. By definition, philosophy
and theology are sciences, using a specialized literary form
understood by their initiates. The Bible's sole aim is to teach
religion to the ordinary man, living in a milieu in which philosophy or theology were not yet heard of. Needless to say, this
question needs more delicate handling than the question of the
natural sciences: philosophy and theology are professedly concerned with and closely allied to the truths revealed in the
Bible. Philosophy deals with the rational principles which

[1] It should be pointed out that this was written before the publication
of the encyclical *Humani Generis*. Cf. Ed. C.T.S. §37. (Tr.)

underlie revelation at its point of contact with the human mind; and theology is the intellectual ordering of the truths which in the Bible are still in a rough-hewn state. Nevertheless it is true to say that, as sciences, philosophy and theology move on a level quite different from that of the Bible.

Interpretation should therefore avoid the common mistake of reducing the inspired text to categories of thought which properly belong to the sciences of philosophy and theology. The truths of faith which are expressed in this way have in fact been drawn from the Bible through the Church. But the framework must not be confused with the content. The content is eternal, the human framework is not, the modern framework in particular being quite different from that in which the truths were first enshrined. The fact that our modern framework evolved from the biblical one only adds to the confusion. To understand that the danger is a real one, we have only to refer to the exegetes of nineteenth century Germany, who interpreted Scripture in the light of their philosophical outlook, and did even more damage than those apologists who try to reduce Scripture to a number of artificial classifications. If we hope to drink at the source of the Bible's revealed truth, we must be prepared to forget our accustomed ways of thinking and adopt those chosen by the Word of God. We must get outside what is to all intents and purposes a Greek mentality and become familiar again with the Semitic mind. We must desert Science for a while in order to acquire Wisdom.

We are not saying that philosophy and theology are of no help in our study of the Bible. On the contrary, they are indispensable guides to interpretation, even in their technical and rational sense. On the deeper level of living religious wisdom and knowledge, the Bible and theology are practically one, as we shall see later. Every experience of faith intensely felt must be a repetition of the experience of the first believers. At this level we could say that the Bible in the Church is the sum total of theology (the study of God) and philosophy (the love of wisdom), since it is the Word of God given to man as the divine wisdom by which he is to live. But on the scientific level, philosophy and theology are distinct from the Bible, and it is misleading to speak of a biblical theology. Technical theology is a scientific elaboration of the truths of faith; the Bible is the transmission of the truths of faith in a living tradition. Technique as such comes into biblical study only in the field of scientific exegesis, where the aim is to determine as precisely as possible the objective biblical truth. The purpose of scientific theology is to rationalize this truth; it lies therefore in a different world.

T H E R E is no doubt that even the scientific exegesis referred to above is foreign to the mentality of the sacred writers. Scripture is its own interpretation, as the Fathers showed when they appealed to the great doctrinal themes as the guides to an understanding of the whole. This does not of course mean that a text must always be interpreted in the sense it is given when it is quoted elsewhere in the Bible, nor that texts can be ripped out of their context and juggled about like algebraic formulas. To disregard their living context is to deprive them of their meaning. To disembody them is to kill them.

When the sacred writers quote each other they are not concerned with scientific exegesis. They follow the literary customs of their time. St. Paul, for example, makes use of the Old Testament in the rabbinic manner, and Christ himself refers to Scripture as any of his contemporaries would. When he speaks of Jonah and the whale, he is not pronouncing on its historical character nor offering a technical exegesis of the book of Jonah. It is true that the Scripture he quotes with special reference to his own claims must be placed in a class apart, but even here he does not rule out a more immediate historical reference, but only illustrates more clearly than ever the homogeneity of the Bible's organic development. Scripture throws light on Scripture as it progressively reveals the framework on which it grows. It is in this living sense, and not in any artificial codification, that the Bible is its own interpretation. There is nothing of the text book about the Bible. It is not a lifeless code where everything is of the same value, but a book which lives and communicates life through the Church.

II

THE BIBLE AND HISTORY

Biblical history not scientific yet real; characteristics of the Bible's historical literary form; miracle, prodigy and provi dence; discord and concord between the Gospels.

AT FIRST sight it would seem that history ought to fall in the same category as the other sciences. Since the purpose of the Bible is to teach religion, then history, too, is outside its scope, and its inerrancy will not apply to the historical data found in the Bible.

There is a certain amount of truth in this argument, and the complex ties between the Bible and history cannot be understood without reference to it. But it obviously needs modification. Where the purely technical sciences are only remotely connected with the Bible, history, which plays such a large part in the sacred Books, stands in a class of its own. It is an oversimplification to say that the Bible is only concerned with the teaching of religion, because the teaching itself is founded on events which claim historical accuracy. If this foundation is taken away, we have lost all contact with revelation.

The relationship between history and the Bible illustrates well that fundamental incarnation which we have mentioned so frequently in this book and which, as we have just seen, plays a part even in reference to the natural sciences. Revelation is essentially supernatural, but it is wedded to nature. Faith is above reason, but it is still reasonable. The Word is eternal and dwells with God, but it becomes temporal and dwells in the flesh. The Bible enjoys absolute truth, but it comes to us in relative terms. Salvation is beyond time and space, but it is worked out on earth and woven into the very fabric of history's evolution. The Bible teaches religion alone, but its religion is based on historical fact.

It is certain then that the Bible contains innumerable historical statements of great import, which share the privilege of infallibility, because they are an integral part of its religious teaching. A safeguard must be made, however. To judge the true historicity of the events recorded, we must always apply the distinction we made in reference to the natural sciences: a picture drawn for the common run of men must not be read as science. The Bible does record history, but not scientific history. When we were dealing with the problem of inerrancy, we said that there were two sorts of truth. There are similarly two sorts of historicity: "scientific" historicity, which conforms as closely as possible to the event considered in itself and for itself, and "empiric" or popular historicity, which conforms to one aspect of the event, considered from the relative point of view to which the writer confines himself. Scientific historicity has only relative truth: it is faced with an absolute it can never achieve. Empiric historicity, if it is to exist at all, must have absolute truth: it is limited by the author's own aims, and it can and must confine itself to those limits. This is the historicity of the Bible. It contains no scientific history or history for its own sake, but only history that is used to achieve a higher purpose. The Bible's inerrancy guarantees the historicity of the events it records to the precise degree in which the writer intends to support his religious teaching on fact.

We see then that the problem of historicity is bound up with the problem of literary forms. If we are to find a solution to the problem we must determine as accurately as we can the laws, limits and procedure of the historical form used in the Bible. It does not follow hard and fast rules, and we can only compare it with our scientific way of recording history in the light of the intentions and the capacities of each individual writer. The author of the book of Chronicles, for example, aims to give a general picture of Israel's religious development. Clearly such a book has less pretentions to our sort of history than has, say, the record of David's reign or the first book of Maccabees, both of which give evidence of great concern for precision. It is true to say in general, however, that there are certain fundamentals common to all the historical books of the Bible, and these more than anything else mark the difference between biblical history and our own.

THE first of these we have already mentioned: the *subordination of history to a religious thesis*. This is always present, in however small a degree. Each of the literary schools which contributed to the production of the Heptateuch has marked it with its own religious stamp. The main theme of the Yahwistic narrative (known as J) is mankind's gradual degradation and the concentration of the promises of redemption on Abraham's clan. This seems to begin in Genesis 2-4, and is continued through to the books of Kings under the form of a chronicle of the " Wars of Yahweh " to show God's faithfulness to those promises. The Elohistic narratives (E) have not the same cohesion, and have come down to us in the form of anecdotes. But they too reflect the religious preoccupations of the oldest prophetic circles. Built on the idea of the Covenant, they are particularly concerned to show God's miraculous interventions. The Deuteronomic (D) writings and the Priestly Code (P) are even more obviously religious in outlook. The first, in the spirit of the great Prophets, sees everything in terms of fidelity to the Covenant, and is typified in the moral tone of the book of Judges. The second is typified in Leviticus, Chronicles and Nehemiah-Ezra, where the emphasis is on the legalistic, ritualistic and theological preoccupations of the austere post-exilic religion.

The history of David's reign affords another example of history presented from a religious angle. It is in a profoundly religious atmosphere that the personality of David is drawn— a man at once human and entirely submissive to the guidance of Yahweh. We are reminded here of the Acts of the Apostles, where the growth of the Church is conveyed through the story of the central figure, St. Paul. The cycle of stories built around Elijah and Elisha reminds us of St. Mark's Gospel. With spontaneity and freshness, both manage to present their powerful personalities, the two prophets in one case and Christ himself in the other. With St. Matthew the religious outlook is more obvious, with its Judaizing thesis of Jesus the Messiah. Finally St. John, far more accurate than the Synoptics from a historical point of view, nevertheless allows his religious presentation of the Son of God to predominate.

All the way through, in varying degrees, the events become a background for religion. Such subordination does not imply that the events are falsified but it does involve an amount of simplification, omission, emphasis and artificiality which would never be allowed in our modern way of writing history. Biblical

history may not be scientific but it is not less truthful for
that.

O T H E R traits which make biblical history so different from our
own can be mentioned more briefly since they flow naturally
from the make-up of the Semitic mind. With its love of the
concrete the Semitic mentality has a great sense of history, but
not speculative history. History for the Semite is the living
memory of his social group, the expression of its traditional
identity. He is at pains to preserve the traditions of his heritage
and all that went to its making because it is through this history
that he becomes part of his clan and united to his "Fathers".
It is in his history that his personal life transcends time and
space and is united to the life of his people. Such a mentality
is the key to the peculiarities of the Semitic historical form.
Primarily history is a record of his oral traditions. It is founded
on living memory in a world where memory plays a far more
important rôle than it does in our bookish civilization. The
oriental memory fixes rather than creates. By the simplest of
techniques it can transmit faithfully vivid and colourful tales
or dry technical records with equal facility.

This emphasis on oral tradition means also that Semitic history has a *popular* character: it remains in close contact with
the people. It takes its rise from a milieu that has itself been
moulded by tradition and where order, coherence and logic are
not so important as imagination, a vivid sense of the concrete,
and an appreciation of the true meaning of things. It is passed
on from father to son, from generation to generation, in the
exact form in which events gave it birth, and it is preserved
whole even when its details are no longer understood. Every
large group has its own traditions, not differing much from each
other, but each bearing the stamp of local interest. Changes, if
they occur, are the result not so much of elaboration as of
stereotype. Details whose meaning is lost are transmitted from
one generation to the next and confused out of sheer concern
not to modify.

Semitic history is equally characterized by its *anonymity*.
The written word is so much of a rarity that it acquires a kind
of sanctity. What is written is written. A Semite will not re-
write a story which has already been committed to writing. He

simply copies it, touching it up here and there to suit the frame-work of a larger work. Even the touching up is reduced to a minimum. If two sources cannot be reconciled, they are not changed but simply placed next to each other as neatly as pos-sible, and the reader is left to make the critical choice which is nowadays expected of the historian. The author of 1 Sam. 16-17 was just as conscious as we are that his two accounts of David's boyhood were inconsistent, even though he included them under his own inspiration by copying them from his sources. The fact that he takes no pains to reconcile them merely shows that his idea of historicity is more flexible than ours, and that God's infallibility is not committed to details as unimportant as this.

These features find their application in the New Testament as well as the Old, and give to its pages that combination of life, directness, realism, simplicity and lack of logical coherence that is its own guarantee of truth. Clearly these pages have not been concocted by scholars: they have been lived. St. Mark's Gospel is perhaps the masterpiece of such oral, popular and anonymous history. We lose sight of the author as we watch this film made up of a medley of cameos taken from life. With his awkward and halting style he has unwittingly caught a port-rait of Christ which is so real, life-like and almost harsh that even the sceptic cannot fail to be captivated by it.

THESE observations have a special significance when it comes to interpreting the *miracles* of the Bible. The believer does not, of course, question the existence of true miracles in the Bible. Nothing could be more in line with the divine plan of incarna-tion, and nothing more calculated to emphasize the transcen-dent power of spiritual revelation than to introduce it by sym-bol into the very heart of the material world. Miracles are the sensible signs of this revelation and the symbols of its effective power to save. Even so they cannot be interpreted outside the context of the religious ideas of the times to which they belong.

We are not here concerned with stories which are not really historical in character. The story of Joshua and the sun, for example (Jos. 10:12-14) is told within the framework of an epic poem, and has every appearance of being a typical example of oriental hyperbole. There are other stories which belong more properly to the realm of popular psychology and can only very loosely be called history. We confine ourselves here to those happenings which are recorded as history pure and simple, and they fall into three categories. The first includes those events which are purely *providential*; the second is made up *prodigies*, where an extraordinary concurrence of natural causes betrays the hand of God; the third is the category of strict *miracles*, where the direct action of God is substituted for natural causes. Although the inspired writers do not generally bother to make the distinctions, they are valid, and have allowed a connection to be established, for instance, between the Plagues of Egypt and the various natural calamities to which the Nile valley is prone, between the crossing of the Red Sea and the behaviour of the tides in the lakes of the Suez isthmus, between the manna and the strange plant that grows in the peninsula of Sinai, and between the crossing of the Jordan and the landslides of the river's marshy banks, which have been known to stop the flow of water.

These comparisons and others which could be made are not vitally important, even when they are made seriously and are not a shabby disguise for rationalism. Clearly, the Bible, in claiming that a given fact has the divine seal, does not do so in the scientific manner of the Medical Bureau at Lourdes. The only thing that interests the sacred writer (and it is the only thing that should interest us) is not *how* these things happened, but *why*. Our concern should be to recapture the deep religious awareness of the ancients, who saw the hand of God everywhere, and recognized his intervention in the course of ordinary as well as extraordinary events. According to the strict letter of science we should relegate many of the things that the Bible calls "miracles" into the first or second of our three categories. It is our faith that helps us to side with the Bible and recognize that even these are signs of God's guidance and guarantees of his revelation. That, in fact, is their only true meaning. We must not allow ourselves to be hypnotized by the miracles of the Bible. They are only signs, and they must not distract us from the reality they signify. We must look in the direction to which they point, to see a power which is truly supernatural, the power of the divine Word in the Spirit.

This approach to miracles is only part of the attitude we

should take towards biblical history as a whole. Generally speaking, the historicity of the Bible is excellent though not scientific. This is especially true of the narratives that deal with events essential to the history of revelation, and of the Gospels in particular. Bitter attacks sustained through a century and a half have only served to throw their calm and honest sincerity into higher relief. The greatest literary genius could never invent a personality so human and divine, so throbbing with life and truth as the Christ of the Synoptics. If we are to appreciate the utter sincerity of their portrait we must rid ourselves of our straightlaced technique. It is possible to be so preoccupied with superficial discrepancies between the first three Gospels (the fourth Gospel stands on its own) that we miss their profound harmony. Anyone with a modicum of good will must see that such superficial disagreement argues strongly to the authenticity of the whole. Witnesses who vary in unimportant detail and agree on the main fact are their own proof of mutual independence. Obviously they have not copied each other but have contemplated the same truth from different angles. "It is on the testimony of two or three witnesses that truth is confirmed." (Matt. 18:16).

III

THE BIBLE AND FAITH

A message that contains faith and arouses faith.

1. The Bible and Tradition: two co-principles of faith, simultaneous, complementary and indissoluble.

2. The Bible in the Church: the Church, mother of the Word incarnate; "catechetical" and "sapiential" rôle of Scripture in the economy of redemption.

3. The Bible Source of Living Faith: the Bible, first Christian experience, communion in the Spirit of the Son, and "total" theology.

IT SHOULD now be clear that to call the Bible a human book does not make it a scientific or historical text book. It remains a divine book, giving faith and divine life. In the introduction to the chapter on the "Word of God" we spoke of the part played by the Bible in the beginnings of faith in the believer. We saw that whereas the Bible furnishes us with one of the most powerful motives of credibility, faith itself is a free gift given to us by God through the Church. We now wish to show that the Bible plays a similar part in the transmission of the object of faith.

The Bible and Tradition

TOGETHER, the Bible and Tradition are generally regarded by Catholics as being the two sources of faith. The distinction is a profound one and goes back to the earliest history of the Church. Modern apologetics has often failed to preserve the true flavour of the distinction by making the Bible and Tradition appear to be independent of each other and by presenting them as two parallel reservoirs which, between them, supply articles for the Creed.

This is not the Church's own mind on the essential relationship between them. The Fathers from the beginning maintained, and the Council of Trent repeated it, that the Bible enshrines the whole of the revelation which is the object of Christian belief. It is true that there are some marginal elements which are not explicitly in Scripture, and it is the oral and written "traditions" of the Church which have preserved them for us, but even these are corollaries to the Bible's message. They are few in number, and follow so closely on the revelation of Scripture as to be hardly distinguishable from it. They must on no account be confused with the oral Tradition which the Fathers and the Church have always looked upon as the indispensable interpreter and living spirit of the letter of Scripture.

The Bible and Tradition are not two distinct things. To be exact, they cannot even be described as two means of transmission, one by writing and the other by word of mouth. They would be much better described as two inseparable components of revelation, of which the written word is the body and Tradition the soul. The book itself has never been anything more than words, print that hits the eye and sentences that feed the mind. As such it is now dead: we no longer speak in this

language or think in these terms or thrill to these events. It is
the musty relic of a past age. As St. Paul said, without the
spirit, the letter can only bring death: it cannot generate faith
or give faith an object of belief. Scholars have been putting
the Bible under their microscopes for over a century, but they
have not been able to restore the life that they destroyed by their
dissection. If it was left to each man to discover the key to
the Bible on his own account, he would have to be prepared to
learn a vast number of sciences and their application, digest
whole libraries of learned works, master the oriental languages
and conduct his own archaeological research. If he were a
genius he might eventually arrive at a few probabilities and a
lot more imponderables. The Bible is a whole world, where
every question has two sides. Its written word cannot be anything but ambiguous. The letter of itself can only bring death
to faith. It is the Spirit that brings life.

The rôle of Tradition is precisely to perpetuate that Spirit and
give life to the letter. It answers a profound human need. God
has thought fit to offer the Word of life to man, but not to let
it go the way of all words. God has spoken his Word to men
of all times, but not to let it rot in the parchment of a literature
doomed to die. God has entered our world, but not to let himself be theoretically discovered for the first time by a handful
of scholars of the sixteenth or twentieth century. The Word of
God must effect what it signifies, and therefore must be infallible and accessible to all men of good will. It comes to them
in the Spirit in which God utters his divine Word.

SOME people think that Tradition was born after Scripture.
The truth is that they were born together. The moment revelation began there was need for Tradition to play its life-giving
rôle. From the beginning, Tradition watched over Scripture
and fostered its growth. It is the progress of Tradition that
Scripture captures in black and white. Throughout the ages
one Spirit has given life to the written body and the living soul.
One and the same virginal womb, fertilized by this Spirit, has
conceived the seed of this body and developed its soul. It was
the constant interplay of living Tradition and its written record
that assured the birth, growth and final flowering of the first
incarnation of the revealed Word.

In the nature of things Tradition did not cease when once Scripture was completed, but continued to guarantee its transmission. The letter which until now had supported the life still needed that life if it were not to become a dead letter. Unless the living Spirit ensured its transmission, it could not live. That same Spirit which first gave life to Israel's written revelation must prosper that life in a new and wider Israel. So it is that the Spirit ensures the fruitfulness of the Bible down the ages by living Tradition. Scripture, Tradition and the Spirit: it is these three that make up revelation.

There are then two stages in the relationship between the Bible and Tradition. For the birth and growth of revelation, it was the Spirit's rôle to act on the living Tradition in such a way that it was gradually crystallized into Scripture. When revelation was complete in its written form, it was the Spirit's rôle to interpret it and continue to give it life by Tradition. Historically the emphasis has shifted but it is the same Spirit that has watched over all.

The Bible and the Church

O N E further element is necessary if the Bible is to transmit faith—the Church. What the written word is to Tradition the Church is to the Spirit. The Bible informed by Tradition is the living body of the Word pre-incarnate; the Church made fruitful by the Spirit is its mother. In order to become flesh, the divine Word had to be conceived in a human body. Only a visible and living society could serve as the womb in which God could generate his Son under the action of the Spirit. The Spirit acts only in the Church. By his action the Church becomes the bride of God and mother of his Word.

Absolutely speaking, the Church was not born after Christ. She came into existence with Abraham, and for two thousand years prepared to give the incarnate Word to the world. After her labour she did not desert the Child she had carried in her womb. The mystery of the incarnation did not come to an end with the death of the last Apostle, but continues down the centuries, until man is brought whole and entire, socially and individually, into the rhythm of the life of God's Son.

At every stage of his life the individual can achieve his end only as a member of society. Similarly he is put into God's plan only as a member of a society big enough to enable him to escape the narrow limits of his own mind. By the same token, the divine plan does not treat him as an individual, isolated from the other members of the social and mystical body in which the life of the incarnate Word is contained. The Church is infinitely more than the necessary passport which permits a man to make contact with the divine will. She is the mother of the mystical body of Christ, with one Spirit and one Thought. This analogy is the source of the remarkable veneration which Christianity has always given to Mary, the mother of Christ, from its very beginnings (cf. the Fourth Gospel and the Apocalypse). Mary is the symbol of the Church which, at the messianic marriage feast, re-echoes the prayer she made at Cana. At the request of his mother, the Word of God changes the water of the Letter into the wine of the Spirit, even though his hour has not yet come.

The Christian finds his faith not in the written word as such but in the living Tradition of the Church and its infallible Spirit. To search for the divine message in the letter alone, without any assistance, is like trying to trace a missing person from a pre-natal X-ray and a photograph taken on his first birthday. The letter of Scripture is a recorded image of the incarnate Word in its gestation and birth. Fixed in form, its picture of the Word must inevitably be an obsolete one, because the Word lives on, unceasingly adapting itself to its human audience and evolving its own inner life. A present picture of the incarnate Word can only be given by the Church of the present, through her Tradition in the Spirit.

IF THIS is so, what further use is there for the Bible? If we can have the message of the Bible direct from the Church in a way we can assimilate, what is the point of searching for it in these outmoded pages? The objection is common enough, and puts its finger on the very heart of the problem, the mystery of revelation. If the Bible without the Church is a body without a soul, then the Church without the Bible is a soul without its body. In normal circumstances, one cannot live without the other. As man risen from the dead, Christ can no longer be separated from his body; as the Word incarnate, he is tied for ever to his verbal expression. The Word of God was given us by the Spirit in human words; the Spirit can only put us in contact with that Word through these human words. Without Tradition there is no Bible; without the Bible there is no Tradition. Without the informing Spirit of the Church, the letter of the Bible is dead—but what has the Church to inform if she no longer has the letter? Basically, Tradition means the inspired and living interpretation of Scripture by the Church. To understand this better we must distinguish two stages in the Church's dispensation of revealed truth.

In the first of these stages, the Church catechizes her newborn children, teaching them the "rudiments of faith", as St. Paul calls it. Here she is careful to suit her teaching to the weak and undeveloped capacity of her children, using words which they can easily digest. St. Paul calls this their "milk". The strong wine of the Scriptures would be too heady for such children.

There is no attempt by the Church to keep the Scriptures from them: her catechism is in fact the letter of the Bible in modern dress. The Bible's own key-words are used so that their minds may be familiarized with it. Before the liturgical decline, which began in the thirteenth century and has become more and more marked since the sixteenth, the Church was bolder still. Her lenten liturgy is simply a course of biblical instruction for catechumens, of which the lessons of Easter Night are a rich and profound synthesis. The recent restoration of this climax of the Christian year, and participation in it by the faithful, have given proof of the interest and the fervour that can be aroused when the Church's catechism is drawn directly from the Bible. The Bible was written by ordinary people for ordinary people, and experience shows that its concrete way of putting the most difficult things has more compelling force in its liturgical setting than the clearest of theological abstractions.

At this first stage, however, the *letter* of the Bible in its fullness is not essential to the individual. In fact much harm could result from its being sown in unprepared soil. The old adage normally applied to the Eucharist: "Holy things for holy people" could be applied equally to the pre-incarnate Word of Scripture. Before a man can take the wine of Scripture and eat the bread of angels he needs to pass through the initiation ceremony of baptism. The same *disciplina arcani* protects both Eucharist and Bible. For both, the Christian is prepared by receiving the rudiments of faith in biblical language, suitably adapted and clothed in set formulas. The pity is that so many Christians go no further. As far as the Bible is concerned they remain catechumens.

We said above that the Bible was not altogether necessary at this early stage of instruction in the faith. For the deepening of that faith into love it is absolutely essential. This is the second stage in the Church's dispensation of revealed truth, and it is so important that it will require emphasis and fuller treatment. The rudimentary knowledge of the faith must burgeon into a living faith, to become an experience, an " epignosis " or super-knowledge as St. Paul calls it. At this level, the Bible and the Eucharist together are the two most indispensable gifts the Church has to offer. We need the Bible not to discover faith but to recover it, not to fix our eyes on God but our hearts in him.

The Bible, Source of Living Faith

THE Bible's unquestioned power to deepen the faith of the Christian cannot altogether be explained by the Spirit which the Tradition of the Church brings to the letter. The full reason lies in the fact that the Bible was itself the original living experience of faith. The actual experience of receiving the Word of God for the first time, under the impulse of the Spirit, was so rich and pregnant that it contained whatever future experiences were to follow. These were but a re-birth of the original experience, the actualization of an original potency. In this sense the Bible goes beyond the horizon of those for whom it was written, and reaches out through them to Christians of all time. True Christian life must always be the personal recapture of that initial experience.

That the Spirit should thus give himself entirely to be the germ of the Word incarnate in the Bible follows a law of human psychology. The history of any movement, religious, philosophical, political or intellectual, and the life of any social or family group, gives clear evidence that they are at their

most vital in their beginnings. Their pristine energy and richness is spent with the progress of time. Age may widen their
scope, but even this springs from the original impulse. When
growth and old age impose their inevitable crisis on a movement, when legalism and the wear and tear of fatigue begin to
threaten its continued existence, then it is that men go back to
the humble beginnings to draw new life as from a fountain head.
A body is strong and vital only if it can renew itself by contact
with its origins. It is precisely in this sense that Scripture, vivi-
fied by Tradition, is the continual source of the Church's faith,
the living mirror to which she must return to see how she compares with her beginnings. "Back to the primitive Church"
has undoubtedly been the slogan of all revolts, but it has always
been the watchword of renewal too. It is true that we cannot
neglect our living evolution and try to find our way back via
archaeology and theory, any more than the grown man Nico-
demus could enter a second time into his mother's womb. But
the Church can return to the living source of her Tradition, to
find there the renewal of her youth and the energy for fresh
advance.

It is the remarkable privilege of Christians that through the
Church they can go back to the very source of their life—the
Eucharist where they are nourished by the Spirit of the incarnate Word, and the Scriptures where they are fed by the Spirit
which vivifies the Word of God. No other unit of society has
such a facility for renewal. A husband and wife who have lost
the first fervour of their love may try to recapture it by going
back over the days of their courtship, but they do no more than
stir the dying embers. A dying nation may look back on its
past glory but it cannot put the clock back one hour. The
Church alone can achieve this miracle of rejuvenation, because
she never loses contact with the Spirit which quickened the
Word of the Father when it became incarnate. Like any other
society, the Church has her charter of foundation. Unlike any
other society she has, in the invisible presence of the Spirit, the
power that inspired the written Word and continues to give life
to her Tradition. The Christian who reads his Bible in the
Church's Tradition possesses not merely the words of Scripture
but the Spirit that inspired them. He is united to the sacred
writer not only through his words and ideas, but through his

spirit, whereby he becomes one with him in the unity of the Holy Spirit.

I F W E look at the Bible in this way, then the whole of Christian theology is transformed. Faith has two stages of birth, and two stages of growth. At the level of technical or scientific theology, where faith must be systematically inventoried and analysed, the Bible is merely the first witness called. But faith cannot be confined to this rudimentary level. Faith is the seed of a learning that must live and be lived. It moulds man after its own image, seeking to develop his conscience, to re-awaken its echoes, to lay open its hidden places, and to achieve the final loving abandonment to the incarnate Word. At this deeper level, which is theology properly so called, or sapiential theology, the Bible has a more vital rôle to play. It no longer merely supplies the object of faith or even its authentic interpretation; here it conforms the believing subject to the object of his belief and forges an affinity between them. Here it lies at the very heart of the matter by supplying a power which is essentially personal, transcendent, and divine: the Spirit.

The Spirit inspired the written word; he inspires the Tradition which quickens the letter; he inspires the Church which preserves that Tradition; he inspires the Christian who receives his faith from the Church; he inspires all human incarnations of the eternal Word of God; he inspires the specifically Christian theology which, based on the Bible and by means of Tradition, develops and hands down the living experience of the incarnation of God's Son. Such is the litany of the various manifestations of the Spirit's inspiration. They are not all of the same order but all come from the same source, which is the Spirit that guards the life of the Church.

What we have said will give some hint of the complex affinities between the Bible and Tradition, Faith and the Church, the Spirit and the Word. Like the Eucharist, the Bible is the "mystery of faith". It is the mystery of death because in putting itself between man and the divine gift it demands a faith that is the death of human pride. It is the mystery of resurrection because in demanding this submission it communicates a faith which is a foretaste of the experience of God. It is the mystery of faith because its depths will never be sounded by

Q

the plumb-line of human wisdom. It is the mystery of faith because it enlightens the eyes which are not closed to the divine Light. It is the mystery of living faith because it demands the mortification of reason's self-sufficiency so that it may be born again to the life-giving Word of God. In short, it is the mystery of the death and resurrection of Christ. He who would accept the Bible must accept the death and resurrection of Christ, the seed of which is contained in the very act of incarnation. To read the Bible means more than the intellectual appreciation of its message; it means the commitment of self.

In this full, spiritual, "ecclesial", faith-inspired and living sense, the understanding of the Bible could be called "total" theology, which is the recapturing of the living experience of faith. Such was the theology of the Fathers, who regarded their own writings as nothing but commentaries on the Bible. Admittedly, to some extent such theology goes beyond the Bible by developing its themes and bringing them to a synthesis. Yet it remains within its orbit, since it seeks not to depart from the faith but only to deepen it.

Above all, such theology is aware that in trying to express the fact of the original experience it may well enlarge certain aspects of it but it will never be able to reproduce its richness. A theology that takes its inspiration from the Bible cannot but be acutely aware of Scripture's living mystery, and, like Scripture itself, yearn for the final vision.

IV

THE BIBLE AND LIFE

The orientation necessary for living from the Bible; the Bible a book of doctrine, not a manual of devotions; a message of love, not a dogmatic treatise; a book for meditation, not a collection of recipes; a source of prayer, not a collection of prayers.

IN SEEING how the Bible affects faith we have equivalently seen how it affects life, because it is not merely an intellectual faith that the Bible imparts, but a faith which gives life as it is lived. The reader might easily expect to find in the Bible a rule of life neatly codified in a set of moral maxims. He will be sadly disappointed. In fact he will get no help at all from the Bible unless he makes a constant effort to re-discover the mentality in which the Word of God became incarnate. It is a feature of our western outlook to draw a sharp distinction between intellectual and moral activity. With us, the head and the heart belong to two different worlds. Where the head can always explain everything with logic, clarity and precision, the heart has reasons which have nothing to do with reason. This dichotomy has had the effect of stunting the natural inter-play of mind and will. Ever since the sixteenth century and more so since the eighteenth, the tendency has been to range the two side by side, to produce a smug rationalism (or a disillusioned scepticism) on the one hand, and a sentimental uneasiness on the other. Thought does not influence the emotions, nor does the heart give any encouragement to the head.

The dichotomy has had its effect on the Christian mind. Dogmatic and moral theology have come to be regarded as distinct if not contrary sciences. The bonds that tie faith to charity are not always so clear as they might be. In fact many of the faithful seem to think that Christianity means subscribing to a code of abstract propositions, and putting into practice a distinct and separate code of obligations. The Bible is approached from these two distinct points of view: from the intellectual angle it is a text book reserved for experts; from the religious angle it is a book of piety. In practice, it is either studied or meditated on. A man can spend hours explaining that *Ego principium qui loquor vobis* (John 8:25) is the Vulgate's mistranslation of the Greek " I have told you from the beginning ", after having spent his morning meditation savouring the pious interpretation " I am the Beginning who speaks to you ", with prelude, three-points and spiritual nosegay. There are even some who have glorified this split mentality into a principle, and no longer seek truth from the Bible, but only subjective " experiences " or pious " attitudes of soul ".

Such an approach to the Bible can never be too strongly discouraged, for it can only bring disappointment, and might even lead to error. Fortunately the Bible is its own best advocate in this regard, since it is so frequently disedifying. Along with the writings of the Fathers, it refuses to be classified as "spiritual", "ascetical" or "mystical" literature. To talk about "the spiritual life according to the Bible" is nonsense. There is no spiritual life in the Bible in the sense in which the word is used to-day. The spiritual life which permeates the book through and through is on a deeper level, where it is no longer distinct from either dogma or morals, from either technical study or living experience, from either mind or heart, from either faith or charity, from either the Word or the Spirit.

We cannot begin to live from the Bible until we have become acclimatized to its atmosphere. The Bible does not divide life into compartments as we do: it will have all or nothing. It is the Word of God, the selfsame Word that creates us for our high destiny and answers the cry that it arouses in us. As a work of God, it bears the divine hallmark of unity and simplicity. Because it is matter and Spirit, it speaks to the whole man, and will have nothing to do with artificial divisions. Since its aim is to refashion us in the image of God, it refuses to be reduced to our measure, and demands of us the renunciation of our ways of thought. If we are to understand its message we must be prepared to accept it in the terms chosen by God, and not try to force it into our own mould. Its demand for faith is a demand for the death of our intellect; and its desire to gather our life into the rhythm of its own is a demand for the death of our judgment and feelings.

ABOVE all else, let it be clear that the Bible is not a manual of devotion, but a book of doctrine. It knows nothing of our need for personal stimuli, "ardent considerations" and "ejaculations". The only prompting it knows is that of truth, the only love it feels is that which lies at the heart of truth. It is the Word of life *because* it is the Word of truth, and for no other reason. Because it instinctively separates the false from the true, it is unflinchingly "intellectual". It is a teaching, a statement that does not argue, a message of light. It is dogmatically dogmatic. It abhors falsehood and will brook no compromise. It is intolerant insofar as it is identified with the truth of God himself. It proclaims the crusade of eternal Light against darkness, of Truth against the father of lies. It is the infinitely truthful Word of God, claiming acknowledgment and demanding adoration.

And yet it is not a dogmatic treatise in the abstract, but a message of love. Its truth is precise enough to give short shrift to any form of scepticism, but it is no mere compendium of lifeless formulas, still less an intellectual exercise in abstract propositions. Its strength is the strength of life, and its precision the fruit of its profundity. Its clarity is that of something which is alive and knows its power and purpose. Its truth is the truth of life, which must be translated into act and can only be known when it is acted upon. It springs from love and leads to love. Its whole purpose is to commit the will to truth, to make it "do the truth" (1 John 1:6) and "complete faith in love" (Gal. 5:6).

This does not mean that it is to be treated as a thesaurus of practical advice. There is no quick solution to be found here: the Bible requires patience. The man who likes his religion in concentrated form, to be taken like a vitamin pill during his half-hour of meditation, will not feel at all happy when he is faced with the stories of the Patriarchs and the genealogies of the book of Chronicles. St. Paul will bewilder him and the high flights of St. John will be beyond him. For the layman there is nothing obvious which he can take to the office with him, for the priest no ready solution to all those matrimonial tangles waiting for his advice. On that level the Bible has nothing to offer. The maxims of the sapiential books and the moral uplift of the Gospels might give him something to go on, but he can find that more accessible in the *Imitation* or the *Spiritual Exercises*. He may be tempted at times to bend the inspired text to suit his needs and make it conform to the mould of these spiritual classics. He may even try to force it into less worthy moulds. . . . The Bible asks a great deal more than this because it is far deeper and far more divine. It does not yield all its secrets at a single reading, but yields only to those who surrender themselves. It is not out of place to point out here that those who advocate a return to the allegorical interpretation of the Bible are sometimes guilty of neglecting this demand of the Bible for mortification and humility. In spite of the sound theology on which they base their claim, their exegesis is often a barely disguised form of private interpretation. The Bible demands that it be received as God made it, in the humility of the letter, otherwise it will remain a closed book.

When Christ said " Search the Scriptures ", he was not giving us leave to let our imaginations run riot, but inviting us to die, and exhorting us to rid ourselves of prejudice, narrow-mindedness and private judgment. It was an invitation to technical study and loving contemplation, to textual criticism and theological reflection, to philological investigation and profound faith. All these human approaches must be consecrated and put at the disposal of the Spirit.

Finally, the Bible is not a treatise on prayer; it *is* prayer. Apart from the formal prayers it contains, it is prayer in its own right, because it is truth in love, the revelation of the Son through the inspiration of the Spirit. The whole point of becoming attuned to the Bible by long and humble familiarity is to reach out beyond technique and understanding (without ever abandoning them), and to be taken up into the " groaning of the Spirit ". The old monks knew no other prayer book, and the prayer of the Church herself is a network of biblical texts. It must be the aim of all critical, intellectual and faith-inspired reading of the Bible to burgeon into the sapiential reading, in which all knowledge and love are surpassed and the son finally embraces his Father.

SUCH an achievement will never be within the reach of anyone who neglects the theandric make-up of the Bible. There is only one right way to read the Bible, and that is to receive the truth as God has given it. It is at the very heart of this human striving that contact is made with God. It is in the actual effort of technical study that the believer is made aware of the divine truth which enlightens his mind and disposes his will to the action of the Spirit. Throughout this long and patient labour the love in his soul grows deeper and deeper, until the book is put aside and the soul is consumed with the breathtaking vision of God. Without this patient concern to penetrate the humanity of the Bible, it will remain a closed book. Unless we become familiar with the atmosphere of the Bible, even the Gospel will not furnish us with practical help, even the Psalms and the *Pater* will not stir up our hearts and make them beat in time with God. We cannot pray the Psalms unless we know how to pray the whole Bible. The listlessness with which many priests say their office is not entirely the fault of the Vulgate Latin, which admittedly is far from perfect. A new version, even a vernacular one, will not help them to pray in the right liturgical spirit until they have acquired a deep familiarity with the whole of Scripture.

To conclude, what we must look for in the Bible is a Light and a Spirit. We must not exaggerate either its human or its divine element. It does not demand intellectual technique, nor does it provide a set of rules for Christian living. Intellectual effort is required, but this does not make it into a text book of science or history. Its claim is to lead us to divine truth, not to be the immediate source of faith, still less to be the only sacrament of our return to God. It takes its place in the living society which is the Church, alongside the Eucharist, at the very heart of the mystery of incarnation and redemption. It does not implant these mysteries in us, but rather encourages their roots to strike deeper, their flower to grow and their fruit to ripen. The Bible gives us a foretaste of what is to come. By its means the Church opens the mind of her children to re-discover the light of the incarnate Word, and their souls to receive the abundant life of his Spirit of love.

CHAPTER IX

CHRISTIAN INTERPRETATION

EVERYTHING that is written about the nature, content and value of the Bible should have only one purpose, to teach us how to read it. So far, we have dealt with its complex divine and human origin. We saw that the apparent duality is resolved by acknowledging the theandric nature of its inspiration. A close examination of this principle showed us precisely what to look for when we read the Bible. We shall find that the same principle and the same facts must guide us in dealing with the more delicate and all-important problem of the Bible's meaning and interpretation.

I

THE ATMOSPHERE OF BIBLE READING

Personal atmosphere of understanding in faith and of commitment through charity; social atmosphere in the spirit of the liturgy and of the Fathers of the Church.

ALL that we have so far said in this book has aimed at convincing the reader that mere ideas, however exact they may be, are not sufficient preparation for reading the Bible. A certain atmosphere and a personal attitude are essential if we are to penetrate its living content.

The Word of God is a living Word. It can be heard only by an attentive ear.

The atmosphere of which we speak is made up of many elements. On the personal level, all the human faculties must be brought to bear—the reason, the will, the imagination and the heart. In our reading of the Bible we must be able to say "This is the best of me". On the social level, the Church must form the constant background to our effort, and keep us in contact, across time and space, with the full life of the Spirit. On both levels, personal and social, there must be faith and charity, because human virtues are authentic only if they are the flowering in nature of that movement towards God which grace initiates at the very root of man's being. Without that supernatural impulse they can never be anything but aimless and stunted habits of mind. Only faith enlivens the intellect, only love energizes the will. Before all else, we must recognize the supernatural character of Bible reading, on every level. Even when it is read from a merely critical or philogical angle, this attitude is essential if biblical study is to be something more than the study of a profane author.

F A I T H then is the root and résumé of all those *dispositions of mind* required for reading the Bible. Even before he takes up his Bible, the reader must believe in its divine content which is Christ, in the Church which gives him this content, and in the Spirit which quickens the letter and sanctifies the Church. He must believe that in the Bible it is God who speaks to him through the Church. There the Son of God is revealed in the life-giving breath of the Spirit. To know such a God the reader must be silent; to be moved by such a Spirit he must put aside his private judgment. Christianity is founded on the law of death, and the primary condition of all communion with God is faith. The Word of God can enter only where pride has renounced its claim to set up its own criterion of truth. At every step of biblical study there must be a humble submission to truth in all its forms. The mind, which is so fond of its own imaginings, must submit and face reality.

Faith is sometimes looked upon as a mere handrail, designed to keep the believer's free investigations within limits. Such a view makes a mockery of faith, as if it were something the mind cannot penetrate. A similar mistake is made, but in the opposite direction, when the articles of faith are treated as so many hard and fast canons, corollaries and conclusions to which all texts and facts must conform. This also is a parody of faith. Faith is an attitude, a profound and flexible driving force which directs without bludgeoning, enlightens without dazzling, and judges without prejudicing. Its aim is to educe and foster the potentialities of the human mind, not to supplant them.

The man of faith is a *humble* man because he acknowledges the majesty of God and his own nothingness. He is resigned to the fact that he cannot understand everything at once, and that there are things which must remain in the shadow of darkness. By the same token he is an *enlightened* man, completely confident in God's truth. He knows that the mind of man was created by God to be the gateway through which eternal truth can enter into him. He is *strong* in this knowledge and fearless. The most embarrassing facts do not disconcert him because he knows that there is a solution, even if he cannot find it at the moment. In fact apparent conflict only serves to strengthen and purify his faith by stripping his mind of encumbrances. He learns to bow to the grandeur of the mysteries of God and to admit his own inadequacy. His horizon is widened, and he becomes a realist. He learns prudence because he learns to know his own weakness. He becomes at the same time bold and daring, because he is not afraid of being found in the wrong. Rather than manipulate the smallest detail of a truth of faith or reason, he will suspend judgment. Faith then is the best school for learning clear-sightedness and *common sense*. Along with simple and bold humility, common sense is perhaps faith's most precious gift. Certainly it is faith's most indispensable contribution to the understanding of the Bible. Common sense is the right appreciation of reality, and nothing is more real than faith. It preserves a man from the scruples of the faint-hearted and the extravagances of the rationalist. Many of the exegetes of the nineteenth century lacked common sense as much as they lacked faith. Having neither, their strenuous labours produced a great deal of nonsense.

THESE dispositions of mind must be accompanied by the proper *dispositions of will*. First and foremost faith is an act of abandonment: it is the beginning and the end of *love*. Intellectual pride cannot be considered fully dead unless self-will dies too. There can be no sincere search for truth unless the will has agreed to act on the truth when it is found, even at the price of crucifixion. The Word of God can dwell in the mind only if his Spirit breaks down the barrier of self-will. True faith requires charity, as true charity requires faith. The Son of God is the source of the Father's Spirit, but the Spirit, in his turn, is the only gateway to the Son's life in his Father.

Intellect and will, mind and heart, faith and charity, they coalesce and enrich each other through the Son in the Spirit, to form the background for a right understanding of the Bible. First of all they must die. Mutually they must strip each other of the demand for autonomy until they stand naked in their need for the light of God's Son, crying out for the love of his Spirit. They can do this only because together they have already heard God's call. Under the impact of revelation the will is stirred to action. Filled with a great surging of the Spirit's love, it throws open to the mind the whole realm of the Word's affinity. The fullness of truth is born of love. Love itself is aroused by the first glimpse of truth, but this glimpse is made possible only by the good will in which the self hears the quiet voice of the Father and agrees to die.

True charity, active charity, submits the will to the Spirit in the same way that faith submits the mind to the Son. The Bible reveals God to us in his incarnate Word: we embrace such revelation by faith. The Bible offers this revelation through the inspiration of the Spirit: we open our hearts to this inspiration by charity. The Spirit shows us the way to the Son. There are powers in the mind which technology and intellectual training cannot reach. Only love can arouse them, and it is this love of God's Son, in which the Spirit lifts up our hearts to the Word of the Father, that the Bible asks of us. To find Christ in the Bible we must be prepared to search for him and want him with as much longing as we wait for his Coming. Love of the Bible is not a private affair or a particular brand of spirituality. It is part of supernatural charity. The object of both is the same —the incarnate Word of the Father; they spring from the same source—the Spirit of the Son of God.

It follows that this kind of love is much more than a sentimental feeling; like supernatural charity it commits the whole will. It is a love that *perseveres*, that does not give in because the preparatory studies are long or because the first steps must be hesitant. It is *patient*, because it knows that God reveals himself slowly, as the Spirit guides the soul step by step. It is a *detached* love, because it respects the infinite liberty of God and knows that he chooses for each the means he judges best. It is a *humble* love, because true love accepts everything about the beloved, the best and the worst. In loving someone, we must love body and soul. No one truly loves the Bible if he has no taste for the detailed study of its letter, or if he is put off by historical or textual criticism. Above all, this love must spring from a *pure heart*. "Blessed are the pure in heart for they shall see God". How often the Fathers insisted on this quality as the *sine qua non* of Bible reading. The Bible will only reveal itself to eyes that are unclouded. In this earthen vessel is contained the light of God, and eyes that are blurred will have no power to penetrate it.

FINALLY we must mention the *social conditions* which form the context for these moral and intellectual requirements. The Bible is directed to mankind as a whole, and therefore must be read in its proper *social* environment, which is the living Church. This environment was a long time forming. It began with the Fathers, and continues in the liturgy, the authentic framework of the Church's life. There the spirit of the Fathers is preserved, and the revelation of the Bible is enshrined. There continuity with the past is a *living reality*, for the liturgy is no artificial re-enactment of the past. It actuates the faith and charity of the Christian by extending throughout time the mystery of the incarnation of God's Son through the sanctification of the Spirit. At its centre lies the Eucharist, without which it is meaningless. But the Spirit who formed the body of Christ in the Eucharist also formed the body of the Scriptures, where the Word of God is expressed under the species of human words. It is this supernatural fact, far more than the fact that it is done as a communal act, that gives the liturgical reading of the Bible its efficacy. The pity of it is that so often the reading is no more than a perfunctory rubric. Surely the liturgy ought to mean that the one Spirit, who inspired the Bible and still inspires the Church, is offering the written Word as food for man's spirit, to prepare him for the Eucharistic Word as food for his body. The two are inseparable. The Church is Christ's body, and shares not only his risen life in the Eucharist but also his thought in the Bible. In short, the Bible is the verbal body of Christ, the Eucharist his fleshly body, and the Church his mystical body. All these incarnations of the Son of God are made one reality in the liturgy, where the Spirit concentrates his life-giving power to unite the Christian, whole and entire, to Christ. The Mass is truly the synthesis of the Christian mystery and eternal life.

It will be seen that the Bible is tied to the liturgy in the same way as it is tied to the *Fathers of the Church*. In both the liturgy and the Fathers it is the spirit that we must look for, not detailed interpretations or principles of exegesis. To base an argument on the mere unanimity of the Fathers and the liturgy would be pointless; to analyse their exegesis literally will give no true idea of their spirit. This is the rock upon which a number of allegorists have foundered. They have gone back to the outmoded methods of the Fathers and have entirely neglected their general biblical attitude—the one thing that gives patristic literature its lasting value. Strictly speaking there is no " patristic " or " liturgical " method of exegesis, and to set it up as something opposed to or different from the historical scientific method is to talk nonsense. Every one of the Fathers had his own method. Some were good, some were bad, many have been superseded by progress in technique. But what has not been superseded is their spirit, their Christian attitude towards biblical revelation, and the foundations which they laid of a truly Christian science of interpretation. This is what we have tried to present in the chapter on the Word of God, though we have translated it into scientific language.

To be faithful to patristic and liturgical tradition does not mean, as some imagine, that we must return to rabbinic exegesis or the neo-platonic artificialities of the school of Alexandria. Nor does it mean that we must reject the scientific and theological progress that has been made since the time of the Fathers. A return to the past, if it is to have any value, must be inspired by the fact that the present needs a new lease of life. In this case the present means modern exegesis with all its technical perfection and, it must be said, its relics of rationalism. The past we look to for inspiration is not the outmoded technique of the Fathers, but their attitude.

This attitude could very well give modern technique its Christian baptism. First and foremost it is an attitude of *complete faith*, which believes in the text and loves it. It is consequently a *sapiential* attitude (" liturgical " and " scientific " fans alike fail to understand this) where the intellect yields to love and the text is lived and not simply read. In this, the patristic mentality is a natural continuation of the Bible's Semitic mentality. In this alone, the Fathers and the liturgy conform more closely to the inner meaning of Scripture than the subtlest allegorical or scientific exegesis of to-day. Both are careful to preserve the true sense of symbolism and mystery which science has neglected and allegory has reduced to something merely mechanical. The Fathers were able to fuse their " prejudice " of faith with this sapiential outlook, and it is this that enabled them to find in the Bible those profound " *constants* " which our science must make into the basis of a true interpretation. In this context, the liturgy of Easter, if it is enacted in a spirit of faith and not mere aestheticism, is a striking interpretation of the biblical message, not only because of the richness of its detail, but because the very purpose of that detail is to plunge the newly-made Christian, heart and mind, soul and body, into the mystery of Christianity.

The present day discussion of the spiritual interpretation of the Bible will come to a dead end if people continue to state the problem in terms of " either the Fathers or Science, either the liturgy or technology ". If people will force the language of the Bible into the same mould as its liturgical or patristic paraphrase, then they run the risk of losing the finer points of the Church's traditional thought, and of compromising the value of the Bible. It is essential to see them both as simply different expressions of the one living Spirit and the one Word of God. They are not meant to exclude each other, nor to be juxtaposed. There is only one way of reading the Bible, and it is that in which the Fathers would have read it if they had modern means at their disposal. What we must do is to marry the unalterable legacy of the past to the undoubted gains of the present. We must search out the revealed truth with all our mind and heart, in its traditional milieu which is the Church, and in the living light of faith.

II

THE MEANING OF THE BIBLE

Variety of meanings in the Bible; ambiguity of the words "spiritual" and "literal"; the Bible's inspired meaning is one because God assumes responsibility for the sacred writer; two perspectives because revelation is inserted into an evolving history; the full sense seen in the light of the historical and typical points of view; related to parable more than to allegory.

IN DEALING with the liturgy and the Fathers we touched on the important question of the meaning of Scripture. It is a problem age-old and forever new. Patrologists who are now reading the Fathers with such enthusiasm are amazed at the number of different meanings they derived from the Bible. They have tried to classify these different approaches. To the well known literal, allegorical and accommodated senses, they have added moral, typical, anagogical, mystical, figurative, and a host of others. They can all be reduced simply and adequately to the "literal" and the "spiritual" sense.

Ambiguous Terms

THESE terms can be very misleading unless we are clear what we mean by them. There is difficulty over the word "spiritual" because it is nowadays applied to different things. It is used not only for the "typical" sense properly so called, but also for a host of subjective pious interpretations. On the whole it generally has a "pious" connotation. A sense is called "spiritual" if it nourishes spiritual life. It is distinguished from the aridity that is expected of scientific exegesis. The word has taken on a modern flavour, and now denotes the subjective affective life of the spirit, with special reference to religion. It is almost the opposite of "intellectual".

To say that this word has the authority of the Fathers to support it can only lead to confusion. "Spiritual" with them does not mean the world of the spirit or of "religious feeling" as opposed to the world of matter or of reason without religion. To denote that spiritual world they used the term "psychic". By "spiritual" they understood what the Bible understands, namely divine and objectively transcendent. Its opposite is "carnal", that which is merely human. It signifies the plane of reality and fullness upon which God moves, the world of "Spirit and Truth", as distinct from the earthly world of phenomena and sensible symbols. There is no conflict between these two worlds except when "flesh and blood" rise up against the Spirit and seek to be independent, thus becoming caricatures of the higher life to which they are meant to lead. The "carnal" world of phenomena was designed to be a support, a tangible expression, an introduction to the "spiritual" world which lies beyond it. This it can achieve only if a higher principle intervenes to begin the process. If this world is to lead to the world of God, the Spirit must move first. "Flesh and blood has not revealed this to you, but the Father who is in heaven" (Mt. 16:17). *For the Fathers, "spiritual" exegesis means the discovery of the profound objective meaning of a text, in the light of the complete economy of salvation.* It starts off from "literal" exegesis, because its aim is to elucidate, with faith as guide, the full value of the writer's obvious meaning. There is nothing subjective, moralizing or pietistic about such exegesis. On the contrary it is entirely objective, doctrinal and didactic. If they were not such barbarisms, the terms "pneumatic" and "somatic" could profitably replace the words "spiritual" and "literal", and all misunderstanding would be avoided. Whatever we call them, the distinction between literal and spiritual lies not in their subjective application (scientific versus devout) but in their objective content, in one case purely human, and in the other illuminated by faith.

The term "literal" likewise causes confusion. Often it is taken to signify the face value of the words. What it really means is the sense that the author intends the words to have, according to the accepted rules of the literary forms in his particular milieu. The literal sense can therefore be moral, typical, figurative, allegorical, or mythical, according to the author's intention. The literal sense of Ecclesiasticus, for example, is moral. That of the fourth Gospel is historical and typical, and that of the Apocalypse is allegorical. Consequently there is never more than one literal sense, although it can take a number of forms according to the writer's intention to express his thought on various levels. To see this we have only to examine St. John's Gospel. There, minute details, besides having a material historical reference, have also a psychological value (they set the stage for a religious interpretation of this history), an allegorical value (they are symbols for the doctrine), and a typical value (they go beyond immediate events and suggest the answer to the doctrinal problems which Christians of all time will have to face). To a lesser degree the Synoptic Gospels do the same. Their intention is to record the life of Christ, but they have a moral and didactic value too. Almost any book of the Bible will show the many forms which the literal sense can take.

The One Meaning

THE accommodated, allegorical and moral senses of the Bible give rise to further ambiguities. In the first place we must be absolutely clear about the fundamental principle which governs any attempt to determine the meaning of the Bible. It is an obvious principle, but it is easily misunderstood. It is misunderstood, for example, when the whole of patristic exegesis is thought to be in opposition to the literal sense. In fact, the Fathers can be appealed to only to the degree in which they intend to give the authentic interpretation of Scripture. When they are merely using Scripture as language, no argument can be taken from them. Confusion on this point could endanger the success of the modern return to the Bible, because it obscures the fundamental principle that the only meaning of a book is the meaning its author intended it to have. The meaning of the Bible is the meaning God intended it to have when he inspired the sacred writer. We may discuss the extent, the import and the depth of that meaning, and the exegete may (in fact must) formulate the laws which enable us to recognize this intention of God. But the only purpose, interest and value of the Bible lies in the objective meaning which God put into it. Whatever cannot be included under this cannot be included in the meaning of the Bible, nor does it share the super-

R

natural value given to the Bible by the inspiration of the Spirit.

In insisting on the absolute sense, we do not intend to condemn the use of an accommodated or allegorical sense. Still less are we saying that the Bible must not have its moral application. We have already hinted many times that accommodation is perfectly legitimate where it is the natural expression of a Christian mentality that is moulded in biblical terms and thoughts. But there is no real accommodated *sense* in the Bible. By definition accommodation means using biblical terms in a way foreign to their objective and divinely intended content. Where accommodation strictly so called is used (it is not often found), the Bible is simply language and not thought.

Much the same may be said of the moral use of the Bible, where the ethical application is outside the scope of God's intention. A mind rightly disposed could gain subjective profit from what is objectively an immoral book. The Bible too can serve as the starting point for pertinent and salutary thoughts which have nothing whatever to do with the obvious meaning of the text. In this case the text is merely the occasion for human reflections, not the source of divine teaching. Such reflections are in no way a sense of Scripture, nor do they share its divine power. Strictly speaking, the Bible has no moral sense. When it sets out to teach a moral lesson (and it does so on almost every page), then that is its literal sense, intended by God. This does not, of course, mean that a text cannot have a personal application intended by God. Many texts do in fact formulate a moral principle, either directly or (as in a narrative) indirectly, and the reader is meant to apply it to himself. The highly moral portrait of David is an object lesson to every Christian, and this lesson is part of the literal sense of the text, however little the writer was aware of its later application. The lesson is, in fact, objectively present in the purpose of his writing.

To sum up, the literal sense is the Bible's only true sense. This does not mean, as we shall see presently, that there is no room for Christian tradition's double perspective, the somatic and the pneumatic. On the contrary, it demands it. But, before we examine this duality, we need to be very clear about the absolute unity of sense. The two perspectives are based on the one letter of Scripture. A book has only one meaning, the one given it by its author. An author may have several intentions at the same time, but this can never mean that there are several disconnected meanings, one beside the other, as there might be in a cryptogram. Indeed, even a cryptogram has only one real meaning: the others are disguises.

The Two Perspectives

IT MAY be argued that the Bible cannot be treated like other books, because it has two authors, God and man. Surely this dual authorship implies two senses? The objection is not often put in so many words, but it underlies any attempt to establish a spiritual sense that is really distinct from the literal. If what we said of the nature of revelation and inspiration seemed rather drawn out at the time, it was because we had this objection in mind. Now we have only to make a corollary. It is perfectly true that the Bible has two authors, but these two authors act in concert to produce a single work. We tried to show how the two activities come together to give birth to the one sacred book. God's part cannot be isolated from the part played by the writer. Theirs is a joint action which results in one book. Though each operates on his own level and in proper order, the effect depends upon both, and must be attributed entirely to each of them, and to each through the other.

Since inspiration is theandric, the meaning of the Bible must be theandric too. The thought of the Bible is not the liaison of two independent thoughts. It is the undivided thought of God made incarnate in human form. Even less than any other book can the Bible have more than one meaning. There is a necessary agreement, not to say identity, between the human expression and the divine thought, the first inevitably limiting the second. Since God speaks to us in human words, we cannot understand the divine message except within the framework of these words. The divine meaning of the Bible is in exact proportion to the thought of the sacred writer. It has only one meaning, the literal meaning as understood by the human author under inspiration. His thought is nothing but the materialization of God's thought.

Whatever duality there may be, it is not based on the objective reality of the inspired writing. Is is perhaps based on the subjective appreciation of the reader, according as he approaches it either with reason or with faith? Some exegetes, Catholic ones included, would make this distinction the starting point of sane criticism. But insofar as it still presupposes that the divine and human elements of the Bible are separable, the distinction is false. It is true that the Bible is offered to man in a form he can assimilate by his natural powers, and on those grounds it demands what any book demands. Man as such can grasp the human term of God's Word. But in fact this term has no independent existence. Its roots strike far beneath what is merely human, and it can never be fully appreciated by the mind which is not enlightened by faith. There are, then, two sorts of approach to the Bible, one carnal, the other spiritual. The first, having at its disposal the resources of science and criticism, will reach some of the Bible's meaning. But so long as it lacks the direction that faith gives, it must eventually come up against something that it will misunderstand altogether. From this angle too, therefore, there is no real duality in the meaning of the Bible. There are only two senses, of which one is true and the other false. The carnal meaning is not something on which the Christian meaning is superimposed. It is the monstrous result of an arbitrary separation between the human expression and its divine principle. Nor is there any distinction between the Christian meaning and the human expression. The one is simply the full and complete understanding of the other, given by faith. So we conclude once more that Scripture has only one true meaning, and that is the literal meaning perceived with faith.

There is a duality in the Bible, and it is a profound one. It is not a duality of meaning, but of perspective. It is not based on a distinction between the human and the divine content, or between reason and faith. The two perspectives lie at the very heart of a reading that is done in the spirit of faith. Far from implying any conflict between two independent realities, this duality springs from the harmony that exists between symbol and reality, between figure and truth, between seed and flower.

The dual authorship puts the Bible in a category of its own. Inspiration guarantees an absolute unity of thought, which is not destroyed by the number or variety of human authors. Each of them conveys some fraction of the whole thought. This leads to what seems at first to be a paradox. The divine meaning of a text is in exact proportion to the thought of the writer, and yet the writer has not understood the full significance of his own thought, which is only part of a whole of which he is unaware. Inspiration has given him no more of the divine thought than he has expressed in his own writing. But God's view is not so restricted. He sees more than the inspired man can see. Each communication he makes to man is only part of the whole body of revelation, one point in a line which spans past, present and future. God defines the position which each of the Bible's inspired authors will fill, and he assigns to each a portion of revelation relevant to that position in the overall economy of revelation.

To understand the Bible therefore, it is obviously not enough to fix on the immediate content of a text and the exact meaning intended by its inspired writer. We must go further than the immediate significance and try to judge it from God's angle, to see it in the fuller setting of revelation as a whole. It is here that the reading of the Bible allows for two perspectives. The *initial* perspective is that of the author. A text must be seen in its own right before it can be seen as part of a whole. This can be called the immediate perspective. The reader starts off from a text which he accepts in a spirit of faith, and he extracts from it, as objectively as possible, the concrete thought of the writer so that he may arrive at the precise divine truth that God has placed there. It is in this process of enquiry that the reader becomes aware of the relative value of this truth; he sees its relationship to the vast body of God's truth which is bound into the covers of the book he holds in his hands. The proper context of the particular truth he is studying is the whole Bible, and so far he has captured only a moment in time, a single stage in a progressive development. Once he has perceived that, he leaves the perspective of the human word made divine, and enters the perspective of the divine Word made incarnate. In this new perspective, which may be called *evolutive*, the truth assumes a new and unexpected value, almost a new meaning, in most cases beyond the inspired author's own realization. His thought becomes transposed in a way unforeseen except by God.

The immediate (initial) perspective has opened out on to an eternal (evolutive) perspective, and the individual text takes on a fuller meaning because it is seen to be a "type" and an embryo of the whole. As revelation unfolds, the realities that go to make it up show us the shape of the finished pattern. They are symbols of the final reality because they point to it and effectively prepare for it. In fact they point to it only insofar as they prepare for it.

We can appreciate this "spiritual" sense only if we appreciate the twofold relationship existing between the successive levels on which revelation is realized. There is a relationship of inner *proportion* between the content of revelation at each of its successive stages, and a relationship of *efficient causality* between one stage and the next. The earlier stage is a "type" or "symbol" of the later one. This symbolism is not merely imaginary, but real and efficacious: it is founded on the onto-logical bond that ties the symbol to the reality it signifies. The transition from one stage of revelation to the next is not merely subjective, in the sense that the people who received it simply became more conscious of it. It is an actual growth, based not on a haphazard conglomeration of unrelated elements, but on a network of internal forces, present from the very beginning and recognizable at every stage that leads to the full realization. An *organic* unity binds all these stages together. This living unity lies at the heart of the spiritual sense. It is the principle of that proportion which the spiritual sense tries to capture in the various forms of revelation's gradual realization. In the Bible a symbol is something more than a mere sign: it is the reality already present *in germ*. This fact is often forgotten by the allegorists. What are really preparations they see only as prefigurations. If something in the Old Testament is to be called a type of something in the New, it must necessarily also be a historical preparation for it. No text of the Old Testament has its fulfilment in the New without having led the mind to it.

It will be seen that the spiritual sense is not really distinct from the literal sense, but is already objectively present as one aspect of it. It is the deepest and most decisive aspect, and can be seen only when the rest of revelation has been accepted. It cannot be separated from the literal sense, still less can it be set up in opposition to it, since it is simply the full realization of the literal sense, even though the writer may not have understood it, even implicitly. It is simply *a new relationship to revelation as a whole*. In other words it is a reference to Christ. There was no necessity for the writer to understand that relationship; by definition he is confined to his limited outlook. Even if he saw beyond (if he was a prophet, for instance) he still saw it from his immediate literal perspective, and not from the eternal perspective of God. Yet the full meaning adds nothing objective to the content of what the writer knew. It only transfigures it by bathing it in a blinding new light. To sum up, the immediate perspective is static and limited to the immediate horizon of the text, the author and the people for whom he wrote; the evolutive perspective is dynamic, and places the historical fact in a living movement. The first is anatomical, the second is vital. The one is analytic, the other synthetic. The one appeals primarily to the intellect, the other to the heart filled with faith. Where one sees the divine through the human, the other gives the human its full divine length and breadth.

Historical and Typical Points of View

ONE further nuance remains to be made. Within the evolutive perspective we may distinguish two further points of view. The first starts with the immediate historical fact and sees it as the first stage of an evolution which, after a series of transpositions, will be finally achieved in the message of Christ. This *historical* viewpoint traces the development of a revealed truth through all its stages, from its first perception to its final realization. The second viewpoint does the very opposite, and starts with Christ in whom the truth is achieved. It traces the course of a truth backwards from him, seeing at each stage an imperfect prefiguration of Christ. This can be called the recapitulative or *typical* viewpoint. In the one case the historical fact is given an eternal context, in the other the eternal is seen in its historical antecedents. The first concentrates on the efficient causality which ties the immediate meaning to its spiritual development, the other emphasizes the exemplary causality that this presupposes. The historical viewpoint makes of the literal sense a *positive and progressive preparation* for the

Christian sense; the typical viewpoint makes of it a necessary *prefiguration*.

It would need many examples to illustrate this distinction clearly. In the chapter on the *Word of God* we tried to give some understanding of it. The analysis we there made of the progressive stages of revelation gave the broad outlines of the historical viewpoint; the preceding summary of the doctrinal themes, with its emphasis on the constancy of the unbroken line which runs from start to finish, gave some idea of the typical viewpoint. The two are in any case inseparable, and unless their mutual interplay is appreciated it will be impossible to understand the "spiritual" import of any given text. We shall say more of this in the next chapter.

The point we wish to make about the "allegorical" sense should now be clear. The word is ambiguous. If it means wrenching texts from their context and applying them arbitrarily to things entirely foreign to their true meaning, then it should be called accommodation, for it is nothing else. If, on the other hand, it denotes that profound proportion which exists between the true literal sense and its development in the rest of revelation, then it should be called quite simply the spiritual sense, because that is what it really is. Perhaps it would be better to avoid the term "allegorical" altogether. Since our minds are necessarily formed in the Greek mould, the word is almost bound to make us think of the merely extrinsic illustrations that Greek allegories are. The typology of the Bible has nothing to do with that artificial world at all. It belongs to the more supple world of Semitic parable. The Greek allegory smacks of geometry; the Semitic parable is something more delicate, built on a profound sense of mystery and a living understanding of symbolism. With the Semite a symbol is never merely a conventional sign, but an objective reality, already containing the higher reality which it effectively prefigures and develops into. The word "allegorical" is redolent of mental gymnastics and a jig-saw puzzle mentality. It should not be applied to the spiritual sense, for which the word "parabolical" would be more suitable, for it is the synthesis of the whole and the spiritual flowering of the seed contained in the letter. This conclusion is so important that we must enlarge on it further below.

III

THE PRINCIPLES OF INTERPRETATION

Primacy of the spiritual sense and priority of the literal sense; the Christian meaning contained in the development of the literal meaning; the nature of typology: nothing can be called a foreshadowing unless it is also a historical preparation; the rediscovery of a sapiential understanding of mystery and symbol.

IN THE light of what has been said, it should not be difficult to marshal the basic principles which must govern a sound interpretation of Scripture. We are in a position now to understand the relationship between the Christian and the historical meaning of the text, and to see how the one must be judged in the light of the other. We can also state the final principle which must dictate the spirit of such an enquiry.

Importance of the Literal Sense

THE reader will not need to be reminded again of the absolute primacy of the " spiritual " sense. It embraces the fullness of the divine sense, and anyone who wishes to savour the richness of revelation must make the search for it his one aim. The primacy is only one of principle. Our anxiety to live from the Word of God should not blind us to the fact that, in practice, the appreciation of the " somatic " or literal sense must be the first object of our study. Before we can rightly estimate the bearing of any given event upon the whole scheme of salvation, we must first understand the event itself. The various bonds which tie it to its proper context are not extraneous to it but are part and parcel of its essence. A single synthesis requires months of analysis. It cannot be too often repeated that the main task of the reader is to apply himself with unflagging zeal, resolute faith and constant love to the letter of Scripture. It is this personal effort alone which the Spirit will reward with the light which reveals the hidden riches of God's Word. Without this mortification of self there is no room for Christ in our hearts. As we share his divine life only by eating his flesh, so we hear his divine word only by listening to its human expression. To refuse to submit to the apparent "poverty" of the literal sense is to find the Cross a stumbling block. The fact is that the true spiritual meaning of Scripture can be found only in the literal sense, just as the Son of God can be found only in Jesus of Nazareth. This *law of incarnation* dominates every aspect of man's life and the mystery of his salvation.

It governs the literal sense also. The Christian mystery of eternal life is a fact of history and belongs rightfully to the domain of reason. It follows that the study of the Bible must involve some use of science. This may vary in degree but it can never be dispensed with altogether if there is to be any religious insight into the Bible. The purpose of the Bible is indeed to encourage the growth of the divine life within us, but this progress depends, like any other progress in life, on *patient study based on technical foundations*. It is true that technique does not of itself guarantee progress: it may even bring about paralysis and death. Technique and spiritual advancement are not synonymous terms. But they are complementary terms, and an intense spirituality will always promote technical progress, just as technical progress must necessarily promote spiritual advancement in anyone who tries to integrate the conquests of science into his personal outlook on life, and who lets himself be led by the Word to the Spirit, and by God's truth to God's love.

The fundamental principle of a spiritual approach to the Bible could best be summed up as follows: the true spiritual sense must always *be based upon and grow out of* the literal sense. It is the full flowering of the seed which is contained in the letter of Scripture, studied in the light of its Christian fulfilment. Every reading of the Bible, even if it is done for an exclusively pious purpose, demands a rudimentary appreciation at least of its literary forms and of the conclusions of biblical science. The deeper understanding given by the Spirit is proportionate to the amount of human energy a man is prepared to put into the study of the letter. The deeper the critical study of the Bible, the deeper will be the appreciation of its thought. Without some effort, there can be no spiritual profit.

We arrive at the same conclusion when we consider that the

spiritual sense is more akin to parable than to allegory. The Christian meaning emerges not from the Bible's individual details, but from its main trends. It searches out the *dominant themes* which constitute the framework upon which all revelation hangs. Whether we are dealing with its historical or its typical aspect, with its gradual growth or its underlying constants, the spiritual sense can be found only in the fundamental themes, and not in isolated texts. Occasionally an individual text will have a timeless application, but this is purely coincidental, and its only purpose is to indicate the presence of a deeper vein which must be mined before it will yield its gold. Under the historical reality revealed in a given book lies a Christian treasure, and this is not to be measured by the ambiguous meaning of an occasional text. David is a type of Christ, but not because the staff he used against Goliath is a figure of Christ's Cross or because the stone he put in his sling is a symbol of the "corner-stone" which would later become a stumbling block to Christ's enemies. A vivid imagination can easily produce plenty of ingenious, or puerile, examples of this kind. The Iliad or Aeneid would be equally suitable for this sort of exercise. David is a type of Christ because he effectively prepared for the coming of the Messiah, and at the same time accustomed the Israelites to the idea of a king who was also the mediator and saviour of his people. Given this basic theme, it is indeed possible to imbue certain features and even details of David's life with a typological significance, but even then their value is entirely dependent on whether or not they exemplify the dominant theme, and whether or not they are rooted in the literal sense.

The Nature of Typology

AFTER insisting, as we have done, on the importance of the literal sense, we are left with the problem of determining the exact value of the spiritual sense and of establishing the principles which govern its use. In recent years spiritual exegesis has quite rightly called attention to the existence in the Bible of a complex network of signs and symbols. It is not our intention to decry the undoubted importance of such typology in biblical study. In neglecting it scientific exegesis has not only cut itself off from patristic tradition, but also deprived itself of the key to the full meaning of the literal sense itself. In fact the progress that has been made in psychology and philosophy has widened the scope of the historical method, and in the light of its new synthesis of patristic tradition and scientific enquiry it is beginning to rediscover the true significance of biblical typology.

Even so, it is extremely difficult to measure the exact function of typology in biblical exegesis. A simple appeal to the authority of the Fathers solves nothing, since they used two kinds of typology, and they themselves would have been the first to distinguish them if they had had a better knowledge of the laws of the historical method. Some of them did have an inkling of these laws, but not the technical equipment to apply them. Their nearness to the events relieved them of the need to make the distinction we find essential. In any event the Fathers were fully aware that their many typological interpretations were not all of the same value. They were careful to emphasize the fundamental themes which form the organic structure and unity of biblical revelation, but in their margin they devised a whole mass of flourishes, variations and improvisations which could be called semi-serious poetic flights of fancy. Their doctrinal interpretation is inextricably mingled with the pastoral use they made of the text, and it is no longer possible for us to determine the dividing line between what was the fruit of a deep knowledge of Scripture and what was a contemporary manner of expression. Sometimes they use the Bible simply as a vocabulary, giving biblical terms an entirely Christian meaning. With these words they fashioned the vehicle for conveying to others an experience they drew, not from the words themselves, but from the very heart of Scripture.

There is no point, then, in saying that a return to the exegesis of the Fathers is the only basis for interpretation. Their biblical thought has a timeless value, but their vehicle of expression is outdated. When we read the Fathers we must in all charity realize this and make allowance for it. If we persist in trying to resurrect their method we shall distort the truth of their message. We must go to them to rediscover their fundamental grasp of biblical typology, but we must go to history, philosophy and theology to learn the laws and the real import of this typology in the light of the progress that these sciences have made. Those who fondly advocate a return to the Fathers and the liturgy are being unfair to both if they try to encase their pliant and vital approach to Scripture in a set of rigid and lifeless axioms.

In practice there are two ways of finding types of the New Testament in the Old. One is to imagine that God has *superficially* imbued certain texts here and there with a typical value undreamt of by the author or his immediate audience. The figurative meaning is superimposed on the obvious meaning and is limited to the few phrases that allow of an ambiguous interpretation. The typical value of a text lies in the secret meaning which the Holy Spirit has given it in view of its future fulfilment in Christ, over and above the meaning intended by the author in view of his contemporaries. Typology in this sense is not to be found throughout the Bible but only in certain isolated texts that relate to particular persons and facts. It becomes a kind of hallmark of inspiration, whose purpose it has been to hide these unexpected Christian portraits in the ordinary backcloth of the Jewish setting, much in the way that the wind and rain could carve a rock which later could be recognized as a portrait of Churchill. The chief aim of the exegete would be to find as many of these silhouettes as possible, in the conviction that they would give him the essence of the Bible's divine content.

This sort of typology will always be at loggerheads with both technical exegesis and the whole patristic tradition at its truest and best. A tremendous feeling for the living unity of all Scripture is manifest on every page of the writings of the Fathers, and lies beneath the apparent arbitrariness of their typological interpretation and paraphrase. To them the Bible is never an ingenious jig-saw puzzle but a vast body with an inner power which gives it life and harmony. Their knowledge of history was too limited to give them our modern sense of evolution, but they had an intuitive knowledge of the divine life which energizes Scripture, and this more than compensated for their limitations. Their typology was evolutive and historical, not static, as is clear from their concern to look for the correlation between the two Testaments in the living continuity of revelation. The unmistakable parallels which occur through revelation have not been superimposed artificially by God. On the contrary they are the natural expression of the fidelity with which the initial seed developed along the lines of its fundamental structure, under the impulse of an inner force that remained constant throughout.

The static kind of typology is reminiscent of those exegetes who were only able to jusify the biblical date of creation by concluding that God must have created the fossils. Every child knows that fossils are only specimens of a past age, sporadic links in an infinitely long chain of evolution. They mark only the more obvious stages of a process whose vastness is as great a tribute to God's power as creation itself. Something of the sort happened in the Bible. The more obvious similarities that can be observed between certain parts of the Bible are only specimens of a life that runs unbroken throughout the whole. A parallel could be drawn from the life of an embryo, where the organs which will develop later can be observed from the beginning, and grow gradually more precise. Such a view of typology does not destroy faith in inspiration: it puts inspiration in its proper context, which is divine.

This sort of typology is something entirely different from that which the allegorists look for. It is neither the goal nor the essence of spiritual exegesis, but simply one of the many means at its disposal. If such typology reveals the obvious Old Testament *prefigurations* of Christ, it is only to invite us to penetrate to the deeper realities which make the whole of the Old Testament a *preparation* for the New. Typology is the flowering of a far more general evolution, and where it has no roots in this evolution it has no place in the study of the one divine sense of Scripture. The principle on which this study must be based should now be clear: for a text to have a precise spiritual meaning, it must be *clearly and objectively related to its fulfilment in Christ both on the historical and on the typical level*. An Old Testament fact can be called typical only if it is connected by both history and inner continuity with the fulfilment it foreshadows. A New Testament theme can be called the *exemplary* cause of an Old Testament theme only if the Old Testament theme is its *effective* cause in fact.

Some examples will clarify the point at issue. The famous text from the book of Isaiah "Who shall declare his generation?" (Isa. 53:8) will almost inevitably call to mind the eternal birth of Christ. The prophet's "unutterable" generation is a natural image of the ineffable generation of Christ, and there is therefore an exemplary relationship between the two ideas. What of the literal sense of the passage? The context deals with the suffering of the Messiah. The prophet is describing the utter tragedy of his life in terms that the Semitic mind will find most compelling: this Messiah will have no son to perpetuate his name. Neither in theory nor in historical fact is there any objective link between this description of the sufferings of the Servant of Yahweh and the divine sonship of Christ. Therefore the text cannot refer to it. Such an interpretation is not the spiritual sense, but a mere accommodation, for all the use made of it by the Fathers. To take another example. The Hebrew name Joshua is the same as the name Jesus and means saviour. It is not a matter of great import but it is the sort of detail seized upon by the exponents of static typology. Now in fact between Jesus and Joshua there is clearly an efficacious link: Joshua's conquest of the promised Land was a real preparation for the conquest of the new "Land" by Jesus. Moreover, the first conquest actually made men look forward to a more perfect Saviour to lead them to a richer "Land". It is this that eventually shows us that there was a divine purpose behind the identity of the names. The name itself is nothing. To be a type of Christ it is not enough simply to bear his name. The external similarity must be based upon an internal and effective relationship of fact.

The theme of blood is of more moment. The scarlet cord that Rahab hung from her window in the walls of Jericho has often been taken as a type of the blood of Christ. The scarlet cord was the saving of Rahab: the scarlet blood of Christ is the saving of man. Does the similarity entitle us to conclude that the Spirit prefigured the redeeming blood of Christ in the scarlet cord? By no means. There is no real connection between them. The one did not lead to the other, nor was faith in Christ born of the contemplation of Rahab's cord. With the blood of the paschal Lamb and the blood with which Moses hallowed the people of the Covenant at

Sinai we come to a different matter altogether. On the subjective level, these rites effectively opened the Israelite's religious conscience to a realization of the true significance of the Passion and the new Covenant. On the objective level, they effectively prepared the historical ground in which the new event was to flower. There is here a true spiritual sense, because it grows out of the literal sense. In contrast, when the author of the book of Joshua wrote of the scarlet cord he could have had no explicit, implicit or even embryonic notion of the blood of Christ. If the scarlet cord is understood as a sign of Christ's blood, it is by sheer accommodation. Such a spiritual sense does not stem from the literal sense. Admittedly it is a legitimate accommodation, and may even be of great devotional significance, but it still remains outside the scope of inspiration's guarantee.

The Sapiential Mentality

THE few principles which we have enumerated on the connection between the initial sense and its final evolution all stem from a wider principle: *the words of the Bible are less important than the concrete realities they stand for.* We have many times insisted on the need for adapting ourselves to the Bible's Semitic mentality. We insist on it again because we believe it to be essential. Our minds feel more at home with abstractions than with concrete images, and we are in constant danger of taking refuge from reality behind our concepts of reality. Clearly we cannot dispense with such concepts, but we must remember that they are messengers and should not be mistaken for the message itself. The Bible demands that we reverse our customary mental approach, and goes so far as to require a complete revision of our epistemology. It will always remain a closed book to minds that do not acknowledge the primacy of life and reality. The climate of the Bible is "sapiential", that is to say it deals with truth in the concrete, bearing a relation to life. In its search for this kind of truth it calls up all the powers of the soul, for the single purpose of encouraging the reader to commit and abandon himself to it. The Bible cannot be treated dispassionately, like a problem from Euclid. This kind of approach has already robbed exegesis and theology of their vitality, and killed philosophy altogether.

The sapiential approach commits the whole man, even if he has not yet learned to see with the eyes of faith. Since it appeals to the complete man with all his receptive faculties, reason becomes a servant rather than a master. This is what provides the foundations required for faith, itself a synthesis between supernatural knowledge and supernatural love. If the reading of the Bible is to be fruitful, there must be complete submission to reality, and the sort of common sense which can support an enlightened faith.

IV

THE METHOD OF INTERPRETATION

Theological exegesis as the exhaustive method: literary, historical and doctrinal criticism must be completed by commitment; meditative reading as an abridged method for the uninitiated: based on a minimum of science, enlightened by the " five senses " essential for the biblical mentality, completed by prayer.

GIVEN the right atmosphere, the essential principles, and a clear grasp of what it is he must look for in the Bible, the reader must still know how to turn all this to good account: he must know something of the method of interpretation that flows from these principles. Not that there is a cut and dried approach that is suitable for all; every man has his own temperament, his own intellectual and moral standing and his own needs, and must find the form which suits him best. But the broad outlines of the method will always be the same, simply because the Bible is what it is—a book both human and divine. The method will take one of two main forms, depending on the technical knowledge of the individual.

Theological Exegesis

THIS is the unabridged method. It involves a long scientific study of the written word. Before a book can be understood it must first be read. If the book is as old as the Bible the very reading of it is a science in itself (*documentary criticism*). The exact text must first be established with certainty (*textual criticism*) and the immediate meaning of the words determined (*philology*) before they can be understood in their particular context (*science of interpretation*). This context is itself part of a more general background, and the character, literary form and style of the whole writing must be understood (*literary criticism*) in order to establish its precise origin (*authenticity*). This abstract study of the circumstances of a book's composition does not yet determine the meaning of its contents: it has still to be put into its living framework, which is the milieu of the people for whom it was written (*historical and psychological criticism*). So far the exegete has remained on the surface of the written word. If he is to go further and discover the inspired doctrine, he must now correlate the particular book he is reading with earlier writings (*source criticism*) and with parallel trends of thought (*study of influences*). Only after this will he be competent to determine objectively the precise import of every nuance of the writer's thought, as expressed in each word of the book (*doctrinal criticism*). It is this exhaustive examination of the literal sense that is the aim of a critical commentary.

Even at this stage the exegete is still only half way. It goes without saying that throughout the process outlined above the reader's faith and reason have gone hand in hand, and science has never been divorced from religion. But now he has to penetrate further still into the divine thought, and discover its ramifications on a level which is deeper than that on which the writer moved. To achieve this he must determine the writer's exact position in the development of revelation. His thought must be seen in relation to those who went before and those who came afterwards to enrich the ideas to which he gave birth. This *study of the evolution of doctrine* will lead him eventually to Christ, who is the perfect flowering of the germinal thought expressed in the text. Finally, having arrived at this term, he must retrace his steps in order to evaluate the original thought in the light of its later fulfilment (*typological* or *recapitulative study*). Then and only then will he discover the full richness which lies hidden beneath the apparent poverty of the text; then and only then will he be able to say that he has drained the text, insofar as man is able to drain it, of its content of divine truth.

This is the task of the exegete as such. But even at this stage he cannot be said to have finished. Knowledge is something more than mere objective perception; a thing is truly known only when it is assimilated. The subject must do more than receive the object, he must open himself to it. It is the subject who is transformed by knowledge, not the object. The Word of God cannot be said to have penetrated until we have laid our fallen and warped nature open to its influence. The one aim of the Bible is to re-make us after its own image. We cannot hope to plumb its depths until we have allowed it to sound ours. It is a commitment of the mind that is required, a refashioning of our mentality until the life, background and ideas of each of the sacred writers have become our own. It involves a refashioning of the heart too, and finally the acquiescence of faith. The Bible speaks its full message only to one who is prepared to make complete and unconditional *surrender* of himself.

When the exegete has learned to crown his labours with such love, then his scientific technique can be said to have blossomed into *biblical theology*, in the sense explained above.

His objective knowledge of the Bible is transformed into a personal experience. God's thought becomes *his own* thought and life. Insofar as this effort is subjective and based on the need for synthesis and a desire to find the Bible's relevance to the present day, the exegete has here gone beyond the scope of science. But he has not gone beyond the scope of his object, since he has done no more than assimilate it. He has tried to do what St. John did in the Fourth Gospel, where his thought is so deeply modelled on Christ's thought that the two are no longer distinguishable. The exegete remains within the limits of the Bible's objective content simply because no individual will ever be able to exhaust the potentialities of the Word.

Through this discipline of mind and effort of love the exegete, without ceasing to be an exegete, must become a theologian. In patristic times the exegete played a vital rôle in the Church. If he is ever to recapture that position, he must be alive to his special function in the Church's life in the Spirit. His calling is a charismatic and supernatural one, rather like that of the "doctor" or "teacher" in apostolic times. His knowledge does not give him the right to retire into the aristocracy of the modern professional wise man. His gift for interpretation is a social function. The biblical theologian is at the service of the Church, and the effort that he puts into reaching a living understanding of the Word of God is pointless if it does not promote the life and movement of Christ's mystical Body. Here lies one reason for the loss of contact between the people and the proper source of their life, which is the Word of God. If the exegete has failed to inform his study with the Spirit, and if the theologian has failed to inform Christian thought with the inspired Word of God, we must not wonder that there is temporary paralysis in some parts of the Church. Materially, psychologically, intellectually and morally, most people are not capable of the effort demanded by the complete method we have described. They are dependent on the expert and must wait for him to put his learning into digestible form. Under the Church's magisterium, it is he alone, with his charism of teaching, who can give them the Word of God.

Meditative Reading

THIS long list of technical requirements is the heritage of the scientific revolution of the last few hundred years. They may well discourage the average reader from taking up his Bible. He may even feel that they constitute the final insurmountable barrier. However much education or leisure he may have, he can hardly hope to master the scientific training which will make him a biblical theologian. Such fears are groundless. The complete method is not the only method. In fact there is a shorter and easier way which will allow the uninitiated, whatever his walk of life, to draw profit from the inspired text and enable him to live purposefully.

Simplification must obviously be made at the expense of technical study. But let us affirm here what we have frequently said before, that technique cannot be dispensed with altogether. The chief aim of this book has been to convince the reader that there can be no fruitful reading of the Bible without a *minimum of initiation* into the main conclusions and findings of technical exegesis. It is for the specialist to make such findings available at a popular level if the biblical movement is to have the far-reaching effects of which it gives promise.

There is no need for the layman to clutter himself up with lengthy introductions and scholarly commentaries. Provided he has the basic requirements, his best introduction to the Bible is the reading of the text. We have tried in this book to point out what these requirements are. They can be summed up briefly as a sense of history, a sense of literary form, a sense of the gradual growth of revelation, a sense of faith, and plain common sense. Anyone who has acquired the instinct for seeing all earthly events against the changing background of history, and for recognizing the relative value of the forms in which human truth may be expressed, will immediately understand that biblical revelation must also be judged by these criteria. Given a firm faith in the Church and a measure of common sense, the difficulties of the Bible should not be insurmountable.

Besides his text he would do well to obtain other books which will provide him with enough technical information to suit his particular needs. A work like Robert and Tricot's *Guide to the Bible* (English transl. by Arbez and McGuire) will not only give him a general introduction and the outline of a solution to basic problems, but also furnish him with a bibliography should he want to go deeper into certain questions. The one thing he must not do is to surround himself with a library of commentaries and introductions. To read and re-read the inspired text itself without ever being discouraged, that is his most important task. Too many people allow themselves to be put off by the first difficulty they meet. They complain that they do not understand and so give up before they have really started. It is essential to read at length, regularly and often, avoiding long intervals and interruptions. It is best not to linger over anything that is obscure, but to by-pass the difficulties and cling to what has been understood. Little by little the mind will grasp the unity of the whole and feel at home in the milieu of biblical thought and ideas. Gradually the broad outlines will become clear, and the reader will be caught up into the movement of the book, feel the rhythm and thrill to the warmth of its touch. Thus his love of the Bible is born, and the first and most difficult step has been made.

This constant reading will take various forms. First of all it should be a *liturgical* reading. The liturgy forms the perfect framework for a simple introduction to the Bible, since it selects readings to suit the sequence of the liturgical seasons. The social, articulate, and above all sacramental character of the liturgy give it an efficacy that nothing can replace.

Since the Bible is not just a series of extracts, it should be read as a whole and in a *continuous manner*. This should be done with some attention, but cursively and without too many breaks. The inspired text should be the Christian's regular everyday reading, at home in the evening or on the train to and from work, whenever he has the chance.

A third way of reading demands more attention but is still fairly rapid. It is the beginning of a study of the Bible and must be done in quieter moments. A particular book or a few chapters are chosen and notes are taken on what is read. A special notebook should be kept and in it recorded all the questions, reflections, queries, attempted solutions, and everything else prompted by a reading done thoughtfully and without recourse to commentaries. This *meditative* reading is without doubt the most beneficial way of approaching the Bible.

A fourth way of reading can be called *doctrinal*. The reader will have become more confident and will want to go deeper into the text. To find its full riches he will need to put aside an hour or two and give his undivided attention to a study of the literal meaning of some rich passage, or of the development of some theme throughout the course of the Bible. Generally speaking, this sort of study will be more doctrinal than critical. It will be helpful to use some of the more specialized works, particularly a concordance, that is to say a kind of biblical dictionary which lists all the words used in the Bible and gives references to the texts in which they occur (Cruden's Concordance can be obtained from many second-hand bookshops, and an abbreviated form of it is bound into many non-Catholic Bibles). The chapter on the *Word of God*, with its outline of the biblical themes and their gradual transposition, will give some indication of the direction this study should take. This approach to the Bible is exacting and requires much patient hard work, but it is by far the most rewarding of all meditative readings.

Finally there is the *sapiential* reading of the Bible. Here the reader goes beyond understanding and faith and comes to rest in love. He learns to make the Bible his prayer. It is not simply a question of praying the words of the Bible, but of being caught up in the whole rhythm of the Spirit who inspired them, to contemplate the Father in his Word. Obviously some pages are more conducive to this than others. The Gospel of St. John and some of the Epistles of St. Paul have a greater appeal than, say, a story from Genesis or a genealogy from the book of Chronicles. It is up to the individual reader to make his own choice of what he knows will help him. In any event it is only a question of degree, since every single page is capable of effecting this union between the reader and God, if only he reads it with faith and love, and is prepared to go beyond the words and their human significance to the Spirit behind them. This was how the monks of old used to pray the Bible, eloquent testimony both to their understanding of prayer and to their belief in the divinity of the Bible. They remind us of the early Christians who spoke in " tongues " without choosing their words. Both understood that the whole movement of prayer transcends what is human in order to gaze at the face of the Father in the Spirit which he pours out on them. Unlike the cursive reading mentioned above, this must be slow and pensive: the words are now only the vehicles of an inner harmony which floods the soul. The letter has become a sacrament of the Spirit.

These various ways of reading the Bible are not meant to follow each other successively. They should be done simultaneously so that one reading may help the other to bear fruit. It may be difficult at first to strike the balance. Familiarity with the Bible comes slowly and much patience is needed at all times. Some would do best to start by reading the Bible from cover to cover in order to get an idea of the whole. Most people would do better to begin with its more accessible parts —the Synoptics are easier reading than St. Paul or St. John, the historical books are less forbidding than Leviticus. But care should be taken to read both Testaments, so that from the outset the reader will grow accustomed to see that each needs the other to complete it. It should be his aim to read *all* the books and find nourishment in each of them, rather than keep to the ones he knows to be richer or personally more fruitful.   Once he has overcome the difficulties of initiation, he should make up his mind to cover the whole Bible in a year or two and map out a daily plan of cursive reading.   He would do best to take the books, as far as possible, in the order of their historical evolution, rather than in the order in which they are printed in the Bible.   The Prophets, for instance, and the Epistles of St. Paul, should be read in chronological order if the movement of revelation is to be properly understood. The reader is not dealing with a succession of detached sentences.   Led by the Spirit, he must go beyond the earthly words and be caught up into the gradual and harmonious incarnation of the Thought of God.

CHAPTER X

THE BIBLE AND CHRISTIAN CULTURE

T HE best way to conclude this book is to give some explanation of the fruits that may be expected from reading the Bible. These can be summed up by saying that the Bible gives a Christian his *culture, human and divine*. The Christian is human, through and through. There is no aspect of human activity to which he is a stranger. And yet he cannot realize the fullness of his humanity until he has risen in God above all that is human. Christian humanism demands the death of all that is merely human. The man who is self-sufficient can never be anything more than his natural fallen self: only the man who lays himself open to God can ever be a man to perfection. Thus while Christian culture is essentially human it is necessarily turned towards God. The Spirit of God alone can give to man's nature its true supernatural harmony. And it is precisely in the Bible that the plan for this harmony has been sketched and its first expression realized, in the written and incarnate Word of the Son of God.

I

THE LITERARY VALUE OF THE BIBLE

The conflict between biblical spirituality and Greek humanism; how it began, how Christianity resolved it, how it has reappeared in modern civilization; the inspiration of the Spirit and literary inspiration.

I N T H E last analysis the literary value of the Bible must be assessed in this Christian spirit. It is possible, of course, to approach it on a purely human level and appreciate it as one might appreciate Homer, Cicero, Chaucer or Shakespeare. In fact there are people who read the Psalms, Isaiah and St. Paul not in any spirit of faith but simply to relish their literary content. Nor can one condemn them for doing so: even on this level the Bible will stand comparison with the literature of any time or place. Nevertheless such an appreciation is a superficial one, and may even be false if it is divorced from the one thing that gives biblical literature its specific character, namely Christian faith.

When we dealt with the Semitic language and mentality we analysed the elements which constitute the Bible's literary beauty. An appreciation of this beauty requires an understanding of the Semitic mentality and of the fact that it is different from our own. To some extent the beauty of the Bible is self-evident. It would be hard not to feel the power of an oracle from Isaiah, or the grace and freshness of some of the historical narratives. Even when they were presented to us in the lifeless form of our Bible History, the stories of Jacob and Joseph, the adventures of Samson and David, the figure of Elijah and the Christ of St. Mark fired our childhood imagination. Those impressions did not last. When we went to College they became a little faded and were submerged under new impressions which were more subtle and precise. There we fashioned other ideas of style and beauty, based on the Greek model. Daily contact with the masterpieces of our western literary heritage took away the appeal of our early love of the Bible, and it was consigned to the dusty corner of childhood memories. The canons of beauty were now in the world of Athens and Rome. Our thought was remodelled on them, and we took easily to them, since we are naturally inclined that way already. The divorce between our religion and our humanities had begun. Religiously we remained children while in every other respect we had begun to grow up.

If we are ever to appreciate the beauty of the Bible we must bring about a reconciliation. It would be useless (and unChristian) to attempt this either by renouncing our Greek culture or by being complacent about our neglect of biblical culture. Both cultures are human and belong therefore to the Christian by right. They are different in that they represent two distinct types of outlook, but they are complementary, and together form a synthesis of thought which is all the more human because it corresponds to all aspects of God's plan. What we need is an understanding of the precise contribution that each culture has to make. Every civilization at some stage of its history absorbs a number of transient elements which it will either modify or reject. Christianity is no exception. All the same Christianity is rooted in far richer soil than any other civilization. Born in the Semitic world, it came to manhood in the Greek world, and so was in an ideal position to synthesize the two most stable and profound of all human cultures.

FROM the very beginning mankind has been moulded by two opposing civilizing influences, which can be summed up under the symbols of *homo faber* and *homo sapiens*. On the surface at least, man's intelligence has always been of a twofold nature, discursive and intuitive. He has a corresponding double sphere of activity, and marks his progress either in the external world of material reality and abstract thought or in the internal world of spiritual reality and reflection. In the first field he is a scientist who analyses, in the second a man of wisdom who synthesizes. In the first he is a mathematician, in the second an artist. These two extremities mark the orbit within which thought moves and has evolved. They are part of man's constitution and to sacrifice one for the other would be to deprive him of part of his being.

Unfortunately that is what has so very frequently happened. Man's history could be told in terms of the struggle between these two aspects. Man has gone from one extreme to the other, from thesis to antithesis, without ever realizing the higher synthesis which Christianity has tried to achieve. In pre-history man was naturally preoccupied with the material side of things: he forged the first industrial age of the *homo faber*. This was followed by the first sapiential culture when Magdalenian man discovered art and religion. This age came to full flower in the civilizations of the ancient Semitic East and reached its finest expression in the Bible. With the rise of

Greece a new age was born. The cave-man had invented the tool, and *homo sapiens* had learned how to think. It was the Greek who made the discovery that thought itself could be a tool which gave access to a world of infinite horizons. Christianity was born at the point in time and place where these two cultures met. For a while it succeeded in establishing an equilibrium. But from the thirteenth century, and even more from the sixteenth, the West has gradually rejected the Church's guiding hand. To-day we find ourselves back in an age that is completely industrialized. Technical advance has been gained at the expense of the things of the spirit. Modern man is faced with the task of effecting, once again, the miracle of the Magdalenian era, and putting his technical achievements at the service of a new sapiential age. The germ of this miracle is already present in Christianity. It is making small progress not because it is in decline but because it is still adapting itself to the modern technological age. But the Spirit will triumph, and it is in Christianity that he will work his miracle.

From a purely human standpoint, our Greek culture needs the culture of the Bible to revitalize it. Even on a purely human level the Bible is man's spiritual masterpiece and therefore his finest achievement. We must look to it for that sapiential mentality which will restore our sense of spiritual values. There we will discover that spirit of finesse and appreciation of the concrete which will teach us to deal with reality rather than with abstract concepts, to delve into the mystery of things rather than remain on the surface of " clear and distinct ideas ". The critical character of our own culture will help us to do this all the more effectively. The New Testament itself was an attempt at such a synthesis, the welding of Semitic thought to the vocabulary and thought-forms of Hellenism. Its masterpieces are those works which achieved this tour-de-force: St. Luke in both his writings assimilated his Semitic sources into a Greek mind; St. John adapted his Semitic mentality to his Greek readers. St. Paul is perhaps an even finer example of the Christian attempt to integrate the two types of human culture. In some ways he failed. Humanly speaking this was only to be expected: it simply is not possible to express what is inexpressible. The force of the Apostle's living thought was something so Semitic that it could not be contained within the technical niceties of the Greek culture to which he subscribed. Yet his very failure to resolve the struggle gives his short writings their extraordinary vigour. They came white hot from the fire of his human genius.

HUMAN genius is all the more human for being committed to the divine. The spiritual value of the Bible is something more than the value which attaches to all sapiential civilizations. It is the quintessence of that civilization, because its truth is the Word of God and its spirit the Spirit of God. Its literary value is unique because it is God's "literature". Men will react to it in different ways according to the measure of their genius, but, whatever the degree of appreciation, the man who is in touch with God by faith will always be more aware of its divine overtones. For us the beauty of human literature consists in the brilliance of expression in which an emotion is enshrined; for the Semite the emotion itself is more important than beauty of form. The beauty of the Bible depends neither on the triumph of created form nor on the poignant inability to express uncreated Beauty. Here the Reflection of God's own face shines on every page, and the Breath of his mouth gives it life. The man of faith and love who enters into communion with the pre-incarnate Word in the Bible is gradually made aware of the divine rhythm which has swept all its various books and authors into one vast melody. The beauty of the central theme is appreciated all the more as it appears in its variations. It develops with such intricate harmony that it might almost be accused of artificiality did it not at the same time breathe such an air of spontaneity and life.

From the beginning to the end of the Bible there sweeps a force as irresistible as the storms of Sinai. It catches men and carries them beyond the confines of the books they wrote, beyond even the horizons of this world. Yet it can be as gentle as the evening breeze of Eden in which God spoke to the heart of man. Strong but gentle, a synthesis of fire and water, of the splendour of God's Light and the warmth of his Fire, the Bible is like the wind for which Elijah waited at night in the cave on Mount Horeb—a raging storm which rends the

mountains and breaks the rocks, an earthquake which destroys
and a fire from heaven which consumes. Yet it finally reveals
its secret in the still small voice after the fury of the storm has
passed (3 Ki. 19). It is a glimpse of the glory of God such
as was given to Moses when he crouched in the cleft of a rock
(Ex. 33:17ff). With his eyes shielded by God's hand, the
believer looks into the divine mirror and sees the reflection of
God's Countenance.

II

THE BIBLE AND ART

*Art that is Christian in spirit or only in form; expression-
istic art and evocative art; the inexpressibility of the Christian mystery; the Bible and its evocative style; Christian
art as a commentary in symbol on the Bible.*

ART is as much part of human culture as literature, and it too
must receive the impress of the Christian synthesis. We are
not speaking here of the vast amount of art that has been
inspired by the Bible, but of the part the Bible has to play in
the formation of Christian art as such. The Bible has provided subjects for artists without number, but the mere fact
that a man paints "Susannah Bathing" does not mean that his
art is Christian art. Some churches are little more than art
galleries, and some sacred oratorios are hardly distinguishable
from the composer's operatic works. It is not the subject
which makes art Christian art, but the Spirit.

To make this clearer we have only to compare the works of
art produced by an age which was thoroughly Christian with
those from other ages. Byzantine religious art is profoundly
Christian, and Romanesque in all its forms even more so. In
contrast, most of the Renaissance work, in spite of its brilliance, reflects a spirit which frequently contradicts the subject
depicted. St. Peter's in Rome is not the prayer in stone that
Chartres is. Michelangelo's Last Judgment has not the overwhelming effect and meditative appeal of the pediment at
Moissac. The Madonnas of Botticelli and Raphael may make
one wonder about the ladies who were the models, but nobody

could possibly mistake a Russian icon for anything other than the Mother of God and her divine Son. For one who is rooted in the Bible and the Church even Bach's St. Matthew Passion has not the power and pathos of the ordinary plain chant of the Good Friday Reproaches.

Art can be Christian in form and spirit, or Christian in form only. The one yardstick by which the difference can be measured is, it would seem, the degree to which the Bible has been its inspiration. The fact is that art has been truly Christian only when the Bible held pride of place in the Church. It could hardly be otherwise: the mind that would create Christian art has no other specifically Christian source upon which to draw but the Bible in its living context, which is the Church. It is the Bible which furnishes the artist with both subject-matter and Spirit. The interior and spiritual mystery which is the true object of his art has already found expression in words in the Bible. It is to the Bible that the artist must turn if he is to give expression to that mystery.

The distinction which we made between the scientific and the spiritual mentality has its bearing, therefore, on art too. Just as there is a literature which is expressionistic and a literature which is evocative, so there is an art which seduces and an art which arouses love. The former seeks to enthrall the emotions, the latter to liberate them. The one relies on virtuosity and skill in imitating, the other instinctively seeks to capture the inner rhythm of the subject, although it knows that the most perfect of techniques will be unequal to the task. The primary aim of one is to express nature, of the other to interpret it. For one, art is something exceptional superimposed on nature, the transcription of reality by a man of genius; the other draws its beauty from the very essence of reality. Both forms of art arise from the necessity of marrying inspiration to technique, of making a synthesis of the spirit and the flesh. But while one relies on technique to express its inspiration, the other knows that no technique is adequate and seeks only to set inspiration free. In one case art is a technique that has been inspired, in the other it is an inspiration that has become incarnate.

IN THEORY the Christian artist is faced with making a choice between these two. In practice he knows that only one choice is possible, because of its very nature the Christian message is inexpressible. The aim of art is to create a reflection of uncreated beauty. From the outset therefore it has set itself an impossible task, an attempt to break the charmed circle of reason and reach beyond the boundaries of the spoken word. Art is born of the powerlessness of reason to give expression to reality, and of the inadequacy of the *anima* (soul) before the self-sufficiency of the *animus* (mind). Art tries to communicate with a God who is incommunicable, to contain a God whom the whole of creation cannot contain. Of its nature, then, art is divine, a reflection of God himself. If this is true of merely human art which tries to evoke the divine as it exists in creation, it is infinitely more true of Christian art which makes God incarnate the theme of its song. Art is essentially a mystery, but it is only a shadow of the supreme Mystery which God gives to man. What distinguishes Christian from non-Christian art, therefore, is not simply the method that is used and the subject that is chosen, but the Spirit that inspires it. The Christian artist is in touch with the supernatural world of revelation, and his art tries to communicate it. He is the herald of the incarnate Word; the living continuation of the Bible. His task is to use his symbols to provide a commentary on Scripture, to evoke in tangible form what has become incarnate in words. Like the Bible in the context of the Church, he has the truly Christian mission of bearing witness to the Son of God made man. Those forms of our spirituality which have abandoned the Bible or lost its living Spirit have either destroyed Christian art or made a travesty of it. By the same token those ages which lived by the Bible and the liturgy were unable to imagine that God could be honoured by refusing him the service of beauty. In short a man cannot be a truly Christian artist unless he is truly a Christian.

If he is true to his art, the Christian artist must realize more clearly than any other that he can never succeed in expressing the blinding glory of God—the sight of God face to face means death. He will instinctively choose, as Christian art has always chosen, the second of the two approaches to art which we outlined above, and try to evoke rather than to express. He gives his talents to paint a canvas upon which the Bible can show its true colours. His task is to fashion a tabernacle for its earthly dwelling. He will naturally go to the Bible to find there not only his ideas but his experience. It is the Bible with its Semitic mentality which will teach him the art of evocation, and the Spirit which transfigures its literary style will fill him too, to enrol him in that company of "craftsmen whom Yahweh has endowed with the Spirit of wisdom to make Aaron's garments". (Ex. 28:3).

III

BIBLICAL EDUCATION

The Bible as the manifesto for Christian expansion; the re-creation of a biblical mentality involves the formation of true witnesses to Christ; the part to be played by religious orders, missionaries, teachers and the Christian family.

As TWO forms of culture, literature and art share with the Bible the task of bringing Christianity back to the world. It was the Bible that first evangelized the world and gave it its Christian education. It is the Bible that must do the same again for the young people of to-day. They perhaps more than any other previous generation are ripe for it, in spite of their mechanized background. Born into a world of disillusioned humanism, they have seen the fruits of excessive technology, and are beginning to hunger for the deeper truth which Christianity can give them, if Christianity can only learn to speak their language.

The return to Christianity demands first of all the unity of Christians among themselves. Here, at the very start, the Bible provides a suitable meeting ground. The Orthodox Churches share with the Catholic Church a common biblical and liturgical background, which is in fact even more integrated into their lives than it is into our own. With Protestantism and its rejection of the living tradition of the Church the rift is wider. Even so there are signs among Protestant thinkers of a rediscovery of the Church and the Sacraments, and of an attempt

T

to meet halfway the effort on the Catholic side to live more consciously by the Bible and the liturgy.

With the non-Christian world there is as yet no real contact. But even here our missionary apostolate must begin from the Bible. The whole purpose of the Bible is to bear witness to the Word of God. If it is enshrined in the living and flexible framework of a sapiential tradition, scriptural preaching is still, as it was in the time of the Fathers, the best way of winning souls. The Far East, Africa, India and the Arab world form in many ways the ideal audience for this type of preaching. Their mentality closely resembles the mentality of the Bible, and they would be less inclined to think of Christianity as a western imposition if a greater effort were made to present it to them in its traditional biblical form. In view of the fact that these people may very well have a decisive rôle to play in the future of the world, a Christianity boldly adapted to their needs could have untold effects.

Nearer home, the dechristianized masses see the Church only as the symbol of an obsolete feudalism. For them too a preaching which is based on the Bible would have the simple and direct appeal it had once before for the humble and disinherited peoples of a decadent civilization, who welcomed it as the "good news". Through whatever avenue the approach is made, literary, artistic or catechetical, the Christian message can only gain in force and sincerity from its contact with the Bible, which will not only make it aware of the real needs of the human soul in distress but also teach it to answer those needs as God answered them. The Bible, in short, is the reservoir from which the Church's dynamism is continually charged, because it knows and respects the basic nature of man and God's commands to him. Renewal can come only from such a reservoir. It is to this hidden treasure that the Church constantly returns "like a learned scribe" to renew her ancient patrimony. She may adapt boldly, but her teaching will always be in line with this authentic tradition. Together with the liturgy, therefore, the Bible is the source of Christian vitality, the leaven which works its way through the whole and ensures that the growth is never false to itself. Like the Eucharist, the Bible is *eschatological* in both senses of that word: it looks to the Kingdom of God in the future, and points to its present realization in the mystery of the Church, the living flower of the seed which was first sown at the incarnation.

CHRISTIAN reform must be based on a return to the Bible. Without the Bible the liturgical movement will degenerate into mediaevalism, and our missionary and social apostolate into a soulless propaganda cut off from its life source. Few Christians yet seem to have any real idea of the fundamental importance of the Word of God. This must again be made clear to them and all prejudice disarmed, so that a *biblical mentality* may be re-created.

This is no easy task. The disease is deep-seated and must be tackled in stages. Before we can hope to reach the masses, we must first approach the intellectual and moral elite who are partly to blame for the loss of the scriptural tradition. They must themselves be convinced of the exact function of the Word of God in the economy of the faith, and see clearly the living bond which ties it to the tradition of the Church. They must be taught to understand the whole mystery of incarnation. The scientific advances of the last century, especially in the fields of cosmic, historical and psychological evolution, are not a barrier but a help to the appreciation of this mystery. The barrier that must go down is the intellectual, moral and psychological one that has been set up by rationalism and pseudo-humanism. Once this barrier is down, the way to the Bible will be open to all instead of only to the few who are capable of scientific study. In short we must re-create the atmosphere in which the Fathers studied the Bible, and transform that atmosphere by putting it in contact with the achievements of the sciences.

For the time being the Bible cannot be put into the hands of all and sundry without preparation. The right atmosphere can be re-created only by means of a carefully planned campaign. This campaign must spread from the clergy to the teaching and missionary orders, from intellectual circles to teaching circles, and so eventually find its way to the family. Its constant aim must be to bring the Bible to every person in every walk of life.

FIRST and foremost, biblical education must have a social or "ecclesial" character. From his seminary days, many a priest has been put off rather than inspired by the Word of God, chiefly because Scripture was another examination to be got through, after Dogma and Morals. It was never made an integral part of his life there, nor was it sustained by a living liturgy. Even the enthusiasts of the modern liturgical and biblical revival are unfortunately often lacking in their understanding of this traditionally social character. There is a great deal talked about the Bible but very little of its life actually lived. Present needs are either ignored in an attempt to resurrect the past, or else they are misunderstood and fundamentals are sacrificed to an over-hasty adaptation. The monastic orders would do well to shake off their mediaeval cobwebs and rediscover their true vocation in this matter. Sacramental life and true Christian discipline achieve a perfect harmony in the community life of a monastery, and offer the ideal conditions for the creation of a really modern centre of the Church's ancient traditions. The Bible, the liturgy, discipline, personal faith and social charity are there welded together to form what could be a typical example of Christianity in action.

Much is demanded from missionaries and teachers too. There is a great temptation for the missionary to become utilitarian, and to overlook the fact that his first duty is to be himself transfigured by the Word of life which he has undertaken to give to others. A great deal of our missionary activity fails because instead of the divine message itself only a temporary and passing expression of it is preached. To learn the way God teaches, a way which never fails, the missionary must return to the Bible and the Christian tradition that issues from it. The same applies to teachers. One shudders to think of the harm that is done in the name of Bible History. Most manuals of Scripture ought to be burned. They are full of ideas which are enough to shatter the children's faith when they grow up. Nuns especially have much work to do in this respect. It is said that women make or mar the world. Certainly what a nun teaches a girl to-day will be what the mother teaches her son to-morrow. If this is mere sentimental piety the boy will reject it as nunnish nonsense. But if it is a direct and living contact with revelation he will make it the leaven of his life and of the circles in which he moves.

The whole problem of the education of our young people is a very delicate one. Both our grammar education and our universities are geared either to the humanities or to the sciences, and our Catholic schools naturally have a bias in the same direction. Yet one could ask whether it is right that our priests and nuns should spend their lives teaching quadratic equations and expounding on the myths of ancient Greece. Are not, in fact, Isaiah and Ezekiel worthy of the attention given to Cicero and Virgil? Are the Acts of the Apostles less interesting than Caesar? The letters of St. Paul and the Fourth Gospel have as rare a power of educating and inspiring a child as any play of Shakespeare. The story of David is as fresh and bracing as any song from his contemporary Homer, and if it has less elegance it has more truth. As for the Psalms and the Canticle, there is nothing comparable in any other literature. As long as we continue to exclude our Semitic and Christian patrimony from the syllabus, it may well be that our education in the humanities is doing more harm than good. Our classical culture cannot possibly form the synthesis it should with our Christian culture if the one has achieved a high degree of polish at the expense of the other.

The ultimate aim of Christian education is to bring the Bible back into Christian family life. No Christian home should be without a Bible and a Missal. Daily Mass and the daily reading of the Bible should be the mainstay of family life. This is not an impossible ideal. Experience shows that a child will adapt himself to the biblical and eucharistic mentality with astonishing ease if he has been accustomed to hearing the Word of God and receiving the Body of Christ daily. A Christian should normally begin his day by communion with the Son of God at Mass, and end it by communion with God's incarnate Word in the Bible. Discretion must be used in the choice of reading, but it should cover the whole range of the Bible, and should form the conclusion and climax of the family night prayers. In this way the child's day will be cradled in the rhythm of the Spirit of Christ. The Bible, after all, was written for children, not for scholars. Christ himself said "I thank you, Father, that you have hidden this mystery (the revelation of the Father in the Son) from the wise and self-sufficient in order to reveal it to little children ". (Mt. 11 : 25).

IV

THE MYSTERY OF THE BIBLE IN THE CHURCH

The Christian sense of mystery is based on a sapiential outlook; the mystery of the Bible as one aspect of the mystery of Christ; Eucharist and Scripture both communicate Christ in the Spirit, Scripture in the realm of truth and Eucharist in the realm of life; both are the mystery of faith, of love and of hope.

THE modern world has lost all sense of mystery. To-day the word mystery denotes either the inconceivable that must be rejected or the unknowable that must be taken on faith. Truth is seen as two-dimensional, where reality is perceived and then given an absolute value by being made into an abstract concept. But there is a third dimension, and real life can only be found by one who is willing to probe beneath this two-dimensional surface to the truly absolute. This is the level of mystery in its Christian definition, which is the very opposite of what the word is generally taken to mean.

Christian tradition, nurtured on the Bible, has a vivid appreciation of mystery. For the Christian, the word connotes not obscurity but divine light. It is not something outside human truth, beyond man's reach, but something at the very centre of human truth and the human mind. In its Christian sense mystery is indeed something that cannot be mastered by a created mind, but if it remains obscure it is because it dazzles. The eyes of man cannot stare into such a blinding light, even though its purpose is to illumine those eyes. If mystery means something hidden, secret and inviolable, it also means divine revelation and life. *The* mystery is God, a God who is in himself incommunicable, but who fills the void of man's nothingness with the gift of himself. All mystery is an incarnation because it is the communication by symbol of what is in itself ineffable. Mystery is the "sacrament" of divine Light.

This book has tried to show that the mystery of the Bible is only one aspect of the Christian mystery. Christianity could be defined as the personal communication of God to man in the revelation of his incarnate Word, through the inspiration of his Spirit. We have tried to show the Bible's place in the economy of this divine plan. We saw how it was a pre-incarnation of the Son of God in words, designed to support his incarnation in the flesh. This double incarnation in time could take place only once, but its eternal repercussions continue through all time. The mystery of Christ is continued in his Church; the mystery of the Bible is continued in Tradition. We saw how the Church's living Tradition is the leaven which ensures that the Bible continues to give life, and to reveal the same incarnate Word under the inspiration of the same Spirit.

When we tried to analyse this life-giving function of the Bible more closely, we saw that generally speaking it is not the source of Christian life. The principle of life is faith, and this is not born immediately from Scripture but from the preaching of the Gospel, just as charity is not first born from eucharistic communion but from the inpouring of the Spirit at Baptism. There is therefore an analogy in the Christian economy between the Eucharist and the Bible, both of which have similar functions. Neither is the source of Christian life but both watch over its development. They assure not the birth of Christian life but its growth. They are not its seed but its food.

WHEN we have once understood this similarity of function, we are in a better position to understand the different spheres in which they operate. The Eucharist is a sacrament in the proper sense of the word. The Bible is a sacrament only by analogy. That does not mean that its part in the economy of salvation is any the less important. A sacrament is an *action* stemming from the divine energy by which we share in the vitality of the Spirit of Christ. But Christianity offers man not only the means of supernatural action; it offers him also the means of supernatural *thought*. It is here that the function of the Bible lies. Christian life is founded on Christian knowledge; charity is founded on faith. The Spirit of God cannot move the will until the Word of God has enlightened the mind. If the sacraments are the channels through which we are given the Spirit of Christ, Christian instruction in all its forms is the doorway through which the Spirit ushers the Word. If God has given us sacraments that we might have life he has also given us charismata that we might have light. If we are to be saved we need both " to believe and to be baptized " (Mk. 16:16); and if our Christian life is to grow we must eat the bread of the Word by our faith in his teaching no less than by our reception of his risen body. Light and Life, thought and action, both go together to make up Christianity. The magnificent discourse in the sixth chapter of St. John is a perfect exposition of this illumination by the Son through the sanctification of the Spirit. There, the Bread of Life means both the teaching and the flesh of the Son of God. The body of Christ is the food of life, and the Word is its light. The Christian goes to the Bible to nourish his faith on the Word that is Light, and to the Eucharist to nourish his love on the Word that is Life.

The Bible and the Eucharist, therefore, have different but related functions. The Bible is the light that leads to life, and the Eucharist is the life that brings light. The Bible is the Word of God inspired by the Spirit, the Eucharist is the flesh of the incarnate Word through which the believer is nourished by the Spirit. We have laboured this similarity and near identity of function, because so many people are surprised and sometimes disturbed when the parallelism is pointed out. In their eyes the Eucharist is all-important and the Bible merely one of the secondary means of salvation. The Fathers, it seems, were not afraid to reverse this order. Because of its personal and intimate character they say relatively little about the Eucharist; about the more observable Bible they are very eloquent indeed. It is the channel through which we receive the Spirit of faith which must give life to the flesh of Christ (Jn. 6:63). It is the invitation to love. It quickens and sustains the understanding and discipline which are inspired by the sacramental presence of Christ. The Bible continues to perform in the Church the task it fulfilled in the unfolding of revelation. As it once announced the incarnation of the Word, so now it leads man by the Spirit to his sacramental presence in the mystery of the Church, and tells of his final manifestation in the Parousia. Once it was the historical pre-incarnation of the Word of God, the cradle in which he was born in the flesh; now it endures to sanctify the mind of the believer and lead him to a loving communion with the body of his risen Lord.

WE COME finally to the conclusion that the mystery of the Bible is at the very heart of the mystery of the Eucharist. The one is the strength and stay of the other. There can be no Mass without a fore-Mass, no communion in the flesh of Christ without communion in his thought, because there can be no true love without living faith. No sacrifice can be offered without the sacrifice of praise. The Bible, like the Eucharist, is a sacrificial meal, where a man must die to his own judgment before he can make the gift of total love. This is the summing up of Christianity—submission to the Word and acceptance of the Cross. The Bible gives us the understanding of it, the Eucharist the love to do it. Together they have only one aim, and each achieves it through the other—to incorporate us, here and now, into the death and the life of Christ.

Both Bible and Eucharist are therefore the *mystery of faith.* Both require the same attitude of faith, and both supply the object of faith which is the incarnate Word of God. Both are a living memorial of the past, the Eucharist of the Word humbled in the flesh and glorified in the Spirit, the Bible of the Word humbled in the flesh of human language. It is the acceptance by faith of this twofold humiliation that separates us from the world and makes us children of God.

But the Bible, like the Eucharist, is more than a memorial of the past. The historical fact that they commemorate they also extend through all time. The Bible like the Eucharist is the continued presence of the incarnate Word. In it he has already returned in an invisible way, in the Spirit. The Bible brings to earth the real presence of Christ's thought, which enlightens every man and leads him to the real presence of his risen body. It is the witness of the Spirit, which is one with the witness of water and blood (1 Jn. 5:8). "Man does not live on bread alone, but on every word that comes from the mouth of God" (Mt. 4:4). Through the Bible which is his Word, and the Eucharist which is his living bread, Christ fulfils his promise to be with us all days until the consummation of the world (Mt. 28:20). The Bible is the seed which must die to produce the hundredfold of the mystical Body of Christ. With the Eucharist, the Bible is the *mystery of love.*

Still it remains a mystery: it is not yet the final revelation. The Bible looks forward to the day when the veil will be drawn. It is an anticipation of the eternal vision, just as the Eucharist is a pledge of immortality. The one gives light and the other life to a present which is always a mysterious becoming. Together they are the leaven of a constant evolution, transforming the Kingdom as it grows. Both belong to that "in-between" time which lies between the two Advents of Christ. Rooted in the past, they are its witnesses in the present, husbanding the seed for the harvest to come. As light and life, they hold the tension between the two extremes of the mystery that is Christianity. This mystery, achieved in principle by the death and resurrection of Christ, continues and grows in the Church until the Kingdom comes, when the written Word will give way to vision, and the appearances will be torn away to reveal the reality of the Lamb that was slain. Both the Bible and the Eucharist are necessarily eschatological, where Faith and Love together form the *mystery of Hope* and of consolation. The two hands of the Paraclete, they point to the invisible presence of the Son in the Church, and will continue to do so until the day when the narrow confines of the human mind and heart are broken open to reveal the living glory of the Only Son of the Father, in Spirit and Truth.

"As often as you eat this Bread, and drink this Cup, you proclaim the Lord's death, until he comes" (1 Cor. 11:26).

THUS DID THE WORD OF GOD
WHO IS DAVID'S SON YET DAVID'S LORD
PLAY THE SONG OF THE HOLY SPIRIT
NOT ON A LIFELESS HARP
BUT ON THE BODY AND SOUL OF MAN
THUS DID HE MAKE HIS MUSIC HEARD
THROUGH ALL THE WORLD
ON THESE LIVING STRINGS
HE MAKES MELODY TO GOD

(CLEMENT OF ALEXANDRIA: EXHORTATION TO THE HEATHEN)